The Economics of Natural Resources

By the same author
Economic Growth versus the Environment

The Economics of Natural Resources

RICHARD LECOMBER

First published 1979 by
THE MACMILLAN PRESS LTD
London and Basingstoke
Associated companies in Delhi Dublin
Hong Kong Johannesburg Lagos Melbourne
New York Singapore and Tokyo

Printed in Great Britain by
Billing & Sons Limited, Guildford, London and Worcester

British Library Cataloguing in Publication Data

Lecomber, Richard
   The economics of natural resources.
   1. Natural resources
   I. Title
   333   HC55

   ISBN 0-333-19140-4
   ISBN 0-333-19141-2 Pbk

CONTENTS

ACKNOWLEDGEMENTS

Warm thanks are due to Esra Bennathan for constant encouragement and to Marjorie Lunt for her great patience in preparing the typescript.

LIST OF TABLES

LIST OF FIGURES

1 INTRODUCTION

1.1 Natural resources and economics

Economics is often defined as the science of allocating scarce *resources*, resources being a general term used to cover all inputs to production, not only land, minerals and fuels but also labour and capital and even foreign exchange. The principles are very general and in some ways the economics of *natural* resources is a not very special case.

The definitive feature of natural resources is that they are provided by nature, not by man. Man uses them and in so doing may deplete and eventually exhaust them. Indeed, some uses, in particular the burning of fossil fuels, are unavoidably depletive. Natural resources can, it is true, sometimes be augmented (for example soil fertility can be improved and fisheries stocked) but depletion is perhaps more common. This gives rise to the fear of exhaustion — bringing disaster. It is widely felt that markets, if they work moderately well in allocating other resources, somehow fail with natural ones, and that common economic principles somehow fail to apply.

A major purpose of this book is to clarify such issues: Is exhaustion of some or all resources likely in the near future or at all? Is the effect necessarily disatrous? What are the principles of resource allocation and how, precisely, do they apply to *natural* resources? What ethical issues are involved? How far are market influences on resource use satisfactory? Can specific failings be identified? Is resource depletion generally excessive? What policies are available for influencing resource use? What are their relative merits? What particular problems are likely to arise and how may they be countered?

1.2 Coverage and approach

In a book of this length it is not possible to cover all aspects of (natural) resource[1] economics. The first limitation is to define resources narrowly to refer to sources of raw materials and food. This corresponds to popular usage. Thus we shall not, as some other writers (see, for example, Herfindahl and Kneese, 1974) do, attempt to cover other services provided by the natural environment, such as a sink for wastes and a direct source of life support and satisfaction. These aspects of the environment will be discussed but only in so far as they relate to resource use as narrowly defined; thus it will be necessary to consider the impact of quarrying on scenery or that of burning fossil fuels on air pollution, just as it is necessary to consider the *social* implications of resource use. Additionally, there are marked similarities between problems of pollution and indeed congestion and some problems of resource use, so that useful analogies may be drawn.

Second, attention will be focused on the longer-term problems of resource use associated with depletion. A wide range of problems associated with the term 'commodities', for example price fluctuations and their effect on producer countries, especially L.D.C.s (less-developed countries), commodity agreements, speculation and forward markets, will be altogether ignored (see Banks, 1976; Rowe, 1967).

Third, no attempt will be made to give a detailed or rounded picture of decision-making problems in any specific resource industry. Problems, such as investment appraisal, which, though crucial, are not unique to resource industries, will be treated summarily; peculiarities of particular industries will be discussed only in so far as this is necessary to develop an example which is useful in exploring a more general theme. The aim is to examine broad principles from the viewpoint of society as a whole. (However, the viewpoint of individual resource owners is relevant, since it is their decisions, albeit influenced by government policy, which   determine resource use in a market economy.)

Finally, examples are drawn mainly from the United Kingdom and the United States and little specific consideration is given to resource problems in either communist countries or L.D.C.s. However, much of the discussion is sufficiently general to apply universally.

The book has been written with economists (or at least those with a good grounding in microeconomics) primarily in mind, in that it draws on various tools and ways of thought of economists, particularly optimisation, market mechanisms and market failure. However, the subject-matter and its presentation are not especially difficult and there is nothing (except possibly the appendices) which is beyond the persevering non-economist. The arguments are developed from scratch, if a little tersely; and references to more extended treatments are given.

The use of mathematics is always a problem. It is of course an aid to precise thought, even if it carries the danger of biasing the discussion to those aspects of the question which are most readily formalised. Each reader will have his own level of mathematical competence; works aimed below this level are apt to seem unnecessarily cumbersome and imprecise; those above it make hard reading and may even be incomprehensible. The latter seemed the greater danger, especially as there proved to be few ideas which could not be expressed verbally reasonably satisfactorily. Where the subject-matter warrants it (Chapters 2–4), there are short mathematical appendices and it is hoped that those with the necessary skills will look at these to gain some idea of the formal work in the field.

1.3 Some terminology

Resource types

It is usual to distinguish two broad classes of resource: *renewable* and *non-renewable*. Renewable resources are those which may be used without depletion; there are two sub-groups. The first, typified by solar energy and sometimes known as a *flow* resource, is incapable of depletion; it yields a flow which may be tapped without affecting the flow available in future years. The second, typified by the fishery, renews itself through biological growth, permitting a constant harvest to be collected without depletion; however, in this case depletion is possible and will occur whenever output exceeds the rate of natural replenishment. Non-renewable resources, typified by fossil fuels, are necessarily depleted by use – use of a unit of fuel in one period precludes its use in another.

The distinction between renewable and non-renewable resources is not altogether watertight. Even fossil fuels are, strictly speaking, constantly being renewed, but the rate of renewal is so slow that for practical purposes it can be ignored. Minerals, though usually classified as non-renewable, are not destroyed by extraction or even by use and are in principle available for recycling. Recycling may not always occur: it may be prohibitively expensive or impossible; it may also involve the depletion of other resources, notably fuels. Similarly, the exploitation of renewable resources (of both types) almost always involves the depletion of non-renewable resources (for example fuel for tractors or fishing boats, inorganic fertilisers). Finally, some resources may be renewable or non-renewable, according to the use to which they are put. Thus quarrying of non-renewable stone may entail the destruction of renewable farmland. Despite these difficulties and qualifications, the broad distinction made is valuable.

Pessimists, Optimists and Conservationsts

As so often in heated controversies, views have tended to polarise. Accordingly, it will be convenient and not too misleading to employ the labels Pessimist and Optimist to refer to two broad schools of thought. Of course it must not be supposed that either school is homogeneous in its opinions, or indeed that every writer on resource problems can be fitted into either school. Indeed, some of the most thoughtful writers (for example, Meade) cannot. The views of the schools may be characterised as follows.

Pessimists[2] emphasise the finiteness of the world and the limits this places on economic output. They insist on the eventual necessity of a stationary state, when all output is derived from renewable resources. Moreover, they consider that severe resource scarcity is imminent: many non-renewable resources are approaching exhaustion and renewable resources (and environmental sinks) are being fully used and in many cases over-used. They emphasise the suddenness of the onset of scarcity and the consequent difficulties of adaptation; they are very sceptical of the adequacy of existing mechanisms, especially the market mechanism, to cope with such scarcity in a satisfactory way. They fear that, in the absence of a carefully planned adaptation to the stationary state, non-renewable resources will be exhausted suddenly and renewable resources will be overworked, with disastrous effects. Many Pessimists appear to advocate an across-the-board approach, for example *zero* economic growth. They blame the materialistic and expansionist ethics of capitalist (and communist) societies and the false optimism of the opposite camp for preventing the taking of necessary measures to avert disaster. They are sceptical of the power of technology to obviate or even significantly postpone the crisis. Some Pessimist writers even see technology as hastening and aggravating the crisis.

Some Pessimists combine their scarcity critique of capitalism with a social critique: materialism, rapid change, advertising and large impersonal work-places and towns are causing disastrous social problems. This line of argument is essentially distinct from the question of resource scarcity, but there may be some overlap between the remedies required.

Nearly all Pessimists emphasise the central role of population growth in aggravating the resource crisis;[3] but, as many who are otherwise Optimists share this view, this is not a distinguishing characteristic.

Optimists[4] admit the physical finiteness of the world but question its significance. Some deny the eventual necessity of an end to economic growth and all question whether such an end is imminent. They argue that the physical measures of scarcity frequently quoted by the Pessimists are misleading in that they ignore new discoveries, substitution possibilities (between resources and, more significantly, man-made capital resources) and technical progress. They point out how, historically, resource scares have been averted in precisely this way.

They emphasise the role of the price mechanism in stimulating the necessary adjustments (and, incidentally, believe that, if and when resource limits to growth do materialise, the price mechanism will play a central role in adaption to the stationary state). They believe, more positively, that the price mechanism allocates resource use reasonably well between different time periods. They admit the great uncertainty that must surround the distant future, but they tend to use this uncertainty to justify a short planning horizon. They are scornful of many of the approaches of Pessimists to resource scarcity, particularly zero economic growth, which they see as unnecessary if not harmful to conservation, besides aggravating unemployment and the distribution of income.

Optimists concede problems, even serious problems, when ownership rights are inadequately defined or externalities are present, for here the market mechanism on which they place such emphasis clearly fails; specific remedies directed to specific problems are indicated. As already remarked, many Optimists also concede the importance of the population issue.

It must again be emphasised that these sketches are caricatures and readers interested in the views of particular members of the schools should consult at first hand the writings of those in question.

Conservation is variously used to denote: (i) protection of the environment, especially preservation in its natural state, or (ii) elimination of 'waste', or (iii) abstaining from using resources, *not* to enhance their availability at a later date. Here, the third usage is adopted. Correspondingly, *Conservationists* are those who advocate an increase in the degree of conservation.

1.4 Plan of the book

Chapters 2—5 represent different approaches to the question 'Are resources being used too fast?' Chapter 2 is concerned with the debate between Optimists and Pessimists. The extent to which an apparently critical resource situation may be transformed by new discoveries, substitution and technical progress is examined, together with the role of the market mechanism in facilitating adaptations to resource scarcity. Chapters 3 and 4 are concerned with optimal resource use, Chapter 3 from the viewpoint of an individual resource owner, Chapter 4 from the viewpoint of society as a whole. Firm conclusions on the shape of the optimal path would have been useful, as these could have been used as a basis for judging the actual path. In fact no firm conclusions emerge, but these chapters are valuable in highlighting some important general principles. Chapter 5 starts from the theorem that 'perfect markets' *promote* 'optimum outcomes' and examines possible sources of market imperfection. The list of relevant imperfections turns out to be a long one and ranges well beyond the resource industries. The general conclusion is that there could be a fairly strong tendency to use resources too fast. Moreover, reasons are identified, suggesting possible remedies. The ethical issue of responsibility for the well-being of future generations is also considered in Chapter 5.

Remedies are considered systematically in Chapter 6. In addition to exploring the remedies indicated by Chapter 5, zero economic growth (Z.E.G.) and *ad hoc* conservation measures, such as recycling subsidies and resource taxes, are examined. More general problems of cutting back on resource use, in particular the transitional problems of moving from a position where resource use is high and rising to one where it is low and static, are examined in Chapter 7.

Finally, Chapters 8 and 9 are devoted to a more detailed examination of what is probably the most critical resource problem (except, perhaps, agricultural land), namely energy. Chapter 8 concerns the prospects for supply, Chapter 9 the scope for conservation in the United Kingdom.

2 THE ADEQUACY
OF NATURAL RESOURCES

2.1 The basic pessimist position

Present reserves of all but a few metals will be exhausted within fifty years if consumption rates continue to grow as they are . . . if current trends are allowed to persist . . . the breakdown of society and the irreversible disruption of the life support systems on this planet are inevitable (Meadows *et al.*, 1972).

This chapter begins from a stark and highly simplified form of the Pessimist position. This form is both convenient for initial exposition and also significant in the controversies in its role as paradigm and a straw-man for easy demolition by the Optimists. As criticisms are introduced, the Pessimist position will be successively refined.

The Pessimist position, thus simplified, may be summarised in the following six propositions:

(i) The world is finite. This places a limit on resource supplies and hence on the level of output that can be sustained.

(ii) 'Nearly all of mankind's current activities . . . can be represented by exponential growth curves' (Meadows *et al.*, 1972). This includes the level of output.

(iii) However, growth in output is necessarily brought to a halt when the supply limit is reached.

(iv) This limit will be reached 'soon'.

(v) The effect of reaching this limit is likely to be disastrous.

(vi) Hence a deliberate attempt must be made to modify the tendency to exponential growth and to limit mankind's activities to the constraints imposed by the finiteness of the world.

These propositions will be examined in turn.

(i) *Resource limits*

Clearly the world is endowed with a finite quantity of physical resources. It is argued that the quantity of *renewable* resources (such as land) sets a finite limit to the *flow* of output (such as food) that can be sustained. It may be possible to exceed this maximum sustainable output (M.S.O.) temporarily by overworking the resource (for example by overgrazing) but only at the expense of a long-term reduction in M.S.O.

In addition, there are *non-renewable* resources (such as fossil fuels) which cannot be used without depletion. When these are exhausted, output is constrained to that obtainable from renewable resources alone which thus in the end determine M.S.O.

(ii) *Exponential growth*

Economic change is generally expressed in exponential terms (i.e. in terms of *proportional* or *percentage* rates of growth) by professional and lay connentators alike; a country will normally regard a fall in its (proportionate) rate of growth with dismay, even if in absolute terms the increment to output is greater than in the previous period. Many key economic magnitudes (though by no means all) may indeed be observed to be following trends which are approximately exponential. Exponential growth is indeed an assumption so standard in these contexts that understandably it is generally adopted by the Pessimists without explicit justification.

However, Meadows *et al*. (1972) provide explicit arguments to support their view that the *natural* process of growth is exponential in a wide variety of key situations. The basic idea will be familiar enough to students of economic growth as well as to demographers. The rate of growth of an economy depends on the proportion of income which is saved (s) and the productivity of these savings ($1/v$). If these two magnitudes remain constant over time, then income will grow at a constant exponential rate ($g = s/v$). Likewise in the demographic field, a population with constant birth rate b, and death rate d, will grow at a constant rate $g = b - d$. As Meadows points out, a change in the *rate* of growth implies a change in one of the underlying parameters of the system. Thus, it is suggested, exponential growth is a natural starting assumption and departures from exponentiality demand explicit justification.

(iii) *The halt to growth*

For the case of production from renewable resources, these assumptions are depicted graphically in Figure 2.1. Output expands along the path *ABC*, and if unchecked reaches maximum sustainable output (M.S.O.) at *D*. This outcome follows inescapably from the assumptions.

(iv) *The imminence of the crisis*

Obviously this is a crucial issue. Distant limits, requiring no current action, are of little more than academic interest. The dramatic impact of *The Limits to Growth* (Meadows *et al*., 1972) and similar Pessimist

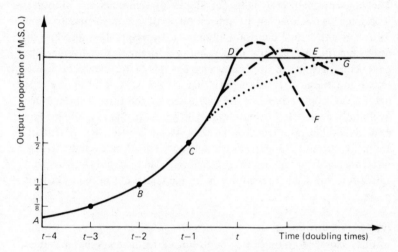

Figure 2.1 Exponential growth in the face of a limit

writings derives almost entirely from their depiction of an *imminent* crisis within the next 100 years or so.

These conclusions stem from comparisons of the level and growth in usage of various resources within estimates of resource stocks. The simplest calculation is illustrated in Table 2.1.

Table 2.1 Global availability of selected resources

(1)	(2)	(3)	(4)	(5)	(6)	(7)
			Annual demand (1970)	Growth rate (% p.a.)	Static index (years)	No. of years to limit
Item	Unit	Supply				
Arable land	10^{12} hectares	3.2	1.5	2*	–	40†
Petroleum	10^{9} billion barrels	455	14.7	3.9	31	20
Natural gas	10^{12} cu. ft	1140	30.0	4.7	38	22
Coal	10^{9} tons	5000	2.2	4.1	2300	111
Aluminium	10^{6} tons	1170	11.7	6.4	100	31
Copper	10^{6} tons	308	8.6	4.6	36	21
Iron	10^{9} tons	100	0.4	1.8	240	93
Zinc	10^{6} tons	123	5.4	2.9	23	18

* Growth rate of world population.
† Ignoring taking of land for non-agricultural uses.
Source: Meadows *et al*. (1972) fig. 10 and table 4.

The conventional static index of stocks of non-renewable resources (column 6) is obtained by dividing estimates of resource stocks (column 3) by current annual demand (column 4). However, the static index is misleading in that the life of a resource is dramatically shortened by exponential growth in use. Allowance for this factor yields the figures shown in column 7. It will be seen that, on the basis of this, petroleum, natural gas, copper and zinc are exhausted by the turn of the century, while only coal lasts for more than 100 years. In the case of land (the only renewable resource shown), only 44 per cent of that potentially arable is currently under cultivation, but if land cultivated increases *pro rata* with population, and ignoring land withdrawn for non-agricultural uses, all the surplus is brought into use in the next forty years.

(v) *What happens next?*

Initially suppose all output to be produced from renewable resources. The economy expands exponentially towards M.S.O., as illustrated by *ABC* in Figure 2.1. There are a variety of possible outcomes, of which four will be considered.

First, output might grow exponentially until *D* is reached and then remain constant at M.S.O. (the solid line in the diagram). This outcome is identified by Barnett and Morse (1963) as optimal and certainly appears attractive. M.S.O. is reached as soon as practicable and is thereafter maintained. But, in practice, such a path is likely to be neither pleasant nor easy to follow. Such an abrupt change in trend will involve all kinds of uncomfortable adjustments. For example, there will be a marked change in the structure of employment (see Chapter 7) and in particular manpower requirements in traditional investment industries will fall sharply. Severe structural unemployment is the almost inevitable result of such an abrupt change. In addition, the population, accustomed to steadily rising standards of living, will be reluctant to accept static ones. The result is likely to be an inflationary scramble for increasing shares of a cake which is, or should be, fixed (at M.S.O.). Government efforts to stem the inflation may add Keynesian unemployment to the structural unemployment already noted. The competitive scramble for resources and employment may take the uglier forms of industrial and class conflict and even sabotage and civil or international strife. Most of these phenomena are indeed familiar enough, if on a relatively minor scale, following the sharp falls in economic growth resulting from recent crises in the supply of oil and other basic commodities.

Another danger is that the scramble for resources will be partly successful and M.S.O. temporarily exceeded. This is particularly likely in that M.S.O. is not known with precision and there will inevitably be disputes about whether, at any point of time, it has, or has not, been exceeded. In any case it may not be in the interest of those responsible for dicisions over resource use to exercise the required restraint. For example, individual fishermen have no incentive to limit their catches, because the benefits of individual abstinence accrue largely to others (for a fuller account of such 'common resource' problems, see Chapter 3). Of course, in principle, fishing can be controlled by government regulations, but suitable regulations are notoriously difficult both to devise and enforce. At times of economic crisis, governments are likely to find suitably tough policies particularly unattractive. Fisheries also exemplify the problems of international agreement.

Further problems stem from *lags* associated with both economic and social decisions, combined with the suddenness with which the limit is approached along the exponential growth path. Lags are involved in diagnosing the need for a change in trend, in reacting to the diagnosis (for example in investment planning) and in the impact of economic activity on resource quality. All these lags impart to the economy a dynamic inertia well known to students of the trade cycle.

Lags can be countered by anticipation, but here the suddenness and unexpectedness of the cases is crucial. Under exponential growth, successive doublings of output take equal periods of time. (The concept of 'doubling time' is very useful in discussions of exponential growth and is much used by the Pessimists.) Thus output, growing at the comparatively modest rate of 3 per cent p.a. doubles every twenty-three years ($1.03^{23} \approx 2$). In a further twenty-three years it doubles again, but the absolute increment is much larger (in fact double). In 100 years it increases more than twentyfold. Thus a mere century before the resource crisis strikes (D in Figure 2.1) output (at A) is a mere twentieth of its maximum sustainable level and the proximity of a crisis will be evident to only the most far-sighted. Even at C (twenty-three years before the crisis) output is only one-half of the maximum sustainable level. Many economic magnitudes are growing at rates nearer 10 per cent than 3 per cent p.a. A 10 per cent p.a. growth rate involves a doubling time of a mere seven years, and in a century such a magnitude increases sixteen thousandfold.

A major purpose of many Pessimists is precisely to alert decision-makers to the imminence of a resource crisis (as they see it) and hence set in motion appropriate responses.

If the economy is allowed to reach D, it is much more likely, then, that its momentum will carry it onward, past maximum sustainable output. By definition this can be done only at the expense of the longer term. Overgrazing, overcropping, overfishing, and the like will deplete resources and maximum sustainable output will fall. This will put a brake on the expansion of output, which will first slacken and then fall (the dashed line in Figure 2.1). Over-use may continue as the population tries even harder to maximise output in the short term in the face of declining resource quality. Such attempts cause further depletion and output plummets disastrously.[1] Alternatively, the population, at last realising the resource crisis, may take steps to eliminate over-use of resources and output may then stabilise at a new level somewhat lower than the initial M.S.O.

If economic growth is accompanied by demographic growth, all these problems are greatly aggravated. Population growth is subject to especially long lags, and in particular past growth will have led to a high proportion of women of child-bearing age, which will persist until those who are then in their infancy pass this age (three to four decades). Moreover, any sharp fall in the birth rate leads to disturbances in the age structure of the population, affecting, for example, the demand for teachers (another phenomenon familiar from recent U.K. experience). In so far as population growth continues, the halt to growth in output will entail an actual drop in living standards, aggravating all the problems considered above.

Introducing non-renewable resources represents a serious aggravation of the Pessimists' position. Current growth is, they argue, sustained not only by increasingly intense use of renewable resources but by increasingly rapid depletion of non-renewable resources (path AH in Figure 2.2). Eventually non-renewable resources must be exhausted — at a time which may or may not coincide with that at which renewable resources are fully utilised. From this point output must be based solely on *renewable* resources and will fall suddenly and substantially (for example from H to C). At worst certain non-renewable resources are essential to production and output ceases altogether. At best living standards do not simply stop rising, they actually fall. Much of mankind has become accustomed to high and rising standards not only psychologically but physically, and a fall on this scale would clearly be calamitous.

(vi) *Implications for policy*
Renewable resources. Given the impracticability of the first alternative

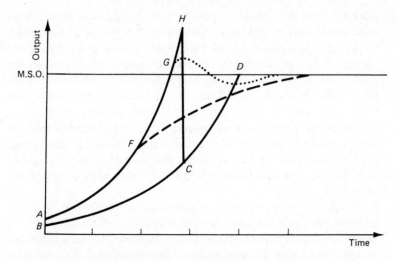

Figure 2.2 Production from renewable and non-renewable resources

in Figure 2.1 (the firm line) and the presumed undesirability of the second (the dashed line), exponential growth should be curbed before the economy reaches *D*. If this is done soon enough, and strongly enough, the economy could adapt smoothly to M.S.O. along, say, the dotted path in Figure 2.1. Some of the problems of adaptation to zero growth will be much muted by the gradualness of the change.

Non-renewable resources. If useage of non-renewable resources is essential to sustain life, then eventual 'doom' is unavoidable; the most that can be done is to minimise usage to prolong life as much as possible (but see Chapter 4). If, however, life can be sustained at an 'adequate' level from renewable resources alone, then a smooth transistion may be achieved by gradually phasing out the use of non-renewable resources (cf. Goldsmith, 1976). If this policy is begun at *F*, then the dashed path may be attainable. If, however, it is delayed until *G*, then an eventual fall in output is unavoidable, and the best that can be done is to make the fall as gradual as possible (for example via the dotted path). Thus earlier action is even more crucial.

2.2 Alleviations of resource scarcity
New discoveries
Clearly estimates of resource stocks are subject to great uncertainty. Those used by Meadows (quoted above) relate in the main to 'proven

reserves', that is resource deposits that are known definitely and recoverable at current cost and technology. These estimates are derived largely as a by-product of the exploration activities of mining companies. These are dictated by commercial considerations and clearly there is no incentive to seek out new deposits far in advance of need. Historically, as old deposits have been exhausted, new deposits have been sought and found and this means that the ratio of proven reserves to current demand (the 'static reserve index') has remained approximately constant for most minerals and fuels.[2] Thus this ratio is perhaps less of a guide to ultimate stocks than to the planning horizons of mineral companies (see Beckerman, 1974; Surrey and Page, 1975; Cole, 1973).

This line of reasoning provides rather limited comfort. While a low estimate for proven reserves is consistent with abundance, it is consistent also with imminent exhaustion. Presumably, for a homogeneous resource and given the exploration policies described, the static resource index would stay constant at, say, t years, until just t years before exhaustion, when it would fall rapidly. What in fact proven reserve estimates provide is a *lower limit* to resource stocks.

It would be useful to have some idea of the gap between proven and total reserves and how much difference this makes to resource lives. A commonly stated view is that 'in view of the paucity of exploration in many parts of the world [it] must be presumed to be large' (Fischman and Landsberg, 1972). While the gap must have declined considerably as exploration has proceeded and geological knowledge improved, this view is to some extent confirmed by reference to geologically based estimates of total or 'inferred' resources shown in Table 2.2 (column 3). The general methodology is to estimate resources in unexplored areas from previous finds in 'similar' explored areas. In principle these estimates, though subject to great uncertainty, are *unbiased*. In practice, however, they exclude from consideration certain possible categories of deposit, for example those contained in so far unknown geological structures. Thus even these estimates are biased downward but to an extent that is likely to be significant only for newer resources whose geology has been little investigated. The ratio of inferred to proven reserves varies widely, being generally greatest for newer resources.

However — a point much stressed by the Pessimists — seemingly large extensions to resource stocks make surprisingly little difference to resource lives 'when viewed against the inexorable progress of exponential growth' (Meadows *et al.*, 1972). This is simply because

Table 2.2 Proven resources and resource base, selected resources

(1)	(2)	(3)	(4)	(5)	(6)	(7)	(8)	(9)	(10)
Resource[a]	Proven reserv[b] (10^6 tons)	Resource base[c] (10^6 tons)	Ratio (3/2 = 7/6)	Growth in demand (% p.a.)	Static index[d] (yrs) using: (2)	(3)	Resource life (yrs) using: (2 & 5)	(3 & 5)	Ratio (9/8)
Chromium	466	2233	4.8	4.55[g]	274	1313	62	81	1.3
Copper	370	1470	4.0	3.76	54	215	29	60	2.1
Fluorine	132	1650	12.5	5.26	54	675	25	70	2.8
Lead	144	1854	12.9	2.15[g]	38	489	27	112	4.1
Manganese	3250[e]	12100[e,f]	3.7	4.70[g]	295	1114	88	97	1.1
Molybdenum	4.7	1132[e,f]	240.9	6.07[g]	78	18790	23	112	4.9
Phosphorus	6614	16534[f]	2.5	5.10	520	1300	66	84	1.3
Tin	4.7	41	8.8	1.00[g]	18	158	16	95	5.9
Zinc	131	5606	42.8	3.69[g]	21	920	15	97	6.5

Notes: [a] estimates for energy resources are given in Table 8.1; [b] known and economic at existing prices and technology; [c] includes, first, sub-economic resources, and, second, 'hypothetical' and 'speculative' resources (see McKelvey, 1972); [d] related to production in 1972, as used by Rajaraman; [e] top end of range; [f] excludes 'speculative' resources (no estimates available); [g] centre of range.

Source: Rajaraman (1976).

each addition to resources lasts less long as usage increases. For example, if proven stocks, R, last 100 years, then at 3 per cent p.a. growth a further R lasts only twenty-two years. Hence exponential growth in use not only reduces resource life below the static index (cols 9 and 7) but also reduces the effect of an increase in resource stocks on resource life (cols 10 and 4).

In conclusion, of itself the existence of undiscovered reserves does not materially affect the Pessimist conclusion that, given exponential growth, lives of most resources are uncomfortably short.

Varying resource quality
So far we have adopted the assumption, dubbed Malthusian,[3] that resources (and output) are homogeneous. Of course this is a drastic simplification, adopted for ease of exposition. The world stock of resources is in fact highly variable: in quality, type and locality. When a particular category of resource is exhausted, the economy will seek out an alternative. As a general rule an economy possessing a range of resources will tend to use the best ones first. It is only when all the best-quality resources are in use, or exhausted in the case of non-renewable resources, that the next best will be pressed into use. Indeed, it can be shown that under certain assumptions this order of use is optimal (see Chapter 3). Ricardo based his theory of rent on this assumption, and this model of resources of varying quality is accordingly referred to as 'Ricardian'.[4]

It should be emphasised that, for this rule to have any wide validity, quality must be interpreted economically, not physically. Thus even highly fertile land may be of 'low quality' because of inaccessibility to markets. In the case of a mineral quality will depend on such factors as ore grade, extent and depth of deposit and other determinants of extraction costs, as well as accessibility to markets and the metallurgical properties of the mineral obtained. Historically this process has been extremely important. For example, in the case of U.S. copper ore (Lovering, 1969; Singer, 1977) the most easily measurable of these characteristics, the average metal content, has fallen from 1.6 per cent in 1932 to 0.6 per cent in 1970.

Pessimist expositions of resource scarcity have generally either neglected these possibilities or dismissed them with minimal discussion. Clearly, the existence of lower-grade ores in no way affects the finiteness of the earth or the limit this places on output, and the simple 'Malthusian' model of constant ore quality is adequate in a discussion of this point. However, other features of the pessimist case, notably the date when limits are reached (considered here) and the problems of adaptation (considered in Section 2.5 below), are affected.

Since exploration has concentrated on profitable, i.e. high-grade resources, less is known about low-grade ones. Nevertheless in the case of most minerals it is thought that as grade falls, availability rises dramatically. Indeed, as a general principle it has been suggested that reserves increase geometrically as ore grade declines arithmetically. The applicability of this principle is disputed, especially at either end of the quality spectrum (see Lovering, 1969). But undoubtedly inclusion of lower-quality ores greatly expands the resource base, though without technical progress (considered below) costs will rise, thus braking economic growth. An *upper limit* to stocks of minerals may be obtained from geological estimates of crustal abundance. These are very great. For example, Beckerman (1972) notes euphorically that 'the natural occurrence of most metals in the top mile of the Earth's crust has been estimated to be about a million times as great as present known reserves. Since the latter amounts to about a hundred years' supplies this means we have enough to last about a hundred million years.' But, leaving aside the prodigious difficulties posed for technology and the severe danger of environmental side-effects, even these resources are inadequate to sustain current exponential growth. For example, at 3 per cent p.a. growth exhaustion occurs in about 500 years.

Substitution between resources
Substituting low-quality for high-quality resources is but one example of substitution responses to scarcity. However, substitution may be at a later stage of the production process and may be extremely indirect, for example aluminium for copper, scrap for virgin ore, oil-based fibres for cotton, vegetable oil for whale oil, clothing or insulation for domestic heating. In these cases, too, it may be presumed that, in the absence of technical change, the substitution will be to a less-preferred alternative, involving a brake on growth.

It remains true that (for constant technology), however varied the resource base, and however varied the output mix that can be derived from it, the finiteness of the total stock places a finite limit on any measure of output. However, this kind of substitution possibility enormously complicates the process of deriving a quantitative estimate of this limit. This is especially the case since account must be taken of resources and processes not currently in use and which are indeed not justified in current conditions of abundance.

Increasing resource productivity
Undoubtedly the most important factor alleviating resource scarcity is increases in resource productivity stemming from capital accumulation or technical progress. (In practice, the two are difficult to separate since the application of technical developments so often requires replacement and possibly extension of the capital stock.) The following examples give some idea of the wide range of possibilities:

(i) *Advances in existing resource industries:* (a) improvements in agricultural techniques (e.g. new strains of plant, such as 'miracle grains', new chemical or biological methods of pest control, or, conceivably, methods of influencing the weather), thus raising yields; (b) improvements in mining technology extending reserves, by making it economic to mine lower-grade ores, different types of ore in difficult situations (e.g. very deep or under the sea).

(ii) *Advances in transport* (e.g. the steam-engine, the internal combustion engine and, more recently, advances in pipe-line technology) make it worth while to exploit resources previously uneconomic because of inaccessibility.

(iii) *New methods of economising on resource use:* (a) use of thinner steel, (b) improved storage of agricultural products, (c) new switching or insulation techniques to save energy.

(iv) *Development of substitutes in resource use:* (a) use of different metals, perhaps completely novel ones (e.g. aluminium), (b) development of man-made substitutes (e.g. plastics, artificial fibres), (c) improved recycling techniques, (d) use of renewable substitutes (e.g. solar energy).

(v) *More complex substitutions:* (a) improvements in mass transit, leading to a reduction in motor-car travel and hence a saving of energy, (b) advances in computer technology, making it more attractive to charge private motorists for the use of congested roads, thus discouraging private motoring and saving energy.

The point is not that technical developments always lead to resource saving. It is not difficult to think of developments, for example in agriculture and transport, which have had the opposite effect. Technical advance is largely the product of research, the direction of which is influenced by scarcity. Often in the past it was labour that seemed the critical factor on account of its scarcity or cost, and hence research was directed to saving labour, often at the expense of greater usage of natural resources. However, if particular resources become scarce or expensive, then research is likely to be directed to methods of alleviating this scarcity. The above list illustrates some of the possibilities. The list also illustrates the connection between technical progress and the other alleviants of resource scarcity considered previously and dismissed as unimportant. Thus technical progress permits the working of lower-grade ores without increase in cost; this in turn stimulates new discoveries; similarly, technical progress stimulates a variety of substitutions.

The importance of technical progress is not in dispute. The difficulty is to make adequate allowance for future developments. The approaches of the Pessimists and the Optimists are very different. The former consider two types of approach. The first involves consideration of specific technical possibilities. Thus Meadows *et al.* (1972, p. 131) suggest that 'we must represent each proposed technology separately in the model' (partly in order to allow for complex side-effects). While such screening of key developments (for example fast-breeder technology) is important, it scarcely meets the more general difficulty of forecasting the over-all impact of future technology.

Loosely, future technology could be divided into the following groups:

(i) technologies already in operation in best-practice establishments;
(ii) those which, while not yet fully operational, are in an advanced

state of development;
(iii) those which are not justified in current conditions but which would be worth while in the face of particular scarcities (e.g. various new-energy technologies, as considered in Chapter 8) – in so far as such technologies have not yet been used, further developments are usually necessary, but these may be considered minor;
(iv) remote possibilities, still requiring major development; and
(v) possibilities not even considered.

Systematic consideration of group (i) technologies is clearly feasible, though formidable. Technologies in groups (ii) and (iii) present more problems in that it is difficult to estimate costs or enviage the full range of side-effects; notwithstanding this, a 'best view' can usefully be formulated. These problems are accentuated with group (iv) and, additionally, it is (in varying degrees) doubtful when, if at all, particular proposals will reach fruition. Inevitably group (v) technologies cannot be considered at all, except in the most general terms. And yet, in the longer term, these can be the most important of all. It is commonplace that a hundred years before their innovation, most of the major technical advances (for example the steam-engine, the telephone, contraception, nuclear power) would not have been included in any list of future technologies. Hence, almost inevitably, this approach underestimates the impact of new technology.

An alternative approach, much used by the Pessimists, is to postulate arbitrarily an apparently large (e.g. fourfold) increase in resource productivity to cover unforeseen developments (see Meadows *et al.*, 1972, p. 51). It is clear that any finite increase does not affect the general 'limits theorem'. Moreover, since an increase in productivity is equivalent to a similar increase in resource stocks, it is evident that the impact on the date of exhaustion is rather small.

Optimists point out that by historical standards a fourfold increase in resource productivity is not especially impressive. For example, in agriculture, even though the major emphasis has been on saving labour rather than land, the yield of U.S. maize-growing land doubled in a mere decade, while in India the introduction of miracle grains has led to an 'overnight' quadrupling of yields on the farms concerned. However, with exponential growth in use, a twentyfold, or even a millionfold, increase in resource productivity makes little difference.

By contrast optimists tend to assume a *continuous* increase in resource productivity. Annual increases in both the capital stock and the state of technology are standard in economic-growth models, which are easily adapted to incorporate natural resources. Some such models are set out formally in the appendix to this chapter. However, the general conclusions are clear enough. In the case of renewable resources , if exponential trends in output are matched by exponential trends in resource productivity, the former may continue unimpeded by resource limitations.

Even in the case of non-renewable resources it is (logically) possible for output growth to continue indefinitely without the resource ever being exhausted. Suppose, for example, that while output increases by y per cent p.a., the productivity of a homogeneous resource increases by x ($>y$) per cent p.a. Resource depletion then *decreases* by $z \approx$ $(x - y)$ per cent p.a. and cumulative depletion is given by:

$$r_0(1 + z + z^2 + \ldots),$$

where r_0 is depletion in the first period. This is a geometric progression with a finite sum, $r_0/ (1-z)$, and, provided initial resource stocks exceed this amount, resources are never exhausted. This possibility of indefinite growth despite resource limitations has been illustrated by the computer simulations of Nordhaus (1974) and Cole *et al.* (1973).

These are very abstract ideas and it will be instructive to consider a concrete example to give some insight into the possibilities of indefinite increases in resource productivity. Consider first the productivity of land. In terms of crop outputs per acre, productivity has steadily increased, largely as a result of irrigation and drainage, increasing applications of fertilisers and pesticides and improved varieties of crops. The growth in yields shows no signs of abating, though certain ultimate limits may be suggested in terms of solar energy conversion. However, land is by no means the only resource used in agriculture. Metals are used in buildings, tractors and other machinery and irrigation, potassium in fertilisers, fish in feedstuffs and energy in running agricultural machinery and in the transport of both inputs and outputs. Crop outputs, while they have generally risen in relation to land (and manpower), have frequently fallen in relation to these other resources, as Table 2.3 illustrates. Thus, if all natural resources used in farming are taken into account, it is not so clear how far, if at all, resource productivity has risen.

As a second example, consider the use of non-renewable steel in producing cars. Again, steel is not the only input, and to form a complete picture of resource productivity in car manufacture one would need to construct a composite index of resources used. However, to

Table 2.3   Growth in output and selected inputs, U.K. agriculture 1965–72

	Growth (%)	Growth in productivity of named resource (%)
Output [a]	12	
Inputs of:		
land [b]	−2	14
energy [b,c]	32	−39
fertiliser [a]	23	−31
capital [a,d]	25	−33

Notes: [a] constant price £; [b] physical units; [c] includes indirect energy inputs, for example energy included in the manufacture and transport of fertiliser inputs; [d] capital stock.

Sources: Leach (1976) for energy inputs; *Annual Abstract of Statistics* for remainder.

concentrate on other difficulties, attention will be confined to steel. Steel productivity could be increased by making cars of progressively thinner steel. This process is clearly limited – an extreme limit is presumably set by the size of the molecules. However, if 'output' is viewed more widely, other possibilities for increasing resource productivity need to be considered. Cars satisfy needs for travel and communication; these purposes may be served in other ways, for example by public transport, by television and telephone, or even by locational policies which reduce the need to travel. Clearly, if these kinds of substitution are under consideration, resource productivity becomes a rather difficult concept. Consider the most straightforward case, the substitution of bus travel for car travel. One might define steel productivity in this context as the ratio of passenger-miles to steel inputs. In these terms the steel productivity of bus travel undoubtedly exceeds that of car travel. But this ignores the important question of quality.[5] Car travel has certain advantages in terms of constant availability, privacy, door-to-door travel, and so on, so that to measure output in terms of passenger-miles would be misleading. However, these quality differences are difficult to quantify and certainly not picked up adequately in the official output measures used in national accounts. The use of locational plans which reduce the need to travel are even more difficult to assess in terms of resource productivity. Clearly there is a saving in terms of the steel used in car construction, but implementation of the locational policies concerned may involve heavier use of other resources (including steel) for other purposes, or involve arrangements that are less satisfying. The full implications for resources are difficult to trace, and a realistic measure of output change virtually impossible to devise.

The implications of this discussion are unsatisfactory, lending little support to either side. While there are clear limits to the simpler (and more easily measurable) ways of increasing resource productivity, these represent but a few of the many possibilities. If more indirect ways of increasing resource productivities are allowed (e.g. the locational policies), the possibilities are so varied that it is very difficult to envisage specific limits.

The role of price
Optimists stress the role of price in triggering the various mechanisms for alleviating resource scarcity discussed above. The basic theory is as follows:

As a resource (for example oil)[6] becomes scarce, its price should rise. Briefly there are two reasons for this (a further account is given in Chapters 3 and 4 below). The first (applicable only to a Ricardian resource) is that successively lower-quality resources must be used, raising extraction costs. The second (which applies even to a Malthusian resource) is that the value of 'oil in the ground' (known as the *resource rental*) should increase *in anticipation* of future scarcity. Specifically, it should rise at a rate equal to the (real) rate of interest. This is because 'oil in the ground' is an asset and if its value is expected to appreciate more/less rapidly than the value of other assets, it will be profitable to retard/bring forward extraction, thus influencing the rate of increase in value.

Thus, *ceteris paribus*, the oil rental, the price of extracted oil and that of all products embodying oil will tend to rise. These price rises should generate all the alleviants of resource scarcity discussed above, for example search for new oil fields, economy in the use of oil, substitution of other fuels for oil, and research into various methods of expanding supplies or reducing demands for oil.

A very important feature of this mechanism is that it generates *current* action in anticipation of *future* scarcity. It does this in two ways: first, current prices, through resource rentals, reflect future scarcity; second, current activities (such as investment or research) which involve long time lags should anyway be geared to expected

future prices. Thus the price mechanism not only stimulates appropriate responses to resource scarcity, but does so in advance.

On the other hand, the mechanism depends on reasonably correct
anticipations. Failure to anticipate scarcity (perhaps due to an un-
warrantably optimistic view of future discoveries) will depress resource rentals and hence prices.

2.3   Evidence from the past

It should now be clear that the issues raised in this chapter cannot be
settled *a priori*. Models can be constructed which fit extreme Pessimist
views; but equally models can be constructed which fit extreme Optimist views; while a variety of intermediate models are also possible.
This is a not unusual situation. The modern economist's normal reaction is to arise from his armchair and test the various models against
real-world data.

There have been two major empirical investigations of past trends in
resource scarcity. The first, by Barnett and Morse, looks at trends in
prices and costs of exploitation of particular resources. The second, by
Nordhaus and Tobin, examines resources as an aggregate factor of
production.

The Barnett and Morse study

Barnett and Morse (1963) tested the implications of resource scarcity
on the extraction costs and prices of resource products. The study
related to minerals and fuels, agriculture, forestry and fishing in the
United States over the period 1870–1957, during which the country
'passed from underdevelopment to an advanced economic state' and the
pressure on natural resources increased enormously.

They begin with the 'strong' test of economic scarcity: in the
absence of various alleviating mechanisms, increasing scarcity, involving
pressing ever more inferior resources into use, 'reveal[s] itself in an
increasing trend of unit cost of extractive products'. For extractive
products as a whole, the trend of unit costs (index of labour and
capital input/net output) fell at about 1 per cent p.a. from 1870 to
1920 and nearly 3 per cent p.a. from 1920 to 1957. Of the many
individual resource products, nearly all showed a decline in unit costs,
the only significant exception being forestry. Apparently the effects of
employing lower-quality resources were outweighed by technical
progress and capital accumulation. Barnett and Morse conclude: 'The
evidence shows increasing not decreasing returns . . . the hypothesis
that economic scarcity of natural resources, as measured by the trend

of real cost of extractive output will increase over time in a growing economy is rejected.'

Barnett and Morse pass to a weaker hypothesis: 'that natural resource scarcity is an obstacle to economic growth which, since it operates more strongly in the extractive sector than in the non-extractive sector, will show the effects in a rise in the unit cost of extractive output *relative* to that of non-extractive output'.

The picture is more mixed. In particular, in the earlier period (1870 –1920) *relative* exploitation costs of several items increased, including agriculture, fuels, bituminous coal, forestry products and resources as a whole. However, in the later period (1920–57) decreases were predominant and in particular over-all extraction costs showed a relative fall.

Finally, Barnett and Morse explore trends in the real price of resource products. They note that price relative should follow cost relative apart from 'differential changes in the degree of monopoly [or in] taxes, subsidies and transport costs.'[7] Broadly, these tests, which rely on a completely separate set of data, confirm the results of the relative- cost tests, though there are significant individual differences.

In view of recent concern over the scarcity of various resources, it is instructive to bring these results up to date. This can be done on a rather crude basis using the *United States Statistical Abstract* and the *Minerals Yearbook*.[8] The results are as follows:

(i) Unit costs of all products examined, except copper and, significantly, fish, fall, mostly faster than in earlier periods.

(ii) Relative unit costs of most products fall. The major exceptions are metals as a group, forestry and fishing. Additionally, petroleum and several agricultural products showed a sharp rise in unit costs over the last few years. It is too early to judge the long-term significance of these rises.

(iii) Relative prices of most resource products rose over the period 1957–75, especially over the last few years. The significance of these rises is not clear and doubtless varies from case to case. They could reflect increased monopoly power, or alternatively an increasing royalty element in the price in anticipation of future scarcity; or they may represent purely short-term imbalance between supply and demand triggered by unexpected demand surges or failures in supply. If high prices are expected to persist, this will eventually stimulate increases in supply — a delayed process, however, on account of the heavy investment characteristically involved. This will cause both a fall-back in prices and a rise in unit costs as lower-grade resources are pressed into use; thus the price rises observed recently could be the first signs of Ricardian scarcity, to be mirrored later on in the more fundamentally significant cost series. On the other hand, cost and price rises will tend to stimulate the various scarcity-alleviating mechanisms, in particular technical advance, thus offsetting or even reversing the cost increases. It is too early to be sure.

The Nordhaus and Tobin (1972) study

This was based on an empirical analysis of an aggregate three-factor neoclassical production function for the United States. The three factors are labour, capital and resources (or 'land').[9] The authors search for particular functions which are broadly consistent with historical values of input—output ratios and factor shares in the national income. They begin with a very general discussion, proceeding through a simulation exercise to econometric estimation of the parameters of the function.

The general discussion starts from certain 'stylised facts' characterising the past. In this context the most important of these are:

(i) resource inputs have declined relative to inputs of labour and capital to output;[10]

(ii) the share of resource rents in national income has declined; and

(iii) growth in output has continued unabated.

(i) indicates increasing relative physical scarcity of resources, while (ii) and (iii) suggest that this has been outweighed by other factors. Nordhaus and Tobin suggest substitution of other inputs, especially capital (which has grown rapidly), and resource-augmenting technical progress as possible explanations.

'In an attempt to make this specification more concrete', they proceed to some more sophisticated exercises designed to determine the form and parameters of the production function. They experiment with four forms of constant elasticity of substitution (C.E.S.) production functions, of which the one eventually preferred is:

$$Y = \left\{ a_1 \left[(A_K K)^{\frac{1}{4}} (A_L L)^{\frac{3}{4}} \right]^{-\epsilon} + a_2 (A_R R)^{-\epsilon} \right\}^{-1/\epsilon},$$

where Y = output, K = capital, L = labour, R = resources, A_K, A_L and A_R represent factor-augmenting technical progress, and ϵ is the elasticity of substitution between (augmented) resources and a composite of (augmented) capital and (augmented) labour. Parameter values are chosen and levels and trends of input—output ratios and factor shares predicted and compared with past observations. The predictions of factor shares depend on the standard neoclassical assumption that factors are paid according to their marginal products. Out of 405 simulations, fifty-one are chosen for their correspondence with these features of the past and all of these exhibit an elasticity of substitution between resources and the capital—labour composite greater than unity.

Finally, the function is estimated econometrically[11] with the following results:

(i) elasticity of substitution between resources and the capital — labour composite is about 2;

(ii) technical change is concentrated on augmenting resources — specifically, the rate of resource-augmenting technical change exceeds a weighted average of capital-augmenting and labour-augmenting technical change by 6 per cent p.a.

Nordhaus and Tobin conclude that on the basis of their studies 'natural resources [will not] become an increasingly severe drag on economic growth'.

2.4   Critique of the empirical studies

Of course, resource scarcity has operated as a brake on economic growth, but these studies suggest that in economic terms this scarcity has not increased. Barnett and Morse show that extraction costs of nearly all resources have fallen absolutely and in most cases relatively to costs elsewhere, despite exhaustion of the highest-quality reserves; likewise relative prices of resource products have fallen and with it the share of national income going to resource owners, a result that Nordhaus and Tobin explain in terms of substitution and resource-augmenting technical progress. Rates of growth have everywhere increased.

What of the future? Norhaus and Tobin conclude from their studies that 'growth will accelerate rather than slow down even as natural resources become more scarce in the future'. Elsewhere, Nordhaus (1973a) is slightly more guarded: 'It is possible that the historical ability to find substitutes for scarce resources will vanish, but this would make the future very different from the past.' But even here one is clearly meant to infer that to countenance such a possibility would be very perverse; after all the assumption that conclusions about the future can be drawn from an investigation of the past is the basis of all policy-orientated econometrics, and indeed of more informal work. Nevertheless such a statement does rather prejudge the central issue. It is after all the corner-stone of the Pessimists' position that the future may differ from the past in crucial respects. If such a possibility is to be ruled out *a priori*, the Pessimists' case can be dismissed without the elaborate econometrics of Nordhaus and Tobin (or the statistical computations of Barnett and Morse), which become every bit as superfluous as the elaborate simulations of Meadows.

However, the matter may be put another way. The outcome of Nordhaus and Tobin's study is prejudged by the *form* of the relationships they choose to estimate.[12] The past may be interpreted in many ways (and it is frequently impossible to discriminate between the various interpretations on statistical grounds). In this case technical progress is inserted as an exogenous factor (or factors) subject to exponential trends. Given this, the outcome is inevitable. Suppose instead one assumed that technical-progress parameters followed log-linear trends; production functions embodying such assumptions would doubtless fit the past just as well (since the initial progress of a log-linear trend is approximately exponential) but would have very different implications for the future — technical progress would eventually slow down and then cease, perhaps because all possible discoveries had already been made. Or again a model could be constructed in which technical progress is endogenous, resulting from the application of investment in research and development (see the appendix to this chapter); 'research capital' is then effectively an extra factor of production, eventually subject (presumably) to diminishing returns. Again the implications of such a model are that the growth rate increases for a time but later slows down. This represents an equally valid interpretation of the past with very different implications for the future.

In addition, Nordhaus and Tobin abstract completely from one of the central problems, namely resource depletion. As they admit,[13] their model applies only to *renewable* resources — and then (as they fail to point out) only on the assumption that their quality is being maintained. Their model could be extended to incorporate non-renewable resources in a variety of ways. The obvious way, perhaps, would be to extend R to denote both renewable and non-renewable resources, and replace the assumption that R is constant by one that R is falling. However, this would be misleading in two respects. First, while total natural resource stocks are undoubtedly falling, *known* stocks are still rising as a result of continual discoveries. Their conclusion, which depended on the increasing relative physical scarcity of resource stocks, immediately breaks down. But, more fundamentally, in the case of non-renewable resources it is resource use (or depletion) rather than resource stocks that should be regarded as a factor of production. Resources held in reserve are valued for their contributions not to present but to future production, so that the marginal-product condition used by Nordhaus and Tobin is inapplicable. The value of reserve stocks will in fact be related to anticipations of *future* scarcity. If, for example, resource owners share Nordhaus and Tobin's optimistic assumptions about future developments, reserve stocks will be accorded a rather low value (see Chapter 5). Further, Nordhaus and Tobin's model is not even applicable to *renewable* resources unless their quality is in fact being maintained. It is possible for the land to be over-worked, fisheries over-fished, forests denuded, pesticides used in such a way as to aggravate future pest problems, and so on. In all these cases the resources are in effect being 'mined' and the above critique applies. In general terms current scarcity can be exchanged for future scarcity, problems pushed into the future perhaps in aggravated form. Certain technical 'advances', it may be argued, are not advances at all, but simply more sophisticated methods of hastening resource depletion. So far these postponed (possibly transmuted) problems have evidently been solved or pushed forward again, and Nordhaus and Tobin, in applying their results to the future, are assuming implicitly that this can always be done and hence growth maintained.

The basic issue separating Optimists and Pessimists should now be clear and is perhaps obscured rather than clarified by the elaborate models which have recently been constructed. Optimists believe that technical progress and substitutions of man-made for natural resources will outweigh the increasing relative physical scarcity of resources as they undoubtedly seem to have done in the past. By contrast Pessimists foresee, or at least fear, the eventual failure of technical progress, the advent of problems for which solutions cannot be found or are not found in time.

The nature of the conflict is indeed clearly perceived by Barnett and Morse (1963, p. 236):

The view that improvements must show a diminishing return is implicit in the thought of those who regard most optimistic opinion as 'cornucopian'.

They go on to expound the Optimistic position forcefully:

Yet a strong case can be made for the view that the accumulation of knowledge and technical progress is automatic and self-reproductive in modern economics and obeys a law of increasing returns. Every cost-reducing innovation opens up new possibilities of application in so many new directions that the stock of knowledge, far from being depleted by new developments, may even expand geometrically.

Later they wax lyrical on future possibilities:

The fact is that the technology of low-concentrate resources is in its infancy and one may be confident that effort to discover replacements for depleting resources will uncover potentialities yet undreamed of . . . . One of the vastest [resources] plateaus of all, the sea, is not simply a great stock of resource substance but . . . a continually augmenting stock. Advancing ocean technology could conceivably lead to a 'steady state' equilibrium of a great circular flow process analogous to, but far more complex than, the carbon dioxide cycle. Equally important are the energy plateaus already created by atomic fission and eventually, perhaps, to result from nuclear fusion and solar energy . . . . Hence the physicist's concept of 'available energy' constitutes a plateau of virtually limitless extent.

This passage is quoted at length because it is so characteristic of the Optimists' view of possible future technologies (see, for example, Maddox, 1972; Beckerman, 1974; Bray, 1972). Pessimists are of course unconvinced and point both to the possibility that undoubted technical obstacles to the developments envisaged may prove insuperable and to the possibility of disastrous side-effects. But of course just as one cannot be sure that specific obstacles will be overcome, equally one cannot be sure that they will not; Pessimists, from Malthus on, have made themselves look silly by confident assertions that such and such an obstacle is insuperable (see, for example, Barnett and Morse, 1963).

2.5 Adapting to limits
The above discussion has supported the position neither of the extreme Pessimists nor of the extreme Optimists. Limits to growth are not a certainty but they remain worrying as a possibility. It may even be that, since resource depletion and population growth are involved, resource limitations do not merely halt growth but involve a fall in living standards (see p. 13). In view of these possibilities it is important to

consider how the world could best adapt to whatever limits may exist.

The Pessimist view is that the crisis will appear suddenly and with little warning; inertia will tend to carry the world past the limits with disastrous long-term consequences. This is the 'overshoot and collapse' path examined above (p. 11). This outcome can be avoided but only by explicit social action stemming from a correct diagnosis of the problem sufficiently far in advance (see, for example, Meadows *et al.*, 1972; Goldsmith, 1976).

The Optimist is generally too concerned with disproving the inevitability of limits to growth to give much thought to the difficulties of adaptation, should this be necessary. However, his position may be inferred from his discussion of adaptation to scarcities of a more limited nature. Broadly, he displays great confidence in the ability of economy to adapt to scarcities in a reasonably smooth and painless manner.

Most Optimists place main reliance on market mechanisms to signal incipient scarcity and provide incentives for early adjustment. Suppose, writes Beckerman (1974), that 'The world did run out of some useful resource and none of the economic feed-back mechanisms [as discussed in Section 2.2 above] came to our rescue in time . . . what would happen? The answer is that far less of the end-products in which the material was used would be consumed. The price would have become too high.' The principle can readily be extended to a simultaneous shortage of all resources: there would be a general rise in the prices of natural resources relative to other factors of production, i.e. labour and capital. Aggregate consumption would be curtailed and its pattern directed away from resource-intensive products.

In view of the difficulties associated with a sudden halt to growth (see pp. 10–13) it is crucial that this mechanism should bite early with steadily increasing severity. In a Malthusian world this will occur only in so far as the crisis is anticipated. If, as the Pessimist fears, the crisis appears suddenly and unexpectedly, then the necessary adaptive behaviour will not be triggered. These dangers are increased by most of the complications emphasised by the Optimists which, while they push back the crisis, make the ultimate limits more difficult to foresee. For example, the possibility of harnessing nuclear fusion is one of the factors which makes it difficult to assess the adequacy of energy resources. If decision-makers expect successful development, then current energy prices will be depressed, permitting continued growth and rapid depletion. The failure of this and other developments could lead to a sudden crisis.

On the other hand, varying resource quality and substitution possibilities provide a mechanism for raising prices and braking growth, which depends much less on a correct view of the future.

As successively lower-quality resources are pressed into use, so (in the absence of technical progress) does the cost, and hence the prices, of products embodying these resources rise. Thus, as the M.S.O. is approached, the prices of resource products may be expected to rise continually, even in the absence of any *anticipation* of future scarcity. The limitations placed by finite resources do not impinge suddenly at the point at which M.S.O. is reached, but bite with increasing severity as M.S.O. is approached. This is just what is required to stimulate the process of early adjustment. But while one can assert that heterogeneity does something to facilitate smooth adjustment, one cannot be sure that it will do enough.

Much will depend on the exact form of the relationship between resources used and associated marginal production costs (see Figure 2.3). The firm line shows the Malthusian case: marginal production

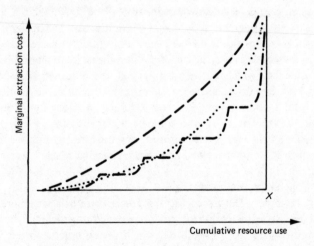

Figure 2.3   **Malthusian and Ricardian scarcity**

costs are constant until, suddenly at X, all resources are in use and costs rise to infinity. The dashed line shows the basic Ricardian case: marginal costs rise slowly and steadily providing with increasing force an incentive to economy and a brake to growth. Clearly a whole spectrum of intermediate cases are possible (for example the dotted line).

The increase in marginal costs may not be steady; rather, there may be a *series* of constant-price plateaus, each higher than the last. In other words there is a sizeable quantity of resources of constant quality and then a sharp drop to another plateau of lower quantity.

For example, in the case of oil, successive plateaus are formed by: (i) reserves below the land, (ii) reserves below the sea, (iii) shale oil and tar, and (iv) conversion of coal. When one is exhausted, production transfers to the next plateau and costs rise substantially. In fact the 'plateaus' do not exhibit constant costs; rather, each type of oil exhibits a Ricardian variation in quality, and the result is the series of broken Ricardian segments depicted by the dash-dot line in Figure 2.3. Crises of adaptation will tend to occur not only as final exhaustion approaches but at each transition between plateaus. It could be argued that the world is currently approaching not the final exhaustion of oil so much as an uncomfortably abrupt transition from low-cost oil beneath the land to higher-cost forms of oil.

Some Optimists (notably Jahoda, 1973, but his comments have been widely echoed) appeal to a second — socio-political — adjustment mechanism: 'It is in the nature of purposeful adaptation that the course of events can be changed dramatically if social constraints are experienced as intolerable . . . . Man's inventiveness in changing social arrangements is without limits, even if not without hazards.' But this, though presented as a criticism of the Pessimists, in no way contradicts their message, which is precisely a call to 'purposeful adaptation' because automatic adaptive mechanisms are considered inadequate. Purposeful adaptation could of course be left until the limits are clear for all to see, but if so one wonders whether Jahoda's optimism is justified. It is at least the Pessimists' view that purposeful adaptation, to be successful, must act well in advance of such a crisis.

2.6   Concluding comments

The only certain feature of the resource situation is its inherent uncertainty. No examination of past experience can yield much insight into future technical possibilities, which are so crucial to any assessment of resource scarcity.

In many ways economic expansion has served to increase the level of uncertainty. First, growth has enormously increased man's capacity to do irreparable harm to the environment. Such harm, the unintentional by-product of modern technology, is increasingly international or global in impact, thus contrasting sharply with the much more local pollution problems of the Middle Ages. One might cite as examples the fears of melting of the polar ice-caps through overheating of the world's atmosphere by excessive energy consumption or diversion of rivers, the possibility of nuclear waste causing widespread genetic mutations or the development of super-germs and super-pests in response to the application of antibiotics and pesticides; while the probability of such horrors is currently in dispute, formerly they were inconceivable. Harm may also be caused by the power of technology being deliberately turned to destructive ends, for example through nuclear war. The benefits of nuclear energy should not be underestimated but neither should the accompanying dangers.[14]

Second, there has, as Barnett and Morse noted, been a marked shift from 'gross mechanical transfomations' to 'chemical processing'. This inflicts on the biological system an increasing range of unfamiliar substances. In many cases living creatures cannot adapt quickly enough and the ecological balance is disturbed. Understanding of these matters is still very imperfect.

Third, the pace of change has accelerated. This aggravates the problems referred to above and makes it more difficult to evaluate the impact. Change will also have a social impact, which even Optimists take seriously. Barnett and Morse, for example, comment that 'The modern resource problem . . . is not diminishing returns, but social adjustment to a variety of adverse indirect effects of technological change and economic growth . . . the capacity of scientific progress to create new problems for society, it appears, has outrun the capacity of social progress to solve them.' Similarly, the Science Policy Research Unit 'put much more emphasis on the political and social limits to growth than on the purely physical limits' (Cole *et al.*, 1973). Moreover, growth acquires its own momentum. People become accustomed to rising living standards and are dissatisfied with static ones. Moreover, if the theory about technology creating new problems for future technology (p. 28) has any validity, then the rate at which new problems emerge increases with the rate of earlier growth, making further technology essential if even current living standards are to be maintained. A pertinent example is the increasing reliance of modern society on abundant energy. The development of alternative sources of energy, at whatever risk or environmental cost, has become almost a necessity.

In short, the possibility that technology *may not* continue to solve all crucial problems is involving the world in increasing risk as a result of the increased scale and rate of growth of man's activity. This can scarcely be disputed. What is less clear is how modern society should act in the face of such uncertainty.

Some commentators, for example Common and Pearce (1973), argue for a *minimisation* of 'survival' risk. This assumes either that 'survival' risk can be minimised without sacrifice of other objectives, for example current consumption, or that 'survival' is of *overriding* importance. Both assumptions seem questionable. Minimising 'survival' risk would involve a very sharp cut-back in all kinds of activities, including, for example, the use of D.D.T. to control malaria in under-developed countries, and the consequences would probably include a marked rise in the current death rate.[15] Their statement certainly seems too strong, and Meade's (1973) vaguer claim is probably more acceptable: 'The disutility of Doom to future generations would be so great that, even if we gave it a low probability and even if we discount future utilities at a high rate . . . we would be wise to be very prudent in our present action.'

But even if this is accepted, it is far from clear, even in general terms, how we may best exercise prudence. Some Pessimists, concentrating on the adverse effects of growth and technical change, suggest that these should be stopped immediately. But, leaving aside the adverse short-run effects, it is not clear that such draconian measures would help even to reduce the risk of Doom. Even current levels of output are leading to a steady depletion of the world's resources and an accumulation of pollutants; to freeze human activity is thus probably not enough to save the world. The allied processes of growth and technical change may not only create serious new problems, but provide essential solutions to existing ones, without which Doom may be inevitable. The policy problem, in this precarious world, cannot be simply one of no change; rather, a more difficult approach is required which aims to decouple predominantly harmful changes from ones which are predominantly beneficial. What this might involve is pursued at length in Chapters 6 and 7.

Appendix: a formal treatment of factor substitution and technical progress

Consider first a conventional two-factor growth model in which output (Y) is related to inputs of labour (L) and capital (K):

$$Y = f(AK, BL). \qquad (1)$$

A and B are technology coefficients rising through time, so that technical progress is factor-augmenting. Differentiating with respect to time:

$$Y = \frac{1}{A}\frac{df}{dK}(AK + KA) + \frac{1}{B}\frac{df}{dL}(BL + LB). \tag{2}$$

Using lower-case letters to denote rates of growth and suffixes to denote elasticities ($f_K = \delta f/\delta K \times K/Y$, etc.):

$$y = f_K(a + k) + f_L(b + l). \tag{3}$$

Assuming constant returns to scale, $f_K + f_L = 1$, and using asterisks to denote *per capita* variables:

$$y^* = (af_K + bf_L) + f_K k^*. \tag{4}$$

The first term represents the contribution of technical progress to growth, the second the contribution of capital accumulation. Along a balanced growth path:

$$y^* = k^* = (af_K + bf_L)/(1 - f_K). \tag{5}$$

With a constant savings ratio, savings $S = \sigma Y$, $s^* = y^*$, k^* tends to r^* and hence to y^*; thus the balanced growth path is approached asymptotically. In the absence of technical progress $af_K + bf_L = 0$, $y^* = k^* = 0$ and output grows *pari passu* with labour.

Now extend the model to include 'renewable resources' (R):

$$Y = f(AK, BL, CR). \tag{6}$$

By analogous reasoning, we obtain (using $r = 0$):

$$y^* = (af_K + bf_L + cf_R) + f_K k^* - f_R l. \tag{7}$$

With a constant savings ratio, y^* tends to k^*, as before, and:

$$y^* = k^* = \frac{(af_K + bf_L + cf_R) - f_R l.}{1 - f_K} \tag{8}$$

If technical progress (the term in the bracket) is sufficiently large relative to the growth of labour (l) and to the elasticity of output with respect to f_R, y^* will be positive. In other words, it is possible for growth to continue indefinitely despite a finite stock of renewable resources. This is the basis of the argument used by the Resource Optimists.

It should be stressed that this argument applies only to a stock of renewable resources. Suppose, instead, resources are entirely non-renewable. There are three cases to be considered:

(i) resources essential to production and exhausted in finite time;

(ii) resources inessential to production (i.e. production possible from capital and labour only) and exhausted in finite time;

(iii) resources not exhausted in finite time.

The first case corresponds closely to the fears of the Pessimists. Clearly, when resources are exhausted, all production ceases and human life ends.

The second case supposes production to be possible without resources. This case seems rather implausible, unless a further class of renewable resources is introduced explicitly, as is in fact done below. Nevertheless it has been investigated by a number of writers (Dasgupta and Heal, 1975; Kay and Mirrlees, 1975; Solow, 1975). When the resource is exhausted, production continues with two factors (capital and labour) and the earlier two-factor model is applicable. Growth in output per head proceeds at a rate approaching the rate of technical progress $(af_K + bf_L)$.

With regard to the third case, the logical possibility that even a finite stock of non-renewable resources may never be exhausted has been demonstrated (p. 20).

If R is used to denote resource *use* (or depletion), equation (1) still applies. However, R must eventually decline, and this $r^* < 0$:

$$y^* = (af_K + bf_L + cf_R) + f_K k^* + f_R r^*. \tag{9}$$

In dynamic equilibrium:

$$y^* = k^* = \frac{(af_K + bf_L + cf_R) + f_K k^* + f_R r^*}{1 - f_K} \tag{10}$$

Once again, if $af_K + bf_L + cf_R$ is sufficiently large relative to f_R and $-r^*$, growth may continue indefinitely.

Renewable and non-renewable resources (R, N) could be distinguished explicitly in a single model. There will be three cases as before. In case (i) non-renewable resources are exhausted in finite time, but since they are also essential to production, human life ceases. In case (ii) non-renewable resources are exhausted in finite time but are inessential to production, so ultimately the model reduces to the three-factor model represented by equations (6) and (8) and the same conclusions apply, in particular that indefinite growth is possible provided technical progress is sufficiently rapid. In case (iii) non-renewable resources are never exhausted:

$$y^* = \frac{(af_K + bf_L + cf_R + df_N) + f_N n^* - f_R l}{1 - f_K}. \tag{11}$$

$f_N n^*$ 0 and, as before, dynamic equilibrium with a positive growth rate is possible provided the term in the bracket is sufficiently large.

So far technical progress has been treated as exogenous. Doubtless some inventions do occur 'by chance' but more typically they are the result of deliberate and costly research effort. This suggests that 'the state of technology', or 'knowledge', might more appropriately be treated as a factor of production (T) which may be augmented by investment in research and development. Without exogenous technical progress $a = b = c = d = 0$, and the condition for dynamic equilibrium is:

$$y^* = \frac{f_N n^* - f_R l}{1 - f_K - f_T}. \tag{12}$$

Since $f_N n^* \to 0$, y^* tends to a negative quantity. Exponential growth is not possible.

The point here is simply that the basic Malthusian argument of diminishing returns to a single factor is being applied to research and development as well as to investment in physical capital. There is no favourable exogenous factor to offset the effect of diminishing returns.

3 FISHERY AND MINE

This chapter investigates the optimal management of renewable resources (as typified by the fishery) and non-renewable resources (as typified by the mine). The analysis is set in a *micro*economic context; the management objective is to maximise the net present value of a profit stream, given the discount rate. The analogous *macroeconomic* problem is treated in Chapter 4.

The analysis is verbal and diagrammatic, although a brief mathematical account using optimal control methods is provided in the appendix. It is also highly simplified, ignoring many features of the fishery and mine which would be vital considerations in real-world management problems, especially those (such as investment requirements) which are common to all industries. This is admissible, since the aim is not to provide a manual for economists in the industries concerned; rather, it is to indicate major principles peculiar to resource industries, to contradict certain common fallacies, and to provide insights which will be valuable in subsequent chapters. The procedure followed is to investigate a simple model rather thoroughly and indicate briefly the effects of important real-world complications.

Each section ends with an analysis of the effects of *common access* (i.e. no restrictions on the number of operators or on the rate of exploitation).

3.1 The Fishery
Simplifying assumptions
Fish stocks can fluctuate wildly and unpredictably due both to climatic variations and in-built cyclical processes resembling models of the trade cycle. Stocks can also follow secular trends as environmental conditions alter. This makes optimal management of a fishery a very complex task. Here attention will be confined to a simpler case in which a constant environment determines a natural equilibrium stock $\bar{s}$ and in which adjustment from a disequilibrium position is smooth. A *logistic* growth process is generally assumed (see, for example, Crutchfield and Pontecorvo, 1969):

$$n = as\,(\bar{s} - s).$$

This embodies, first, the idea of proportionate growth ($n = as$) as exemplified by the dependence of births on population size and, second, the idea that the environment (e.g. food supplies) places a steadily increasing brake as the equilibrium stock is approached. This relation has been found to be a reasonable approximation to a wide variety of biological phenomena (see Pielou, 1969) except at low stock levels. Below a certain critical value of s, stocks will often decline to zero due, for example, to inter-species competition (see Beverton and Holt, 1957). The relationship thus modified is shown in the bottom half of Figure 3.1(a) ($OA\bar{s}$).

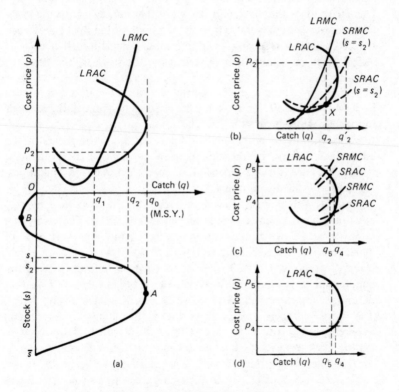

Figure 3.1　The theory of the fishery

Initially no account will be taken of the age structure of the stock or the possibility of selective culling by, for example, the use of large mesh nets. This important complication is considered later (p. 43).

Price is assumed given in competitive markets (the analysis is, however, easily modified to allow for monopoly) and price and cost conditions both assumed invariant over time. The objective is to maximise the N.P.V. of the profits obtained from the fishery *as a whole* (the case of sole ownership or integrated management).

Constant-yield programmes

First, consider fishing at a *constant* rate q. Provided q is not too large, a new equilibrium relationship is reached, such that subtractions from the stock (q) equal natural additions (n). Thus the curve $OA\bar{s}$ represents also the equilibrium relationship between stocks (s) and catch (q). The *maximum sustainable yield* (M.S.Y.) is at A. The associated stock (s_o) falls far short of the maximum stock $(\bar{s})$; the maintenance of the stock at this lower level maximises the rate of growth of the stock, and hence the catch that can be taken without causing depletion. If q exceeds M.S.Y., then no equilibrium is possible and the stock will be fished to exhaustion.

M.S.Y. programmes have received considerable attention, partly because they are often mistakenly assumed to be optimal. In fact their optimality depends on rather special conditions, specifically that both the *discount rate* (i) is zero and fishing is costless. More generally, the curve $OA\bar{s}$ defines the range of possible constant-yield programmes, choice amongst them to depend on cost and demand conditions, together with the discount rate.

Consider fishing costs. For given s (call this the *short run*), average costs may be assumed to be a U-shaped function of q. There will be a family of *SRAC* curves, each corresponding to a different stock level, of which one is drawn in Figures 3.1(b). From these a long-run equilibrium cost curve (*LRAC*) may be derived as follows: in long-run equilibrium, q is functionally related to s ($OA\bar{s}$ in Figure 3.1(a), thus defining a point on each *SRAC* curve (for example X in Figure 3.1(b). The locus of these points gives the unique long-run relationship between average costs and output (Figure 3.1(a) and (b)). Corresponding to these average-cost curves are the marginal-cost curves as shown.

The shape of the *LRAC* curve is unusual: s and hence *LRAC* are two-valued functions of q; thus for each q there are two possible values for *LRAC*, the lower corresponding to the larger stock, the higher to the smaller stock. Accordingly the average-cost curve bends back on itself. Points on the upper branch are apparently inefficient, in that the same constant yield may be achieved at lower cost on the lower branch. Correspondingly the *LRMC* curve rises to infinity at M.S.Y.

The *LRAC* curve may be expected to have a minimum as shown as, at low fishing levels, economies of scale will tend to outweigh the adverse impact of fishing on stocks, while at high levels the converse is true. Thus fishing costs are minimised at q_1 but this will be optimal only if price $(p) = p_1$. If $p < p_1$, constant-yield fishing is unprofitable.

The maximum sustainable profit (M.S.P.) is obtained by equating p with *LRMC* giving the point X (as shown). Evidently $q_1 < q_2 < q_0$. Early economic analyses of the fishery (for example, Gordon, 1954) identified this point as the optimum and concluded that when costs are taken into account, catches should be held below the maximum sustainable level. Notice that, in general, $p > LRAC$ and the fishery earns a rent. This indicates neither inefficiency nor monopoly in the product market (p is assumed given). It is a return to physical scarcity, and as such performs a useful function. It should not be dissipated, though arguably it should be distributed differently.

However, this conclusion is valid only for a zero discount rate. Suppose s and q have been adjusted to obtain M.S.P. as above. Now consider a permanent increase in q to, say, q_3. Stocks fall to a new equilibrium s_3 and average fishing costs are increased. What has so far been established is that once stocks have fallen to s_3, the new programme is inferior to the M.S.P. programme. *With a zero discount rate* (and an infinite time horizon) this is indeed sufficient to establish the superiority of the latter. But while stocks are falling from s_2 to s_3, the benefits of increased output are being reaped without bearing the full costs of the ultimate fall in stocks. There is an initial period during which the former effect dominates, i.e. the new programme earns higher profits initially but lower profits later on. *With a positive discount rate* the new programme may be preferred and generally it may be concluded that with $i > 0$ it is optimal to *raise* output above the M.S.P. level. With a customary 10 per cent p. a. discount rate (cf. Chapter 5) the effect can be highly significant (see Clark, 1976).

It may even be optimal to raise q above M.S.Y. This may be seen by considering the other polar case, $i = \infty$. It is then optimal to equate p with *SRMC*. Suppose, initially, $q = q_2$, $s = s_2$. This is the zero discount rate optimum and $p = LRMC > SRMC$ (because the latter neglects the adverse impact of fishing on stocks). Hence equating p with *SRMC* implies an increase in q and consequently a fall in s, and an upward shift of the *SRMC* curve. A new short-run equilibrium is chosen. The process continues until the q that is optimal in the short run is consistent with the associated stock, and *SRAC* = *LRAC*. Two long-run equilibria, corresponding to alternative prices, are illustrated in Figure

3.1(c). For $p = p_2$ fishing remains on the 'efficient' lower branch. However, for high p (for example $p = p_3$) it is optimal to fish on the 'inefficient' upper branch. In this case, while the cost of landing this catch could be reduced by fishing on the lower branch, to do so would involve a short-term reduction in catch while stocks were being built up which is not judged worth while at an infinite discount rate. Thus the conclusions that it cannot be optimal to fish on the upper branch is not valid for an infinite, or indeed any positive, discount rate.

Before leaving the inifite discount rate case, consider the implications of constant short-run costs. Then $p = SRMC = SRAC = LRAC$. There are no profits (above 'normal profits' which are assumed to be included in costs) once equilibrium has been reached. Sustained profits have been sacrificed to the short-run gains associated with heavy fishing initially.

For a positive but finite discount rate it is probably clear (a proof is given in the appendix) that the optimal programme is intermediate between the two polar cases. In other words, stocks are maintained at a lower level than the zero discount rate optimum, but at a higher rate than the infinitie discount rate optimum. The higher the discount rate and the higher the price of fish, the more likely it is to be optimal to fish on the upper branch.

So far attention has been focused on the long-run equilibrium. The problem of the optimum approach to this point has been considered only in the special case of an infinite discount rate. The general problem is more difficult, though normally the following marginal condition will be satisfied: price equals *SRMC* plus marginal *user cost*, where the latter denotes the impact of q on future profits via the level of stock. The analogous expression for mineral extraction is discussed further below (p. 49). It may be shown (see appendix) that under a wide variety of conditions it is optimal for q and s to converge smoothly and monotonically to the long-run optimum found already.

Other possibilities

Eventual constancy is not inevitable, however, even supposing no changes in the underlying economic or biological conditions. First, if p and/or i are sufficiently high, it may be optimal to fish the stock to exhaustion. This could be optimal even for a zero discount rate: the optimal constant-yield programme could be a point of minimum loss (i.e. $p < p_1$), while at the same time, if there are strong economies of scale, it may be possible to gain transitory profits by heavy fishing until the stock is exhausted. In practice fishing will be abandoned before literal exhaustion occurs; however intense fishing is in the 'final' period, some fish will escape. If the resultant stock is greater than *OB* (Figure 3.1 (a)), the stock will recover and fishing will then resume; but if it is less than *OB* even the abandonment of fishing will be insufficient to save the stock. In the case of most fish fertility is so high that the critical level is rarely reached, but several species of animal have been hunted to extinction.

More gernally, if economies of scale are strong, it may be optimal to alternate between periods of heavy fishing and periods of zero fishing during which stocks are allowed to recover (see Hanneson, 1975). The chief obstacle to this programme is the heavy cost associated with varying activity, but this may sometimes be avoided by the rotation of fishing fleets between different fisheries. (Such a programme is analogous to the agricultural practice of leaving fields fallow in rotation.)

Selective culling. For any size of catch the growth of the stock can be increased by selective culling, for example by the avoidance of breeding seasons or grounds or by the use of large mesh nets which allow the smaller, faster-growing fish to escape. An interesting problem is the optimum size of net.

But consider first a simpler problem, the optimum rotation period (i.e. the period between planting and felling) in forestry. Trees and fish both follow the growth curve shown in Figure 3.2. Growth in weight, and hence in economic value, increases absolutely at first and then slows as maturity is reached at *B*. Felling at *A* yields timber of net value *OA* every *ON* years, i.e. an average annual income given by

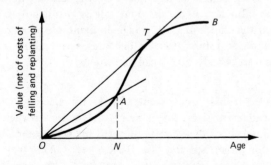

Fig. 3.2 The optimal culling age

the slope of the radial *OA*. Hence annual income is maximised by felling at *T*. This is the maximum sustainable profit (M.S.P.) and is optimal for a zero discount rate. Notice that trees are not allowed to reach full maturity. It may seem surprising that trees should not be left standing while the value is increasing faster than the (zero) discount rate. However, early felling allows the space to be occupied by new trees which will soon be growing much more rapidly.

An *immediate* increase in income can be obtained by reducing the age of felling. At a positive discount rate this consideration shortens the optimum rotation period. Consider a shortening of the rotation period from t to $t - \delta t$. There is an immediate gain. δG, but a reduction in the N.P.V. of the sustained yield of $\delta Y/i$. In the optimum position these must be equal, i.e. $dY/dt = idG/dt$. The higher the discount rate, the more weight will be attached to G, and hence the shorter will be the rotation period.

In its essentials this analysis applies to the fishery, but with two complications stemming from the uncertainty of catching any particular fish. First, since some fish in the 'eligible' age classes will always escape, mesh size will determine the age *structure* of the catch; thus, in place of the rate of growth of the age group (*OT*), consideration must be given to the average rate of the growth of the various age groups caught. Second, the size and age structure of the catch depends both on mesh size and intensity of fishing effort. Thus this analysis must be integrated with our earlier analysis (see Beverton and Holt, 1957; Clark, 1976).

Artificial regeneration. Some fisheries are restocked artificially. Likewise, pheasants are bred and forests and other land crops planted. Such artificial regeneration is an investment activity and the normal criteria apply. The influence of the discount rate is worth noting. The main effect is on the choice of stock: a high discount rate encourages species offering a quick return; thus it encourages agriculture rather than forestry and softwoods rather than hardwoods.

Stock value. It has been assumed that fish are stocked solely as potential catch. However, they may be valued also for their beauty or scientific interest or their contribution to the ecosystem (for example as food for other species). Similarly, trees and other renewable resources may have important values as stock. This consideration will tend to militate against depletion, and especially against exhaustion.

The common-access problem. Most fisheries are bedevilled by *common access,* that is any one or any firm may catch fish. In many cases there are restrictions of various kinds, though these are generally inadequate and inefficient. Before considering these (in Chapter 6) it is useful to examine the case of totally unrestricted access. It will be shown that under such circumstances:

(i) catches are socially excessive;
(ii) exhaustion of the stock is much more likely than under sole ownership; and
(iii) catches may be taken at unnecessarily heavy cost – i.e. production may be on the upper branch of the cost curve even when production on the lower branch is optimal.

To begin with a digression – on *road congestion* – an example which will be familiar to many economists, and which illustrates part of the problem. The number of cars (assumed identical) wishing to use a stretch of road depends upon the journey time and is given by *DE* in Figure 3.3(b) Figure 3.3(a) shows how the journey time depends on the density. Up to *A* traffic flows freely. Beyond *A* congestion increases until, eventually, traffic comes to a standstill. Noting that the number of cars per hour = density × length of road/journey time, and is thus inversely proportional to the slope of the radial in Figure 3.3(a), this relationship may be translated into Figure 3.3(b). *B* is the point of maximum flow, and if more cars than this attempt to use the road the flow is actually reduced. As with the sustained-yield fishery, the cost curve bends back on itself. The equilibrium is the point *X* in Figure 3.3(b). However, this exceeds the optimal use. The marginal driver takes into account his own journey time (the average journey time at *X*) but ignores the effect of his journey on others. The total increase in journey time is in fact:

$$\frac{d}{dn} \text{ (Total journey time)} = \frac{d}{dn} (nt) = t + n \frac{dt}{dn} = t (1 + \text{elasticity } t (n)),$$

1 + elasticity $t(n)$ is the external cost of the marginal journey in terms of time. The social optimum is the point *Y*, where the net benefit of the marginal journey as indicated by the demand curve equals the marginal impact on journey time.

It may be noted that if demand is higher, at *D'E'*, the equilibrium is on the upper branch of the curve (*X'*). Not only is the flow socially excessive (the optimal flow is *Y*) but the associated journey times are unnecessarily large since the same flow could be accommodated at *Z'*.

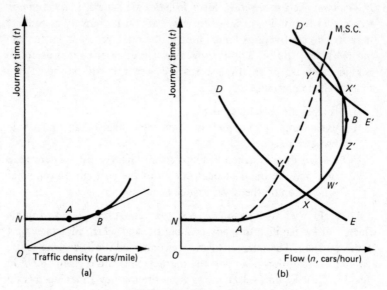

Figure 3.3   Road congestion

In this example congestion is an instantaneous phenomenon and there is no lasting impact on the resource (road space). Now consider the case of the fishery.

Reference back to Figure 3.1(d) reveals the formal similarity of the problem. However, while the essence of the problem is the same — that individual fishing units fail to consider the non-priced impact of their activities on other units — the analysis is complicated by the time dimension.

Here the external effect is precisely the long-run impact on the stock (if there are n units, then $1/n$th of this impact, a negligible proportion when n is large, falls on each unit), and hence operation under common access will be identical to the operation of the sole owner using an infinite discount rate. Specifically, individual units will maximise short-run profits by setting $p = SRMC$. Common access implies profits, i.e. $p = SRAC$. This yields the familiar result that each unit will be of optimal size and that $SRAC = SRMC$, i.e. constant costs. Also, for equilibrium, $SRAC = LRAC$. Hence, as before $p = SRMC = SRAC = LRAC$ (Figure 3.1(d)). For a finite discount rate, fishing activity exceeds, and stock falls short of, the optimal level, and production in the upper branch is more likely than under single ownership (it occurs whenever $p > p^*$). Clearly also, since future impacts are ignored, exhaustion is more likely. The distortion is the *user cost,* which depends on the impact of fishing on future profits via depletion.

Notice also that common access destroys all incentive to practise *selective culling,* or *artificial regeneration,* or *culture,* the benefits of which accrue via long-run impacts on the stock. Small-mesh nets will be used, and fishing will occur in breeding seasons and breeding grounds. In forestry, trees will be felled without reference to age (provided only that price exceeds felling cost), and it will not be worth while to plant, weed or fertilise.

As demand grows, overfishing becomes increasingly common. In fishery after fishery catches have plummeted, despite increasingly sophisticated gear, reflecting mainly the decline in stocks (see Table 3.1). The first signs of falling catches at a world level are evident in the final column.[1]

Table 3.1   Time series of catch, selected species (annual rate)

	Blue Whale (thousands)	Fin Whale (thousands)	Sperm Whale (thousands)	Pacific Sardine (10^8 lb)	New England Sea Herring (10^8 lb)	Mid-Atlantic Menhaden (10^8 lb)
1931–5	22	8	1	7	0.5	1
1936–40	15	22	2	*12*	0.4	1
1941–5	3	4	1	11	0.8	2
1946–50	5	13	2	7	*1.5*	4
1951–5	2	*23*	10	3	1.1	6
1956–60	1	*23*	18	1	*1.5*	7
1961–5	0	10	26	0	1.1	5
1966–70	0	6	25	0	0.7	0
1971–	0	2	20	0	0.7	1

	England and Wales				Scottish	
	Cod (10^6 cwt)	Haddock (10^6 cwt)	Halibut (10^6 cwt)	Herring (10^6 cwt)	Halibut (10^6 cwt)	World (10^6 tonnes)
1938	6.4	*18*	0.6	2.6	0.33	22
1948	6.1	14	0.5	2.4	0.67	20
1951	*6.8*	15	0.5	1.5	*0.70*	24
1960	5.3	15	0.5	0.3	0.39	41
1970	5.9	8	0.1	0.3	0.13	*71*
1971	5.1	7	0.2	0.2	0.12	*71*
1972	4.7	8	0.2	0.2	0.09	66
1973	4.7	10	0.1	0.1	0.09	67
1974	4.2	9	0.1	0.2	0.07	70

Note: the maximum values in each column are italicised.
Sources: *Statistical Abstract of the United States*; *United States Historical Statistics*; *Sea Fisheries Statistical Tables*; *United Nations Yearbooks of Fishery Statistics*.

3.2   The mine

Turn now to non-renewable resources represented by the mine. Begin by considering the simplest possible case in which there are no capital costs, only operating costs, and these depend solely on the current rate of extraction (see Figure 3.4).

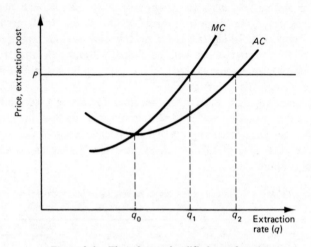

Figure 3.4   The mine: a simplified cost function

Consider two extraction plans with some intuitive appeal. The first is to extract q_1, following the standard profit-maximising rule, $p = MC$. Evidently this neglects the essential feature of the non-renewable resource that each unit can be extracted only once. In deciding whether to extract a marginal unit of ore now, the mine-owner must satisfy himself not merely that current profits are thereby increased but that this increase outweighs the reduction in future profits arising from the associated reduction in future extraction.

The second attractive-looking plan, at least in conditions where price and the cost functions are constant over time, is to minimise the *total* cost of extraction over the life of the mine. Such a policy is the basis of the 'maximum efficient recovery' programmes widely used in the regulation of petroleum extraction in the United States (Wunderlich, 1967). It is achieved by producing at the minimum average cost point, q_0. This indeed is the appropriate policy in the special case where the interest rate, i, is zero; but for a positive interest rate it neglects the advantage of deferring costs to later time periods.

In fact the optimal plan is characterised by two conditions. First, *the discounted value of marginal profits (λ) nust be constant, i.e. the marginal profit must rise at a rate equal to the rate of interest (i),* for if marginal discounted profits in period t_1 exceed those in t_2, then the N.P.V. of the profit stream could be increased by transferring marginal extraction from t_2 to t_1 and the extraction plan could not be optimal. There are several alternative ways of looking at this important result: firstly, the opportunity cost of current marginal extraction includes the impact on future profits (λ), variously referred to as the *user cost* or *depletion cost*; second, the condition may be expressed in terms of *resource rentals* — since the value of the last unit extracted equals the value of the first unit not extracted (assuming a continuous marginal-cost function), the value of the marginal resource in the ground must also rise with i. Resources in the ground are, after all, *assets* which must, at the margin, earn a return equal to that obtainable on other assets.

The analysis is so far restricted to times at which output takes place. Clearly this will only be when a positive profit can be earned. This condition is determined by another, that the (discounted) profit earned must exceed the alternative (discounted) profit that could be earned by transferring the units of extraction to other periods. Thus we have the second condition, i.e. *extraction takes place at time t if and only if the average discounted profit (for at least one rate of extraction) exceeds the opportunity cost of extraction, i.e. the (constant) marginal discounted profit in other periods (λ).*

Together the two conditions determine the optimal plan uniquely, and throw light on our initial assumption that all the stock is mined ultimately. For any *given* value of λ, the levels of production (sometimes zero) are determined from the demand and cost conditions and hence total extraction found. This may be plotted against λ (see Figure 3.5).

Clearly the higher is λ , the lower will be total extraction. There are two cases to consider:

(i) Total resources, $OX \leqslant OZ$ (as shown). The resource constraint is binding, i.e. it would be profitable to expand production beyond that permitted by resource limitations. *A fortiori,* profits are maximised by extraction up to the permitted limit. The appropriate value of λ is immediately derived (λ_x).

(ii) Total resources, $OX > OZ$. In this case the resource constraint is not binding. Thus much of the resource is left in the ground because there is no time at which it is profitable to mine it. In this case $\lambda = 0$. In each period price is simply equated with marginal extraction cost, since user costs equals zero.

Does this analysis allow conclusions to be drawn about the path of

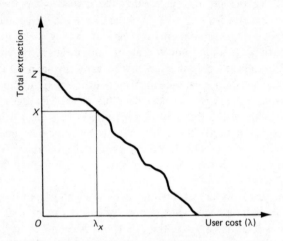

Figure 3.5   User cost, total extraction and resource stocks

q_1 or about the effect of a change in the interest rate? Consider, first, a rather special case in which both price and the cost function are constant over time. (for example Herfindahl, 1967). Costs *exclude* normal profits.

Marginal profit at time t is given by the distance between p and the appropriate points on the *MC* curve (Figure 3.4). Now this magnitude increases exponentially through time at the same rate as i, implying a steady *decrease* in the rate of extraction through time. Extraction finally ceases when the discounted average profit equals the discounted marginal profit, i.e. when q_0 is reached. Again, there are an infinity of extraction paths consistent with these conditions and that one must be chosen which reaches q_0 just as the resource stock is exhausted. (Note that under these assumptions, if extraction takes place at all, exhaustion will occur and $\lambda > 0$. Why?)

A lowering of the interest rate will slow the fall in *MC* and hence in the rate of extraction. Since the final rate of extraction is unaffected it is easily seen that the life of the mine will be extended (see Figure 3.6). In the extreme case, $i = 0$, output will be constant at q_0.

While this is a special case, the conclusions may be readily extended to cover curves in which price (or marginal revenue) and the cost function vary over time, provided the marginal profit function does not rise as fast or faster than i. If it does, then it is easy to see that the rate of extraction will rise over time.

In this connection it is interesting to note that mined products are

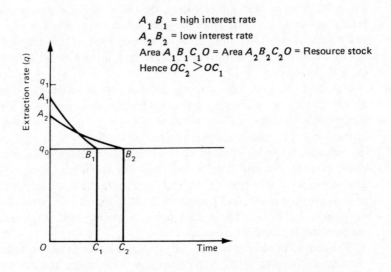

Figure 3.6 The effect of the interest rate on the extraction path

also assets and, in the absence of storage costs and possibly deterioration, their prices too should rise at rate i. This implies that marginal extraction costs rise at rate i in the optimal plan. In this case the rate of extraction rises over time. This conclusion would be reinforced by a similar fall in the cost function. However, the qualification is important: storage is expensive and quite unnecessary when storage in the ground is costless; it is normally undertaken only to meet short-term fluctuations in demand or to take advantage of short-term fluctuations in product prices.

Monopoly.

Before leaving this simple model, consider the effects of monopoly on the extraction plan. The elementary result, that the monopolist will restrict output below the competitive level, is often unthinkingly applied to mineral resources (for example, Kay and Mirrlees, 1975). However, the analogy is somewhat misleading and the result, though not wholly false, must be qualified.

The simple argument that if $p = MC$, $MR < MC$ is, in the resource case, not conclusive. For this is equally true in *all* periods in which production takes place; it is thus not clear that production will be transferred from earlier periods to later ones. For example, if, under the perfectly competitive plan, $a = MR/p$ (degree of monopoly) and

$\beta = p/MC$ are constant through time, then monopoly ownership will involve no such departure from the competitive plan. While a and β will doubtless vary over time, there is no presumption that they will change in such a way as to retard, rather than bring forward, output (Stiglitz, 1976).

However, there are two other possibilities to be considered. The first is that the production span is extended into new periods, in particular ones *beyond* the competitive production span. This could happen only if the stock constraint is binding. In the period immediately following exhaustion the maximum average discounted profit is only just less than $p-MC$ (also discounted) in periods of production. But this latter considerably exceeds the marginal profit to the monopolist in these periods ($MR-MC$). Hence the monopolist can raise the N.P.V. of this profit stream by holding back output and hence extending the production span.

The second possibility is that some of the resource extracted under the competitive plan is left in the ground, not for later extraction but permanently. This will occur whenever the production constraint is not binding, even under competition, or when it ceases to be so under monopoly. If, for example, $\lambda = 0$ and hence $p-MC = 0$ under competition, then $MR-MC < 0$, and output should be reduced. These two possibilities are not mutually exclusive.

In short there is no presumption that monopoly will shift output from earlier to later periods of the competitive production plan; but production may be extended to new, typically later, periods and more of the stock may be permanently 'conserved'.

Variable ore quality.
We establish the important result (used in Chapter 2) that it will generally be optimal to extract the highest-quality ores first.

Consider, first, a mine with two grades of ore, denoted by subscripts 1 and 2. Suppose each ore is extracted under constant costs. If price is also constant the problem is trivial since output is confined to the period in which the discounted value of price minus unit cost is a maximum. Suppose, however, that the mine is a monopolist. This constrains output of the two ores together. We first show that the higher-quality ore will be exhausted before mining of the lower-quality ore begins. To see this consider the contrary case where some of grade 1 ore is mined at time t and some of grade 2 ore is mined at the earlier time T. Suppose a little more (Δq) of period t's output is taken from grade 2 ore and a little more (Δq) of period T's output is taken from grade 1 ore. The total output and hence revenue in each of the two periods is unchanged, but the discounted cost is reduced by $(C_1 - C_2)(1 + i)t - T$. Thus keeping the time profile of total output constant, discounted costs can be reduced, and hence discounted profits increased, by bringing forward extraction from grade 1 ore until this is no longer possible, i.e. when grade 1 ore is exhausted.

The same result may be derived under perfect competition when costs are constrained by some factor operating on *total* output (for example the supply of labour, or finance for investment) according to some function such as:

$$C = C^*(q_1 + q_2) + C^{**}(q_2).$$

The reader may work through this case for himself.

These are special cases, though important ones. In other cases it is possible for both grades to be mined simultaneously. For example, if demand is perfectly competitive and cost a separable function of the extraction of each ore. $C = C^*(q_1) + C^{**}(q_2)$, outputs in any period will be chosen to equate marginal costs (including user costs) from each ore.

These results generalise readily to n grades of ore or to a continuum of ore qualities. Under certain circumstances, then, the mine-owner will work steadily through the sequence of ore grades from the best to the worst; extraction costs will depend on the grade of ore currently mined, which depends in turn on cumulative prior production.

It has been suggested (Nordhaus, 1973b; Heal, 1976) that varying ore quality provides an important exception to the principle that resource rentals rise at rate i. It is important to understand why and in what sense this occurs. Consider two ore grades. $A_1 B_1$ and $A_2 B_2 C_2$ (Figure 3.7) represent the time paths of the resource rentals of the high- and low-grade ores respectively. Both rise exponentially according to the standard principle (the reader should refer back to the third paragraph of this section and satisfy himself that the principle is not undermined by the coexistence of two or more ore grades). The higher-grade ore naturally commands the higher rental and is used first. The lower-grade ore, though not mined, is still of value on account of its future potential. At t the higher-grade ore is exhausted and the lower-grade ore begins to be worked. Now consider the time path of the rental of currently worked ore: this rental rises exponentially along $A_1 B_1$, falls discretely to B_2 and then rises exponentially along $B_2 C_2$. If, however, the variation in ore quality is *continuous*, the exponentially rising segments are obscured by the depressing effect of the continuous decline in ore quality. If the latter is sufficiently strong, the over-all trend could even be downward. Nevertheless it remains true that the rental associated with any particular unit of ore rises exponentially at rate i.

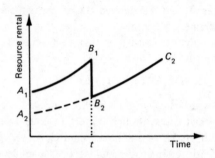

Figure 3.7   Resource rentals of two grades of ore

Costs dependent on cumulative prior production

If a bore-hole is sunk into a field of oil (or gas), the oil will be forced up by the natural pressure in the field. The more oil is extracted, the more the pressure falls and the lower the rate at which oil rises to the surface. The initial rate can be maintained by pumping oil to the surface or by filling the field with fluid to maintain the pressure. However, both these expedients are costly. Thus the greater the quantity of oil previously extracted, the higher the costs associated with any given flow.

Again, consider a large body of ore extending deep into the ground. Under these conditions the depth of mining and hence the cost of bringing the ore to the surface continuously increases. In this case, too, extraction costs depend on the quantity of ore previously extracted.

A third example is the mine containing varying ore grades just considered. Extraction cost depends on the quality of ore currently worked, which depends on cumulative prior production.

Of course, the basic principles are not affected by this complication. Account must still be taken of the *user cost* of extraction, but this must be considered more widely in terms not only of eventual exhaustion but in terms of the higher cost of obtaining subsequent units. The analysis is too complex for verbal treatment. It remains true that the higher the interest rate, the more the extraction plan will be tilted toward the present, but otherwise there are no simple intuitive results.

Capital costs

Mining is an unusually capital-intensive industry and the ratio of capital to operating costs is unusually high. Some writers are correspondingly scornful of the kind of theory presented here. For example, Adelman (1971) writes 'user cost is [not] a helpful concept because it assumes the unknown we should be solving: the future price which itself depends on future user cost . . . let us turn to a more important aspect: investment decisions'.

In defence of the standard theory three things may be said. First, user cost and investment decisions interact, and a full theory would include both. However, explicit treatment of investment unnecessarily complicates the exposition without adding much of value, at least at this level of generality.

Second, user cost is unimportant only if an optimistic view is taken of technical progress, and so on, so that extraction cost may be expected to fall and/or if the discount rate is high. On other assumptions user costs are high and important. It is a crucial role of this analysis to bring out this point.

Third, this kind of theory is not intended to illumine individual decisions in the mining industry, for which a thorough grounding in investment analysis (under uncertainty) would be essential. Rather, it is intended to illumine broad issues in resource economics. Investment decisions, under varying degrees of uncertainty, are in no way peculiar to extractive industries; the unique feature of the latter relates to *exhaustion* – of particular mines or particular grades of ore, and arguably of the whole stock – and hence the user cost.

But it is necessary to consider what effect the introduction of capital costs has on the analysis. One obvious effect is that output is not continuously and costlessly variable: the scale of plant determines the optimum scale of operation, departures from which are costly; a large increase in output could perhaps be achieved by further investment but often with a gestation lag of several years. The result is that plans exhibiting secular trends in output will not be optimal (especially for individual small firms); the optimal plan is more likely to consist of a series of steps, or even a constant output level. Nevertheless the direction of the theoretical trend is likely to indicate correctly the direction of the steps.

A much more important point, which has received near-universal neglect by resource theorists, concerns the impact of the interest rate. The standard result that an increase in the interest rate brings forward extraction depends crucially on the absence of capital costs.

The rate of depletion is closely related to the scale of plant installed. A higher interest rate both encourages depletion *per se* and at the same time discourages investment in the plant which is essential to economical extraction. The over-all impact is uncertain. At one extreme suppose, either because of a high interest rate or a very high level of stocks, the conservation motive is very weak. Then the dominant effect of a rise in the interest rate is to increase the opportunity cost of investment, and hence the scale of equipment and the rate of extraction are reduced. At the other extreme suppose the interest rate is low, exhaustion is imminent and at the same time capital is shortlived, thus barely distinguishable from operating costs. Now the dominant effect of a rise in the interest rate is to reduce the opportunity cost of extraction, the rate of which is therefore increased. It is frequently the case (though this does depend on the other parameter values) that, as the rate of interest increases from 0 to ∞, the optimal rate of extraction first falls and then rises.

Common access

Any motive towards conservation depends on property rights. If, as is usually the case, rights to mine a particular deposit are vested exclusively in a single owner, then the opportunity cost of extraction, i.e. forgoing profits from later extraction, are borne by the owner.

However, there are some important cases where property rights are not defined so satisfactorily. The best-known example is a gas or oil field tapped by several (say w) independently owned bore-holes. Rights to extract from any particular bore-hole are singly owned but since the oil (or gas) is *fugacious*, that is (like fish) it flows freely through the field, it goes to the owner who gets it out first. The bore-holes are effectively competing for the same oil, competing without proper mediation by the price mechanism. The opportunity cost (or user cost) of extraction from each bore-hole is not now borne by the owner of that bore-hole but is shared amongst all those with access to the field. Each, instead of producing where:

p = marginal extraction cost plus marginal user cost,

produces where:

p = marginal extraction cost plus $\frac{1}{n}$ marginal user cost $\approx$ marginal extraction cost, for large n.

Certain costs are ignored. Hence production is overstimulated, the field is exploited too rapidly and the total quantity of oil extracted is reduced by the increase in the rate of extraction.

If we take the argument one stage back and examine the incentive to sink bore-holes, it is clear that this decision is also taken without reference to the effect of a new bore-hole on the profitability of existing bore-holes. A new bore-hole will be sunk (by anyone with the necessary rights, for example an owner of property above the field) whenever such an investment earns a positive private return. Since this rate of return is calculated without reference to the user cost of additional extraction, the result is an excessive number of bore-holes. Typically the same quantity of oil could be extracted more cheaply from fewer, larger bore-holes (see Davidson, 1963).

The demarcation of an oil *field* is not as clear as this analysis may suggest. Frequently oil is borne in rock of varying permeability (See Adelman, 1971). This complicates considerably the quantification of common resource distortions and complicates the problem of devising a remedy. However, the general principles are clear enough: the individual producer produces where:

$$p = \text{marginal extraction cost plus } a \text{ user cost.}$$

where a is the fraction of the user cost which falls on him and depends on the degree of permeability between his bore-hole and other parts of the field. The external cost is $(1 - a)$ user cost.

The effect of common access may be illustrated using Figure 3.4 (p. 48). It has been shown that, under single ownership, extraction falls from below q_1 to q_0. Under common access whenever $p > AC$ it will be profitable to increase extraction. Hence extraction is at q_2 and remains at that level throughout.

Oil fields are the best known but by no means the only case. It is frequently the case (for example in the United States: see Krutilla and Fisher, 1975) that the initial assignment of mining rights on public or otherwise 'unowned' lands or waters is determined by the 'law of capture' or 'finders keepers'. Clearly this establishes a strong motive to search, to pre-empt other searchers. An opportunity cost of finding minerals is that these minerals are no longer available to be found by someone else at a later date.

Deep-sea nodules, especially those rich in manganese, may be an important resource of the future (see Leipziger and Mudge, 1976). The legal position is obscure. If exclusive mining rights to particular areas of the ocean are not established, then there will clearly be a problem of common access. Even if rights are assigned to finders of the nodules (and companies are beginning to lodge claims with international courts), exploration will be subject to common access. There is the further problem that nodules are partially fugacious and may cross any boundaries that may be assigned; moreover, it may be possible to influence such movements, for example by suction.

3.3   Summary and conclusions

The operator should normally equate price (or marginal revenue) with marginal extraction cost (*MEC*) *plus* marginal user cost (*MUC*)[2]. The latter reflects the impact of current extraction on future profits via depletion. In the case of the mine *MUC* or royalty rises with the discount rate. Neglect of user cost will lead to over-exploitation.

In the case of a renewable resource, a maximum sustainable yield (M.S.Y.) policy is generally not optimal, for it neglects extraction costs. At a zero discount rate it will generally be optimal to produce at a lower level and a higher stock, but with a positive discount rate no general conclusion can be drawn. If the stock is initially above that associated with the optimal yield, a period of depletion is of course indicated. Exhaustion of the stock cannot necessarily be dismissed as non-optimal (even at a zero discount rate).

In the case of renewable resources, there is no virtue in indefinite conservation unless extraction is too costly to be profitable or the stock has a value *per se*.

Except in special cases no conclusions can be drawn concerning whether the rate of exploitation should rise or fall over time.

The optimal rule of depletion is generally *very* sensitive to the discount rate. Typically the higher the discount rate, the greater the optimal rate of depletion. However, it is not sufficiently appreciated that this conclusion may be reversed in the presence of heavy capital requirements.

Many resource activities are bedevilled by common access. Typically this leads to a total neglect of user cost, equivalent to using an infinite discount rate. Depletion is correspondingly excessive. Further, there is no incentive to practise selective culling or to enhance the stock, for example by planting or fertilisation.

Appendix: an optimal control formulation

This appendix is written primarily for those NOT versed in optimal control methods, but familiar with elementary calculus and Lagrange multipliers (see Dorfman, 1969, for a fuller account). Mathematicians may consult Intrigilator (1971) for a fully rigorous treatment and Smith (1977) for survey of the application of the theory to resource problems.

Notation

q = catch, s = stocks, $c(s, q)$ = total cost, p = price, i = discount rate, t = time, q and s are functions of time but the time subscripts are omitted where there is no ambiguity. The cost function $c(s, q)$ and the price p are assumed constant over time.

Problem

Maximise the *objective function*, discounted profits:

$$W = \int_0^\infty [pq - c(q, s)] e^{-it} dt, \tag{1}$$

subject to the *constraint* (expressing the growth of the stock):

$$Z = \dot{s} - f(s) + q = 0. \tag{2}$$

It is this relationship, through which a decision in one period affects the whole future profit stream, which is the essence of optimal control. The problem is formulated in continuous time, which, when the principles have been grasped, is more convenient and natural than the more familiar discrete time analysis.

Approach

The stages in the solution are:
   (i)   form a 'Lagrange-like' expression, $W + \int \lambda_t Z \, dt = 0$;
   (ii)   after some manipulation to eliminate s, differentiate to obtain marginal conditions for a maximum which can be given an economic interpretation;
   (iii) eliminate λ and $\dot{\lambda}$ to obtain expressions for $\dot{q}$ and $\dot{s}$ in terms of q and s;
   (iv)   set $\dot{q} = \dot{s} = 0$ to obtain the *phase equations*, investigate the form of these equations, and plot them on a *phase diagram* (glance ahead at Figure 3.8); and
   (v)   hence find any *stationary point* where $\dot{q} = \dot{s} = 0$ and investigate the paths of q and s from other points on the diagram.

Solution
(i)   Define:

$$L = W + \lambda \int_0^\infty Z \, dt$$

$$= \int_0^\infty [H(q, s, t) + \lambda \dot{s}] \, dt, \tag{3}$$

where $H(q, s, t)$ (known as a Hamiltonian) $= [pq - c(q, s)] e^{-it} + \lambda[q - f(s)]$.

λ is known as the *costate variable* and is a function of time. Its significance is analogous to the more familiar Lagrange multiplier, i.e. it represents the value of cost of the constraint (2), in this case the marginal value of the stock or the marginal user cost of culling.

(ii)   Now follows the 'trick' for eliminating s. Integrate by parts to give:

$$L = \int_0^\infty [H(q, s, t) - \lambda \dot{s}] \, dt + \text{a constant.} \tag{4}$$

Differentiating and equating to zero[3] gives the first-order conditions:

$$L_q = H_q = (p - c_q)e^{-it} + \lambda = 0 \tag{5}$$

$$-L_s = -H_s - s = c_s e^{-it} + f'\lambda - \lambda \dot{s} = 0. \tag{6}$$

Equation (5) states that, *along the optimal path*, the immediate value of increasing fishing just balances the effect on the value of fish stock $(-\lambda)$. (Recall that λ is the discounted marginal value of the stock.) Equation (6) states that the discounted marginal return to the stock, comprising the impact on costs $(c_s e^{-it})$, on physical growth $(\lambda f')$ and stock appreciation (λs), is zero.

(iii) Differentiating (5) and eliminating λ, $\dot{\lambda}$ gives:

$$-c_s + (p - c_q)(f' - i) - s\dot{c}_q = 0,$$

and hence, using (2) and $\dot{c}_q \equiv c_{qq}\dot{q} + c_{qs}\dot{s}$:

$$-c_s + (p - c_q)(f' - i) - c_{qq}\dot{q}s - c_{qs}(f - q)\dot{s} = 0. \tag{7}$$

(iv)   Setting $\dot{s}$, $\dot{q} = 0$ in (1) and (7) gives the phase equations. Their shape depends on the functions f and c, and to proceed rather stronger assumptions are needed. For illustrative purposes assume: (a) f is the logistic function, *as* $(\bar{s} - s)$, discussed on page 38. Hence $f' = as - 2as$; (b) c_q is U-shaped and independent of s. Hence $c_{qq} > 0$, $c_{qs} = 0$; (c) c_s is a negative constant. Assumptions (b) and (c) give:

$$\dot{q} = - [c_s + (\dot{p} - c_q)(f' - i)] / c_{qq} s, \qquad (8)$$

and for $\dot{q} = 0$:

$$f' = i + c_s / (p - c_q).$$

As q rises, c_q first falls, then rises. Hence, remembering assumption (c), f' falls, then rises, and, from assumption (a), f' rises, then falls, giving the shape of $\dot{q} = 0$ shown in Figure 3.8. The exact position of $\dot{q} = 0$ depends on the parameter values and there are three possibilities (as illustrated).

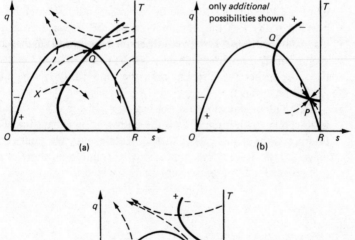

(a) One intersection (b) Two intersections (c) No intersections

Figure 3.8 Phase diagrams

(v) Also, from (8), $\dot{q} < 0$ to the right of $\dot{q} = 0$ and $\dot{q} > 0$ to the left. Similarly, from (1) $\dot{s} < 0$ above $\dot{s} = 0$ and $\dot{s} > 0$ below. This information, summarised by the *signs* shown on the diagram, allows us to find the direction of movement at any point. For example, at X in Figure 3.8, $\dot{q}, \dot{s} > 0$ as indicated.

There appear to be, at most, two equilibria (P and Q). Further investigation shows that the paths converging on P to be minimising rather than maximising profits (this will not be proved, but notice that there are strong economies of scale here). Q is known as a saddle-point. Just two paths terminate at Q; other paths, though possibly passing near Q, then diverge leading either to $q = 0$ or $s = 0$. (However, the paths ending in $q = 0$ are also profit-minimising.) This leaves two possibilities: *either* the fishery converges to Q, after which q and s are constant; *or* stocks are fished to exhaustion.

There will be one other piece of information, i.e. the opening stock (for example if the stock is previously unfished, the starting-point must lie on RT). Even so there remain an infinite number of possible paths and the optimum cannot be deduced from the marginal conditions. For a zero discount rate type (a) paths, converging on Q, clearly dominate type (b) paths ending in exhaustion: the higher the discount rate, the more likely is a type (b) path to be optimal.

If the phase equations do not intersect (Figure 3.8 (c)), there is no stable equilibrium and all the paths end in exhaustion. The interpretation of this case is that all sustainable yield policies involve a loss. Hence, even at a zero discount rate, there is no (commercial) advantage in maintaining the stock.

Limitations and extensions
Most of the assumptions are not central to the qualitative conclusions of the analysis. However, the following extensions are relatively straightforward:

(i) *Monopoly.* replace pq by $r(q)$ in equation (1) (Clark, 1976). This tends to reduce the equilibrium catch and renders exhaustion less attractive.

(ii) *Productivity growth.* Replace $c(s, q)$ by $c(s, q, t)$ or $c(s, q)e^{-\lambda t}$ in

(i) (barely treated in the literature). Productivity growth increases the value of conserving the stock, making paths ending in exhaustion less attractive.

(iii) *Costs of varying fishery activity or 'effort'*. Write effort $y = y (q, s)$ and $c = c (y, \dot{y})$. This effect is important, particularly where sudden large changes in effort are involved, as, for example, with paths ending in exhaustion, which would be rendered particularly unattractive. This conclusion would be reinforced by considering the resultant social costs of unemployment in the fishing industries.

(iv) *Value of the stock (e.g. scientific interest, food for other species: cf. forestry)*. Write $W = \int_{o}^{\infty} u(\pi, s)dt$, where $\pi = r (q) - c (q, s)$ cf. Vousden, 1973). This consideration militates against depletion especially exhaustion of the stock.

(v) *Selective culling*. For example, by employing large-mesh nets, catches can be restricted to larger fish with obvious advantages. This is straightforward provided it is assumed that all fish of age n are caught (cf. Figure 3.2). However, a more realistic stochastic model is more difficult (see Clark, 1976).

(vi) *Behaviour near exhaustion*. In a stochastic world the 'last' trawl will miss many fish which will then not be worth catching (unless as the accidental result of fishing for other still abundant species). This may occur sufficiently early to allow recovery of the stock when fishing will recommence.

The main implication of these extensions is to militate against exhaustion in the privately owned fishery.

The mine
The mine may be treated as a special case of the above theory, with $f (s) \equiv 0$. The cost function $c(q, s)$ caters for varying ore quality, etc. Clearly depletion is inevitable and interest centres around such issues as the path to exhaustion (for example, does q fall monotonically?) and the effect of monopoly. Extension (ii) is particularly intesting as it may allow mining to be continued indefinitely (cf. p. 20).

4 THE SOCIALLY OPTIMAL
USE OF RESOURCES

The last chapter was concerned with the maximisation of profits, given prices (or demand schedules in the monopoly case) and the interest rate. Now, prices and interest rates become internal to the system. The object is to maximise *utility*, given a *social-welfare function*, together with conditions of supply. Initially the fundamentals of the problem are explored through the so-called 'cake-eating model' originally developed by Hotelling (1931). The model is later elaborated to embrace various real-world complications.

4.1 A simple model

Consider a man whose sole means of subsistence is a cake. When the cake is eaten, he starves. (The intended analogy with non-renewable resources is evident.) How should he plan his consumption? First, if consumption is subject to diminishing marginal utility ($d^2 U/dC^2 < 0$), then clearly he will consume at a *constant* rate, for if consumption were higher at t_1 than t_2, utility could be increased by shifting some consumption from t_1 to t_2. But the man still has to choose between a life that is glutonous but short and one that is eked out near subsistence. The slower his (constant) rate of consumption, the longer his life (see Figure 4.1). This illustrates in the starkest possible form, shorn of all complications, a conflict which, according to the more pessimistic writers, lies behind all decisions about resources. Life is an objective to which we attach very great importance, something which many are reluctant to weigh explicitly against other objectives. Yet many men knowlingly reduce their life expectancy by smoking, overeating or motoring. It is not obvious that, faced with this choice, our cake-eating man would opt for the long austere life; and if the example is translated into mankind consuming non-renewable resources, it is unclear how race survival should be weighed against the level of consumption.

However, there are several reasons why such a conflict might not arise. The first is that there might be a planning horizon:[1] the man might expect to die at 70, the current generation might not care what happened after it had gone, or mankind's tenure on earth might be ended by an exogenous climatic disaster. If (see Figure 4.1) this occurs at t_1, then man can achieve his allotted span by restricting consumption

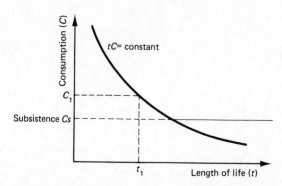

Fig. 4.1 The conflict between consumption and longevity

to C_1. However, shorter, merrier lives remain possible and perhaps preferable.

The second possibility is that there is an alternative renewable resource that can support life near subsistence indefinitely (Dasgupta and Heal 1975). By eating up the non-renewable resource, future consumption is pushed down, but life itself is not endangered. It remains optimal to spread consumption of the non-renewable resource evenly over the allotted span; if this is infinite, then it must be spread infinitely thinly.

Finally, if account is taken of the fact that the resource is not consumed directly but is first converted into consumption goods, then it may be possible to increase the efficiency of the conversion process. If this can be increased without limit, then, conceivably, the life of the resource may be extended indefinitely while maintaining or even increasing consumption (see p. 20).

Consider the optimal plan under these circumstances. First, to fix elementary ideas, consider the two-period case (Figure 4.2). The optimal plan is the point of tangency of the production frontier FF' and one of the indifference curves II'.

The position of the production frontier is determined by the size of the resource stock, and its shape by the increase in productivity over time. If productivity increases by g, the slope of FF' is $1 + g$.

The shape of the indifference curves is determined by the relative preference of the community for present and future *utility – not* consumption. This idea is captured in the *utility discount rate, j*. If society has no intrinsic preference (*pure time preference*) for either time period, then $j = 0$ and the indifference curves are symmetric

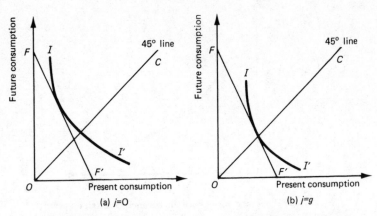

Figure 4.2   The choice between present and future consumption

about OC (Figure 4.2(a)). In this case the optimum point is necessarily to the North-West of OC; future consumption is greater than present consumption,[2] and the ordinary (consumption) discount rate $i > 0$. This arises because of the favourable production trade-off between present and future consumption.

Figure 4.2(b) illustrates the special case where $j = g$. Both the production frontier and the indifference curves are equally skewed, and present consumption equals future consumption, and resource extraction falls by g.

Now extend these ideas to the many-period one. To maximise the net present value of *profits* it was shown (p. 48) that the marginal profit obtained from resource extraction must rise at i, the ordinary discount rate. Analogously, to maximise the net present value of *utility, the marginal utility from resource extraction must rise at j, the utility discount rate*. Now the former is the product of resource productivity (which rises at g) and *MUC*, the marginal utility of consumption. Hence *MUC* rises at $j - g$.

In the special case where $j = g$, the marginal utility of consumption. and hence consumption itself, is constant (cf. Figure 4.2(b)); resource extraction falls at g and cumulative resource extraction is R_0/g, where R_0 is the initial extraction level. Provided R_0 is set sufficiently low (g times total resource stock), this programme may be maintained indefinitely.

If $j > g$, consumption rises and resource use falls by less than g and may even rise. Provided resource use is falling, the programme may be sustained indefinitely. Finally, if $j > g$, consumption falls (at least until subsistence is reached) and resource use falls faster than g.

In every case there are an infinite number of programmes consistent with the marginal conditions. Each path is defined by the opening level of consumption; the higher this is, the higher will be the whole consumption path and the earlier the date of eventual exhaustion, except that if $C_0 \leqslant C^*$, say, resources are never exhausted and the path is sustainable indefinitely. Clearly there is no virtue in $C_0 < C^*$, but a choice exists between the indefinitely sustainable path characterised by $C_0 = C^*$ and the shorter higher-consumption paths.

4.2 Investment

Not all output is consumed, some is used to add to the capital stock. At the same time output is produced not from resources alone but by combination of resource capital and conventional man-made capital (and indeed labour). As resource capital is depleted, man-made capital is accumulated and hence output maintained or even increased. Resource productivity (i.e. output/resource input) steadily increases and qualitatively the results are broadly similar to those derived earlier for one factor (resources) and exogenous productivity growth. But certain special features are worthy of note. First, this view is much 'richer', in that a variety of forms of production function can be considered — and in fact most of the results are crucially dependent on the shape of function assumed. In particular there is the formal possibility (implied by some forms of production function, for example Cobb—Douglas) of the output being produced from capital alone. This provides a fourth means of escape from Doom and it will then be optimal to deplete resources fully in finite time (Dasgupta and Heal, 1975): but compare the comments on this possibility on p. 36. Secondly, it can no longer be assumed, as in the single-factor case, that time paths in resource use and consumption are monotonic; this depends *inter alia* on the production function. Dasgupta and Heal prove that if the production function is linear homogeneous, consumption may (i) rise monotonically, or (ii) fall monotonically, or (iii) rise and then fall; at any event, it will have at most one maximum and no minimum; if the production function is Cobb—Douglas, resource use will fall monotonically.

Finally, this model brings out an important relationship between resource use and capital accumulation. Along the optimal path the price of resources in the ground will appreciate at a rate equal to the rate of return on investment.

4.3   Other complications

Ricardian scarcity

This may be introduced by including the resource stock in the production function. Provided an over-all resource limit is maintained (or marginal depletion costs rise eventually to infinity as the stock is exhausted), the results are little affected qualitatively; the only significant point (important if costs of change are introduced — see below) is that abrupt changes of direction tend to be eliminated.

Environmental effects

The effects of resource extraction and use are usually adverse and often important (see p. 32). Although such effects are often overlooked by resource economists, several models have been constructed in which utility is made to depend on environmental quality as well as consumption (for example Vousden, 1973). The conclusion is, as expected, that the presence of adverse environmental effects lowers consumption, output and resource use in all periods (except where output is used to enhance the environment) and that, even under Malthusian production assumptions, it may be optimal to leave some resources permanently unextracted.

Endogenous wants

Galbraith (1958) and others have suggested that consumer preferences are influenced adversely by past consumption. The implications of such a model have been explored, though in a model which did not include resources, by Ryder and Heal (1973). However, the model and its results are complex and not very illuminating. The presence of an adverse effect might be thought to depress consumption, and hence resource use, but since consumption in *all* periods is subject to this effect it is not in fact clear how inter-temporal choice will be affected (cf. the discussion of monopoly, p. 51). However, if resource use has environmental effects *not subject to the Galbraithian effect*, consumption is likely to be reduced over the whole path. Also, the effect is likely to be assymetric, i.e. *falls* in consumption are likely to be particularly unpleasant. Such a consideration, which has not been modelled,[3] will tend to reject such paths (which are otherwise frequently thrown up in resource-depletion theory).

Population increase

Clearly population increase is an important factor aggravating resource scarcity. In so far as population increase (*n*) is given, independently of economic conditions and societal choice, it seems probable that the effect is to raise the increase (or slow the decrease) of resource use. This is confirmed by analysis.

Some care needs to be taken over the welfare function. Specifically it is disputed whether utility ought to be weighted by the number of people affected (N) (see Dasgupta, 1969). With rising population such weighting produces a more future-orientated resource policy. Provided population increase can be regarded as exogenous, i.e. independent of living standards and deliberate policy, the case for a weighted *maximand* is strong.

Thus marginal utility of resource extraction remains MUC times resource productivity (though both terms will be affected by population growth) and the basic condition that MUC^x rises at $j - g$ still holds. However, since resource extraction depends on *absolute* rather than *per capita* consumption, it will tend to rise more rapidly (or fall less slowly) as a result of population growth. Living standards will be depressed by the additional future population; the effect of the weights is to spread the burden towards the present.

Without weights the marginal utility of resource extraction is reduced to MUC x (resource productivity/N) because of the sharing of the increment. Thus the marginal condition is that MUC then rises at $j - g + n$. Thus MUC rises faster, and consumption and resource rise less fast than in the weighted case.

However, population growth cannot be regarded as exogenous. There is considerable evidence that it depends on the standard of living and some that it may be influenced by government policy (for example Hawthorn, 1970). This has several implications for resource policy. First, resource policy not only affects living standards directly, but also indirectly via the effect on population growth (the dashed lines in Figure 4.3). Since living standards can also be influenced by population policy, it becomes necessary to consider the joint optimisation of

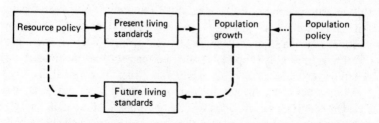

Figure 4.3   The interaction between resources and population

population growth and resource use. This is a difficult problem, raising unresolved conceptual and empirical issues. It is worth sketching the main issues.

First, the question of weights must be reconsidered. The weighted *maximand* recommended above implies that, for any given standard of living, $2N$ people is to be preferred to N and, moreover, that a fall in the standard of living is outweighed (in welfare terms) by a sufficiently large increase in numbers. Most commentators reject this judgement and, when population size is at issue, adopt, explicitly or implicitly, a *per capita* (i.e. unweighted) criterion.

However, Dasgupta (1969), putting the opposite view, objects that an unweighted *maximand* tends to imply the unacceptable conclusion that population should be reduced as rapidly as possible to the lowest feasible number. But the undesirability of this policy surely stems from other factors: (i) production involves the co-operation of resources and *labour*, and increasing returns to labour are likely to become important at low levels of population: (ii) population decreases entail reductions in family size and hence in the satisfactions of child-bearing; (iii) family-planning programmes necessary to effect reductions in the birth rate themselves involve resource costs; and (iv) vigorous programmes would entail an undesirable degree of coercion. An optimisation exercise which neglects these factors is likely to give very misleading results.

The customary procedure (usually implicit) of adopting an unweighted *maximand* where population policies are at issue and a weighted *maximand* otherwise is invalidated, however, by the inter-dependencies discussed above. The debate raises a fundamental and difficult issue (Lecomber, 1974): What is the effect on welfare of an addition to the population? To highlight the source of difficulty. ignore birth-control costs, parental satisfactions and all other impacts on the rest of the population. Then, on the weighted criterion, total welfare is always increased by a new arrival (since standard of living is necessarily positive); on an unweighted criterion, it is increased only if his standard of living exceeds the average. Interestingly the same question arises in the costs-benefit analysis of birth control where yet a third assumption is (implicitly) adopted, namely that this impact on welfare is zero. This is also the assumption generally adopted in every-day life: when deciding not to have a child, one does not generally consider the lost satisfactions which the hypothetical child misses through not being born. Thus, of the three assumptions, the last seems the least unsatisfactory, though its application in a macro context is fraught with difficulty.

Much empirical work also remains to be done. For example, it is not clear whether living standards raise or lower population growth. Theoretically a relaxation of the income constraint might be expected to raise family size and expenditure on death prevention; on the other hand, the value of the time sacrificed in bearing and bringing up children will also rise, leading to substitution against child-bearing. In addition, rises in consumption may have effects on attitudes and preferences altogether outweighing the income and subsidititution effects just referred to (see Leibenstein, 1974). Empirically, over a wide range, population growth is observed to fall as consumption rises both over time and on a cross-section basis; however, it is not clear how far the correlation should be attributed to the effect of education and other correlates of consumption levels rather than consumption *per se*. Moreover, near subsistence, higher consumption is likely both to reduce death rates and increase fecundity so substantially that population growth is increased. Similarly, at very high (e.g. American) levels of consumption, the income effect appears to dominate.

Further uncertainty surrounds the impact of population policies on population growth, while investigation of the welfare side-effects referred to above has scarcely begun.

Uncertainty

All the results so far derived relate to a certain world in which resource stocks, production and preference functions are known. Uncertainty raises two important issues. The first is simply that unanticipated developments will shift the optimal path. Theoretically this point is trivial and so obvious that it is rarely mentioned. But in comparing actual developments with optimal developments it is possibly crucial. For example, unanticipated resource discoveries or technical developments will expand the whole path of consumption and resource use. This may help to explain the historical rise in resource use, which conflicts with the optimal paths derived in so many of the models. But the point must not be exaggerated: while *specific* developments are doubtless unexpected, most resource owners and users do anticipate further discoveries and technical developments of some sort; only thus can one make sense of their otherwise culpable profligacy. It is to the extent that developments exceed (or fall short of) these general anticipations that there is a shift in the optimal path.

The theoretically more interesting issue is how uncertainty of the future should be allowed for in deriving the optimal path. Exploration of this difficult branch of growth theory has recently been extended to embrace natural resources. One important result (not dependent on the inclusion of resources) is that, contrary to the common view, uncertainty does not provide any general justification for reducing the weight to be attached to future utility. If, for example, one follows the rather inferior procedure of working with 'expected outcomes' and adjusting the discount rate to allow for uncertainty, the proper adjustment to the discount rate may be *downward* (see, for example, Dasgupta and Heal, 1975).

4.4   Conclusion

This chapter began with a simple cake-eating model; this was valuable in exposing the essence of inter-temporal choice and the possible optimality of a path ending in exhaustion. But otherwise its simplicity is misleading. As Optimists emphasise, it neglects increasing productivity through capital accumulation and technical progress. It also neglects a variety of other important factors, which are indeed rarely given adequate consideration, particularly in more formal work. Over all, the characteristics of the optimal path are not obvious, and few general statements are possible. This rather negative conclusion is confirmed in the mathematical treatment given in the appendix.

Appendix: mathematical models of optimal resource use

Three models will be considered. The first is a one-factor (resources) model incoporating exponential growth in resource productivity. The second is the simplest possible two-factor (capital and resources) model; this illustrates the simultaneous depletion of resources and accumulation of capital and shows how the optimal path depends in crucial respects on the parameters of the system. The third brings in labour as a factor of production and incorporates population growth and a simple form of technical progress; this model is much richer and the optimal outcome is even more dependent on the complex interplay of the parameters; one possible outcome is convergence to an equilibrium growth path, along which output, capital, consumption and resource use change at constant exponential rates.

Model 1

$$Max \qquad W = \int_0^\infty e^{-jt}\, U(C) \qquad (1)$$

$$X \geqslant \int_0^\infty R\, dt \qquad (2)$$

$$C = e^{gt}\, R \qquad (3)$$

where C is consumption, R is resource use, X is the resource stock, j is the utility discount rate. The first-order conditions are obtained as:

$$\lambda = e^{(g-j)t} U_C. \tag{4}$$

That is, the marginal utility of consumption grows at $g - j$. If $g = j$, consumption is constant, and resource extraction falls at g. Otherwise consumption rises or falls and resource use rises faster or slower than g according as $g \gtreqless j$. The consumption path is monotonic, but if $g < j$ resource use may rise over part or all of the path. For some parameter values ($g > 0$, and X sufficiently large), an indefinitely sustainable path is possible.

Model 2

$$Max \qquad W = \int_0^\infty U(C)e^{-jt}\, dt \tag{5}$$

$$C + \dot{K} = Q = Q(K, R) \tag{6}$$

$$X \geqslant \int_0^\infty R\, dt \tag{7}$$

The first-order conditions are:

$$U_C e^{-jt} - \psi = 0 \tag{8}$$

$$\psi Q_K + \dot{\psi} = 0 \tag{9}$$

$$\psi Q_R - \lambda = 0 \tag{10}$$

where ψ and λ are the values of the accounting and resource constraints (6) and (7) respectively (see p. 60 for techniques).
Differentiating (8) and substituting in (9) gives:

$$Q_K = j - U_{CC}\dot{C}/U_C , \tag{11}$$

i.e. *the marginal rate of transformation via capital accumulation equals the marginal rate of substitution.*
Substituting for ψ in (10) gives:

$$\lambda = Q_R\, U_C e^{-jt}, \tag{12}$$

i.e. *the discounted marginal utility of resource depletion is constant.*

Differentiating (10) and using (9) gives:

$$Q_K = \dot{\psi} / \psi = \dot{Q}_R / Q_R , \qquad (13)$$

i.e. *the return on capital equals the rate of appreciation of the marginal return on resources, that is the rate of increase in the (marginal) value of the resource stock.*

Now introduce somewhat stronger assumptions. Assume a constant utility function and a Cobb–Douglas production function:

$$U_C = \frac{1}{v} U^{v-1} \qquad (14)$$

$$Q = K^a R^{1-a} \qquad (15)$$

Then we can obtain simple relationships governing growth in C, K, Q, R (denoted by g suitably subscripted). Differentiating (14) and substituting in (11) gives:

$$g_C = \frac{1}{1-v}(a\frac{Q}{K} - j). \qquad (16)$$

From (6):

$$g_K = \frac{Q}{K} - \frac{C}{K}. \qquad (17)$$

From (15):

$$g_Q = a g_K + (1-a) g_R , \qquad (18)$$

and differentiating (15) and substituting (13) gives:

$$g_Q = a\frac{Q}{K} + g_R. \qquad (19)$$

From (17), (18) and (19):

$$g_Q = a\frac{Q}{K} - \frac{C}{K} \qquad (20)$$

$$g_R = -\frac{C}{K} \qquad (21)$$

We thus have four expressions for the four variables g_C, g_K, g_Q, g_R (16, 17, 20, 21). From (21) R declines *monotonically*. To investigate the paths of the other variables, define the output-capital ratio:

$$\beta = \frac{Q}{K} \qquad (22)$$

and the average propensity to consume:

$$\gamma = \frac{C}{Q} \tag{23}$$

Then g_β and g_γ can be found in terms of β and γ and the paths found by looking at a phase diagram in β and γ:

$$g_\beta = g_Q - g_K = -(1-a)\beta \tag{24}$$

$$g_\gamma = g_C - g_Q = \frac{va}{1-v}\beta + \beta\gamma - \frac{j}{1-v} \tag{25}$$

From (24) the *output-capital ratio (β) falls monotonically at a declining rate*, i.e. K rises relative to Q. Such a rise offsets the fall in resource input. The progress of γ is less obvious. The 'stationarity' condition is:

$$\gamma = \frac{v}{1-v} + \frac{j}{1-v}\left(\frac{1}{\beta}\right). \tag{26}$$

The dotted lines in the phase diagrams (Figure 4.4)[4] indicate possibly optimal paths. Thus γ may rise or fall monotonically or first rise and then fall — depending on initial endowments and parameter values.

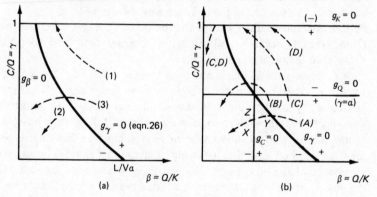

Figure 4.4   Phase diagrams

Now consider the signs of the original variables C, Q, K, R (equations 16, 17, 20, 21):

$K : g_K = \beta(1-\gamma) > 0$ provided $\gamma < 1$. g_K (dissaving) is presumed impossible (allowing for some dissaving does not materially affect the ensuing analysis).

$R : g_R = \beta_\gamma < 0$ always.

$Q : g_Q = \beta\,(a - \gamma) >$ or < 0 according as $\gamma <$ or $> a$.
$C : g_C = (a\beta - i)/(1 - v) >$ or < 0 according as $\beta >$ or $< 1/a$.

These conditions are marked in on Figure 4.4(b). It is evident from equation (23) that $g_Q = 0$ and $g_C = 0$ intersect on $g_\gamma = 0$, as shown.

Confine attention to paths beginning in the bottom right-hand quadrant. The path need not begin here but other paths will simply consist of the latter part of the type of path investigated. For example, a path beginning at X will follow the latter half of path A.

On all four paths (A, B, C, D), R and β fall throughout while the other three variables, Q, C, K, rise initially.

Path A: from Y on, γ falls; Q and C continue to rise but now Q rises faster than C. From Z, C begins to fall. It is idle to investigate what happens as the path approaches the origin. In practice the fall in consumption is bounded by a subsistence minimum (not explicitly represented in the model). When this is reached consumption would remain at this level, though the efficiency condition (10) still holds. The path could be terminated by Doom before or after subsistence is reached. Doom may be unavoidable (depending on the production function, the subsistence minimum and the initial resource endowment) and even if avoidable may be deemed desirable. This issue was adequately investigated in the one-factor models (p. 65).

Path B resembles path A except that before γ changes direction, first Q and then C begin to fall. Q in fact changes direction twice, first rising, then falling, then rising again.

Path C: as on path B, first Q and then C begin to fall. But γ continues to rise so that consumption takes an even larger share of output. Ultimately γ reaches unity. Consumption equals output. Assuming dissaving to be impossible, γ can rise no further. (If dissaving is possible, γ may rise further, but ultimately the phyical limits to dissaving are, or may be, reached and the following analysis applies.) To investigate rigorously what happens now, the constraint $K \geqslant 0$ must be added to the model. In fact it is fairly clear that consumption will be kept as high as possible, i.e. equal to output. The economy will move leftwards along the ceiling $\gamma = 1$ as resource utilisation falls. At W, however, γ begins to fall and the constraint ceases to be binding. Since the path cannot reach $\beta = 0$ (except asymptotically) it must cross into the bottom left-hand quadrant as shown – that is, Q will eventually rise again (unless subsistence or Doom intervene).

Path D resembles path C except that C continues to rise until the constraint $K \geqslant 0$ is reached.

Conclusions. Applicability of the model? It ceases to apply (without modification) when $\dot{K}$ falls below zero and at subsistence. The model also embodies some highly specific assumptions which limit its applicability.

Optimality conditions? Note the important conditions (11), (12), and (13).

Avoidability of Doom? It is not clear whether Doom can be avoided. This depends on the production function, on initial resource endowments and on the subsistence level. Even if Doom is avoidable, it is not clear that to do so is optimal.

Resource use? This definitely falls monotonically.

Physical capital? It has been assumed that disinvestment is impossible. It certainly is possible for this constraint (or whatever weaker constraint may be adopted) to be binding (paths A and B).

Output? This may follow a variety of paths. For example, it may rise throughout (path D), fall throughout (path A, beginning above $g_Q = 0$), or rise, then fall, then rise (path C). However, one can say that there are at most two turning-points, of which the first must be a maximum. No definite statement can be made about the final direction of Q.

Consumption? This may rise initially but must ultimately fall (this conclusion of course stems from the exclusion of technical progress from the model); there is at most one turning-point (a maximum). Like consumption, the consumption ratio (γ) may rise initially but must ultimately fall.

Influence of discount rate? A low discount rate results (as expected) in a more future-orientated policy — less rapid resource depletion, more rapid capital accumulation, consumption beginning lower and rising faster (or falling slower). This is reflected in Figure 4.4(b) by a leftward shift in $g_C = 0$ and a flattening of $g_\gamma = 0$.

Model 3

This model is due to Stiglitz (1975) and the reader may consult this source for a full account. The aim here is to indicate the approach and results and comment in the light of earlier discussion. The model embodies the following ideas:

(i) *Utility*: an iso-elastic utility function $U = \frac{1}{v} C^v$, and a weighted criterion (cf. p. 69):

$$W = \int_o^\infty \frac{1}{v} C^v e^{(n-j)t}. \tag{27}$$

(ii) *Production function*: Cobb–Douglas in capital, resources and labour (no distinction is made between the population, N, and the labour force):

$$C + \dot{K} = Q = K^{a_1} R^{a_2} N^{a_3} e^{\lambda} \tag{28}$$

where $a_1 + a_2 + a_3 = 1$ and:

$$c + \dot{k} + kn = q = k^{a_1} r^{a_2} e^{\lambda t}, \tag{29}$$

where lower-case is used to denote *per capita* variables.

(iii) *Resources:* homogeneous and finite as before:

$$X = \int_o^\infty R \, dt = \int_o^\infty Nr \, dt.$$

The procedure is, as usual, to obtain the first-order conditions and, after some manipulation and using g, suitably subscripted, to denote growth rates we obtain:

$$g_c = \frac{q_{k-j}}{1-v} \tag{31}$$

and

$$\frac{\dot{q}_r}{q_r} = q_k \tag{32}$$

Equation (31) is an expression for the equality of the marginal rate of substitution and the marginal rate of transformation through capital accumulation. Equation (32) states that the rate of return on capital equals the rate of return on resources (cf. equations (16) and (13)).

As before, the next step is the derivation of phase equations not in the original variables but in the output-capital ratio $\beta = q/k$ and the average propensity to consume $\gamma = c/q$. The main difference from the previous model is that g_β can be negative and $g_\beta = 0$ is a curve with a positive slope (see Figure 4.5).

These are shown to intersect provided:

$$j \geqslant n + \frac{\lambda - a_3 n}{1 - a} v. \tag{33}$$

The point X, then, represents a (unique) dynamic equilibrium of the kind familiar to growth theorists: β, γ are thereafter stationary; q,

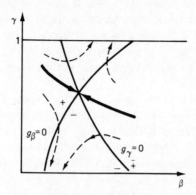

Figure 4.5   Phase diagram

c, k change at a constant (equal) exponential rate and it may also be shown that r declines at a constant exponential rate, so that a constant fraction of the resource stock is used up in every period. The equilibrium is a saddle-point and is approachable from the directions indicated by the broken arrows.

Stiglitz suggests that such a path, if feasible (i.e. if the phase curves intersect), is optimal and that otherwise there is no optimal path. It should be clear from our earlier discussion (p. 65) that these conclusions are too strong. The dotted paths also satisfy the first-order conditions and could be optimal. It is true that they appear to involve consumption falling to zero or rising to equal output — which may be considered infeasible. But then the behaviour of the economy when such constraints are reached must be modelled before such paths can be rejected (cf. the discussion of model 1). An alternative possibility is that the path consists of *part* of such a trajectory, ending in Doom when the resource stock is exhausted. Indeed if $g_\beta = 0$ and $g_\gamma = 0$ do not intersect, one of this possibilities must be optimal.

Further extensions and references. This model still omits vital real-world complications:
Ricardian scarcity? Include $Z = \int_0^t Rd\,\tau$ as an argument in the production function.
Technical progress? More elaborate formulations involving biased progress (Nordhaus and Tobin, 1972).
Environmental quality? Include E as an argument in utility and possibly production functions. E would be given by, say, $\dot{E} = (E - E') -$ function (Q, R, N). The first term is a logistic recovery function, the second a

general damage function (cf. Vousden, 1973; d'Arge and Kogiku, 1973). An environmental enhancement activity could also be included. Endogenous wants? Include $\dot{c}$ as an argument in the utility function (see Ryder and Heal, 1973). $\partial U / \partial \dot{C} > 0$; $\partial U / \partial \dot{C} \gg 0$ for negative $\dot{c}$ (p. 68). This important refinement has not been treated in a resource model.

Endogenous population growth? $\dot{N}$ becomes a control variable and the welfare function needs to be reconsidered (p. 69) (see Ingham and Simmons, 1975; Dasgupta, 1969).

Family planning? $\dot{N}$ a function of lagged C and family planning policy F. Include F as an argument in the utility function. These are difficult but important extensions which have not been attempted.

Uncertainty? Important uncertainties surround technical progress, the shape of the production function, especially for low R and high Z, and both parts of the environment function. Some stochastic models have been constructed (see Dasgupta and Heal, 1975).

Rawlsian utility function? Instead of discounting, some models following Rawls (1971) maximise the minimum level of utility (see Ingham and Simmons, 1975; Solow, 1975).

Ideally all these features, since they interact, should be combined in a single model. This would be a very formidable task. Short of this, one hopes that the 'insights' provided by more limited modelling are not posibively misleading.

5   RESOURCE DEPLETION AND THE MARKET MECHANISM

Resource use is determined largely by the market mechanism. Economists have stressed the role of markets in allocating and adapting to resource scarcity — the various mechanisms were discussed in Chapter 2. However, the question arises as to whether markets provide *sufficient* incentive to conservation — or, alternatively, as some critics (for example Kay and Mirrlees, 1975) allege, too much. It is a standard piece of economic theory that a perfect market mechanism guides the economy to a social optimum in which the 'best' combination of goods is produced according to the most efficient processes: no one can be made better off without at least one individual becoming worse off. The conservationist critique of resource use implies misallocation and this must be attributable to some form of market failure. Both to assess this critique and to devise appropriate remedies it is useful to identify specific sources of market failure.

We begin with a brief exposition of the allocative claims of the perfect market mechanism, and the assumptions on which it rests and then pass to a consideration of the ways in which market failure may affect resource use.

5.1   The Theory of the perfect-market mechanism

The theory will be sketched in a brief intuitive fashion. Those desiring more detail or rigour are referred to Lancaster (1969) and Graaf (1957).

Initially we abstract from time, and consider a static situation.

The basic idea is that individual decision-makers express their preferences in the market. The interplay of preferences determines what is produced and how. More precisely, relative prices provide *signals* of relative marginal costs and at the same time an appropriate *incentive* to follow these signals. Thus an individual, if he imposes a cost on others, pays a price equal to this cost, while if he confers a benefit he receives an appropriate fee. Thus the impact of his activities are exactly compensated (at the margin) and he may proceed to maximise his own welfare without damage to others.

The attainment of a social optimum through these mechanisms depends on six conditions:

(i) The preferences of individuals are taken as given. They are exogenously given and accepted as the proper authority for social decision-making.

(ii) These preferences are reflected in market behaviour, i.e. people do *not*, through ignorance, inertia or other causes, act contrary to their true preferences.

(iii) All individuals are 'price-takers', otherwise the price signals/incentives are distorted. In general this means that there must be a large number of participants in each market. This ensures that no individual can influence the market price.

(iv) All costs and benefits which one individual imposes on another must be subject to the market or some equivalent mechanism. Only then is the individual properly penalised or rewarded for his impacts on others.

(v) Preferences and production constraints are well-behaved. As noted, the price signals reflect marginal costs/benefits and hence guarantee a local optimum *per se*. Cost discontinuities, increasing returns to scale or peculiarities in preference functions can mean that the local optimum obtained is not a global optimum. One kind of discontinuity problem necessarily arises at zero production of each good. A consequence of this is that the market mechanism provides no guarantee that the right goods are produced, only that those that are produced are produced in the right quantities.

(vi) The distribution of income resulting from market forces is 'acceptable', or can be adjusted by 'lump-sum' transfers. This issue is given more extended consideration below.

Allocation over time

In resource economics we are particularly concerned with allocation between different points of time. Broadly the same market principles apply, with the rate of interest or discount, i, playing the role of a price; the relative price of future and present consumption is, in the absence of other price changes, $1 + i$. This price provides a signal and an incentive to savers, investors, mine-owners and all others taking intertemporal decisions. The influence of the interest rate on resource decisions was explored at some length in Chapter 3. The interest rate is determined by the interaction of these decisions and (ideally) the process of matching individual marginal-benefit ratios against a common yardstick $(1 + i)$ ensures optimality. With perfect capital markets and ignoring risk (considered below), there will be a single uniform interest rate connecting any two time periods.

If other price changes are introduced, the picture is a little more complicated. First, assume all prices change by a common factor, $(1 + p)$. Then a sacrifice of £1 today yields £$(1 + i)$ next year, but the command of money over goods rises by only $(1 + i)/(1 + p) = (1 + j)$, where j is known as the 'real' interest rate.

If price movements are not uniform, then each will have its *own* real interest rate, or simply 'own interest rate', j_k, given by $(1 + i)/(1 + p_k)=$ $(1 + j_k)$. This may also be expressed as:

$$\frac{1 + i}{1 + p} \bigg/ \frac{1 + p_k}{1 + p},$$

which is the over-all real interest rate divided by the change in the price relative to the general price level.

In Chapter 3 we saw how these considerations impinge on mining. The mine-owner organises his extractions plan in such a way that the value of the marginal unit in the ground rises with the (own) interest rate. Such a plan not only maximises profits but, in the absence of the various imperfections considered below, is socially optimal.

5.2 A critique of the perfect-market paradigm

Widespread failure of assumptions

It is evident that the claim of the market to guide the economy to a social optimum depends on a variety of heroic assumptions. In fact preferences are strongly influenced by the economic system itself, and they are not always well expressed in market behaviour. Markets are seriously imperfect — monopolies, restrictive practices and externalities abound, and economies of scale are widespread and important. It may legitimately be asked whether an analysis based on such assumptions has any claim on our attention.

However, such criticism runs up against a major difficulty — the provision of an alternative mechanism. The issue is often discussed in terms of *incentives*: Are prices necessary to motivate prople to follow the public interest or can one appeal to altruism or group loyalty? But equally important is the question of knowledge: How are people to know what constitutes the public interest and what actions are required on their part? *Informed altruism*, not merely altruism, is essential. Small groups (most notably one family) may be expected both to be knowledgeable about each other's preferences and motivated by altruism, family loyalty and informal pressures; but even here monetary transactions and rewards and punishments are not uncommon. Large groups may succeed in special circumstances, generally on a rather limited front; in particular a strong cause can provide homogeneity of interest and the required motivation. But, in general, large groups, such as large firms or countries, face acute difficulties in guiding individual action (Olson, 1965). Thus firms introduce elaborate market incentive schemes and in some cases systems of interdepartmental pricing; collectivist economies, despite initial doctrinal objections, rely on a system of prices and bonuses widely noted for its similarity to the capitalist system (see, for example, Keizer, 1971). A widely favoured alternative approach (for example Goldsmith, 1976; Schumacher, 1973; Hall, 1977) is to encourage the development of small communities. But while this idea, which finds limited application in China, Israel and elsewhere, has undoubted merit, there are severe difficulties. There is, in many spheres, a serious conflict between smallness and economies of scale (see Chapter 7) and inter-community externalities are likely to cause problems. Schumacher acknowledges that many activities would need to be carried out on a wider basis than the small community, but if so, then large-group problems re-emerge. Also, forces such as coercion or economic pressure are necessary to bind the small communities together, otherwise, if it is easy to leave the community altogether, group loyalty is greatly weakened (see Hirschman, 1970).

In summary, in a complex interdependent world, a fairly formal system of signals/incentives is required. To complain that the signals/incentives are distorted is a negative and irrelevant criticism. The aim must be to improve them, i.e. to diagnose and hence eliminate or at least reduce the distortions.[1] Hence the perfect market, which by definition provides perfect signals, acts both as a target and a benchmark. By the same token any unsatisfactory outcomes must be explicable in terms of one or more of the inadequacies noted above.

Distribution

The market mechanism produces a particular *distribution* of welfare depending, *inter alia*, on initial endowments of skill and wealth. Of course the market treats labour just like any other commodity, rewarding it according to its marginal contribution to production. Such treatment is indeed necessary to secure an efficient use of labour. Property income is determined similarly. Unfortunately the resultant distribution may conflict with ideas of *justice*. In particular the stupid, the weak and the ill may expect to receive very little, possibly not even enough on which to subsist.

The classic answer is of course 'lump-sum' transfers, that is taxes and subsidies which are independent of human choices (for example subsidies to the congenitally stupid might qualify). By such transfers any desired distribution of welfare could be achieved without interfering with the allocative conditions — the economy is moved from one Pareto optimum to another. In practice, however, lump-sum redistribution is infeasible and redistributive taxes/subsidies interfere somewhat with allocative efficiency (for example income taxes are a disincentive to work and to acquire higher skills). Thus in practice there is likely to be some conflict between allocative efficiency and distribution.

Some writers, faced with this conflict, dismiss the virtues of allocative efficiency as irrelevant to the greater goal of distributive justice. However, it should be remembered that even the poorest groups will suffer from excessive concern with equality. For them income is a product of national income and their share of this magnitude. Broadly allocative efficiency is concerned with the first magnitude, distribution with the second.[2] The cost of achieving more equal shares may indeed be so great a fall in national income that the income of the poor is reduced absolutely (Mirrlees, 1971).[3] The possibility of this outcome is reduced if care is taken to ensure that any desired distribution is achieved in the most efficient possible way. Those measures which are primarily redistributive should be screened for their allocative side-effects; measures which are primarily allocative should not be rejected out of hand because of their distributive side-effects — it may be possible to ameliorate these through special compensation or through the general fiscal system. In short concern with distribution in no way renders allocative efficiency irrelevant.

5.3 Market failures
Common access
Many resources can be exploited by several operators, perhaps by anyone who thinks it worth while. It was demonstrated in Chapter 3, using the particular examples of the oil field with many bore-holes, representing the non-renewable resource, and the fishery, representing the renewable resource, that common ownership leads to excessive exploitation. This arises from the adverse impact, especially via depletion of the stock, that each operator has on the profits of the other operators. The scarcity rent is dissipated by unlimited entry, which ensures that each operator earns only normal profit. However, although the *immediate* losers are the operators themselves, the losses are spread, through the market mechanism and through taxation and inheritance, throughout society. In particular, since excessive depletion occurs, the losses fall in the future and on future generations.

Common-ownership problems are many and varied, as the following examples show. In many parts of the world, tree-felling in unowned forests has led to complete deforestation. If conditions are favourable, the forest may regenerate naturally, but frequently the loss of forest cover leads to erosion, making re-establishment of forest, or indeed of agriculture, impossible (Dale and Carter, 1955). In primitive tropical areas forests may also be cleared for temporary cultivation. Tribes clear small areas and cultivate them intensively for a few years before moving on. If the site is abandoned sufficiently soon, the forest quickly regenerates, accumulating nutrients to support the next slash, burn and cultivate operation. However, if a site is cultivated for too long, or if insufficient time is left for the forest to regenerate, then there ensues a process of progressive deterioration, through erosion and lack of nutrients, until very soon the land is incapable of supporting either forest or agriculture (Ehrlich and Ehrlich, 1970). Again, since the forests are commonly owned, there is no incentive to refrain from excessive cultivation. In fact the main villain of the piece is population increase, since such societies are so near to subsistence that there is little scope for reducing cultivation at any given level of population. However, child-bearing may, in such conditions especially, be looked on as a common resource problem (see p. 105 below). Other examples include common grazing, hunting of wild animals, gathering of wild plants and persistent damage to beauty spots through excessive visiting.

In all these cases individuals not only cull excessively but refrain from taking action to enhance the stock. Where resources are owned in common, no trees will be planted, no fish or pheasants bred, nor will water be pumped into an oil field to increase the pressure.

Certain pollution and congestion phenomena may also be regarded as common resource problems. For example, excessive holiday boating may result in progressive fouling of the water; here water purity is the resource and boating depletes it. More seriously, widespread use of biocides results in the development of resistant pests. The private optimum use of biocides, which ignores the impact on other people's crops, exceeds the social optimum.

Most mineral and fuel deposits are privately owned, though the legal position regarding resources under the oceans is still unclear. But frequently extraction rights go to the discoverer of the resource. In such cases undiscovered minerals are effectively in common ownership, thus providing an excessive incentive to exploration. This activity is itself a misallocation of resources, and, moreover, leads to earlier extraction. However, in this case there is an important offsetting factor, namely that exploration generates *information* on the probability of finds in other places. Such information is a public good, its benefits accruing to others besides the generator of the information.

In principle common resource problems may be remedied by limiting access by assigning property rights or limitations on exploitation, or by providing a fiscal disincentive equal to the externality. In practice regulation is often difficult, for example in poor countries where regulatory institutions are poorly developed or where the problems cross, or are altogether outside, national jurisdictions. Control measures will be considered further in Chapter 6.

Externalities in resource-based industries

Common resource problems are a special case of the more general problem of *externalities*. The common resource is over-exploited because each operator imposes an externality on all the other operators, a social cost for which he makes no payment and therefore disregards. The effects are mutual, all operators both inflicting and suffering external costs. The social losses are borne initially by the exploiters of the resource, though they are partly transferred to others, for example via market mechanism.

In other cases, not so amenable to the common resource analysis, externalities are inflicted on other groups (see Rothenberg, 1970). Often the resource has a value in its unexploited state. Thus a hillside, as well as being a potential source of rock, may provide beautiful scenery and habitat for wild-life. Typically, however, the owner of the hillside gets no financial benefit for providing these amenities and their destruction through mining involves no cost to him. Furthermore, mining activities may involve the errection of unsightly buildings, pollution, noise and dust.

Transporation of the extracted resources may result in congestion and the other characteristic problems of road use, and the processing and use of the products may result in further externalities. Arguably such externalities are better regarded as connected with particular ways of using resources rather than with extraction as such; certainly, direct regulation of the activities concerned is in general the most promising method of social control. However, since resource-using activities have a high propensity to generate pollution and similar externalities, appropriate regulations would probably tend to reduce extraction activity. By the same token inadequate regulation of the externalities of extraction and use is a source of excessive extraction.

Distortions due to externalities are generally difficult to measure but in many cases are likely to be very substantial.

Monopoly

Some important resource products, for example copper, bauxite, potash and, most notoriously, oil, are marketed by monopolies or cartels. Monopoly is commonly cited as a cause of under-utilisation of resources, particularly in the context of oil (see, for example, Kay and Mirrless, 1975). The theoretical arguments were examined above (p. 51). In practice the effect of the OPEC oil monopoly is difficult to assess. The cutback in world oil cunsumption has so far been, at most, 20 per cent, and most of this is attributable to the world depression. However, since fuel consumption is strongly related to habits and equipment (see Chapter 8), the long-term elasticity is probably considerably greater. Moreover, the oil price rise called forth a vigorous search for alternative oil supplies and energy substitutes as well as less oil-intensive production techniques.

A further problem concerns the proportion of the oil price rise that is attributable to monopoly power. The divergence between average extraction cost and price is often cited as a measure of the monopoly distortion. However, it should be borne in mind, first, that it is marginal not average extraction costs that are relevant, and, second, that some allowance should be made for user cost. Certainly, pronouncements by OPEC leaders stress the investment value of oil in the ground, implying that they attach importance to this aspect. The allowance that they *should* make for user cost is very difficult to determine depending on what expectations are appropriate regarding future discoveries and technical developments, what allowance should be made for uncertainty and what discount rate should be used (see Chapter 3). Oil is the only case in which anyone has suggested that monopoly distortion is quantitatively important.

Uncertainty and the absence of futures markets

Decisions affecting the future must be based on future prices, but these are unknown and, as the time horizon recedes, so the margin of uncertainty increases.

It is helpful to distinguish two types of uncertainty. The first, known as *primary* or *environmental* uncertainty, is associated with factors external to the decision-making system, for example the weather, the outcome of a proposed research programme, or the preferences of future generations. The other, known as *secondary* or *market* uncertainty, stems from the absence of a mechanism for coordinating decisions affecting the future. Markets co-ordinate decisions relating entirely to the present, prices adjusted to balance supply and demand. (Ideally the adjustment is instantaneous and no transactions take place at disequlibrium prices. Indeed, in so far as this is not the case, failure occurs.)

There is generally no comparable mechanism for making decisions affecting the future mutually consistent. For example, investment in mining capacity in iron-ore mines may not match investment in the steel industry, so that in future years the demand for iron-ore fails to match supply *at the prices anticipated*. Of course, the market mechanism will bring supply and demand into balance, but at prices which had they been anticipated would have called forth very different levels of investment. What is required is a mechanism for balancing demand and supply in advance. A system of *futures markets* (such as in fact operates for national currencies and for certain primary products) is such a mechanism. Under these, contracts are entered into now to trade specified quantities of goods at specified future dates at specified prices. There would thus be a market operating today, for example, iron-ore sales, ten years hence. 'Ten-year-forward' prices would bring supply and demand into balance in exactly the same way that current prices balance supply and demand today. Investment plans would be geared to these forward contracts. In a completely certain world all prices and quantities would in fact be settled once and for all at the outset.

However, in practice the operations of futures markets make a very modest contribution to the problem – for they are confined to a few commodities and very short time periods. As such they perform a useful role in smoothing out cycles or the impacts of short-term disturbances, but make no contribution to the kind of long-term decision-making which is our primary concern. The prospect of substantially extending their operation seems remote.[4]

However, the virtual absence of futures markets certainly constitutes market failure, a possible reason why extraction decisions, in common with other decisions affecting the future, might be sub-optimal. As it is mine-owners and others must base their decisions on their own *expectations*. Clearly, at the very best, decisions can only be as good as the expectations on which they are based. As Coddington (1972) suggests, 'if the market system "works", it works just as well at reflecting and transmitting incentives based on error and facile optimism as on anything else'. This criticism is logically coherent but somewhat lacking in conviction. The individual critic may proclaim that his pessimistic expectations are the correct ones, but unless some more specific reason for bias is suggested the dispassionate observer may well be more inclined to trust the hunches of mine-owners and other operators in the field.

One possible such bias arises from the manner in which mine-owners are known to form and utilise expectations. Price expectations are not formed very explicitly beyond the next few months or perhaps years. Partly this reflects the rate of time preference, of which more will be said later, but largely it reflects the feeling that in the face of such enormous uncertainty regarding ultimate resource stocks and technical developments, elaborate forecasting is not worth while. Hence the mine-owner is likely to operate on an implicit assumption that prices are likely to move much as they have in the past. As we saw in Chapter 2, most resource products have fallen in price, a situation which has led many commentators to predict that resource prices will continue to fall in the future (see, for example, Barnett and Morse, 1963; Nordhaus and Tobin, 1972). It is likely that resource owners will take a similar view.

However, let us look a little more closely at the expected development of resource prices as exhaustion is approached. Adopt initially the Malthusian assumption of uniform ore quality. Product prices are the sum of resource rentals and extraction costs. The former should rise at a rate equal to the interest rate — which is taken as 10 per cent p. a. in the example which follows. On the other hand, extraction costs may be expected to fall due to technical progress and economies of scale. If, over the past, product prices have fallen, this indicates that the increase in resource rentals has been outweighed by the decrease in extraction costs. However, one effect of these divergent trends is for resource rentals to constitute an increasing share of product prices, so that the fall in the latter is first moderated and then reversed, as illustrated in Table 5.1.

Table 5.1   Resource rentals, extraction costs and prices

(1)	Year	0	100	110	120	130	140	146	150	160	170
(2)	Resource rental	—	1	3	7	17	45	80	117	300	780
(3)	Extraction cost	7660	999	816	667	544	445	393	363	298	243
(4)	Product price	7660	1000	819	674	561	490	473	480	598	1023
(5)	Growth in (4)	−2.0	−2.0	−2.0	−1.9	−1.6	−0.9	0	0.9	4.0	7.2
(6)	Ratio (2)/(3)	—	0.001	0.004	0.01	0.03	0.1	0.2	0.3	1	3

Extraction costs are assumed to fall at a constant 2 per cent p. a. Initially these costs dominate, so that product prices fall by very nearly

2 per cent p. a.; resource rentals may be ignored. The impact of rising rentals is first observable in year 120, though in practice such a small change would be altogether obscured by short-term fluctuations. The situation now begins to change rapidly: twenty-six years later product prices begin to rise, slowly at first, but at 4 per cent p. a. by year 160, 7 per cent p. a. by year 170, and at a rate approaching 10 per cent p. a. asymptotically. Over the space of some three decades (say year 120 to year 150) the situation has been transformed to one in which product prices are steadily falling, as they have been for centuries, to one in which they are rising at an increasingly rapid rate; during the same period, resource rentals, previously negligible, have become a factor of overriding importance.

It seems at least possible that mine-owners in year 120 will fail to spot the coming change in trend. They may well expect prices to continue falling and plan accordingly. Specifically, the anticipated price fall will stimulate overproduction, which will have the perverse effect of depressing prices, thus fulfilling expectations and increasing the stimulus to overproduction. Eventually resource owners will discover their error and cut back sharply in production. But by this time there will have been a substantial departure from the optimal path and, moreover, the sharp cutback now indicated will entail difficult problems of adaptation (cf. Chapter 2).

It is worth emphasising that this bias in price expectations occurs only for a very short period in the lifetime of a resource. Fundamentally this is because a 10 per cent discount rate[5] accords very little weight to the distant future (a point taken up in detail below) so that the possibility of exhaustion is not considered until it becomes imminent. The period of bias, when it comes, is by the same token a very critical one, one followed by very sharp increases in product prices, entailing, in all probability, equally sharp cutbacks in production (even on the optimal path). Departures from optimality at this stage are thus very serious, especially if applying to a number of resources simultaneously.

Before leaving this topic consider briefly the effect of a more realistic (i.e. Ricardian) assumption about resource quality. It has been shown (p. 31) that product prices rise most (or fall least) immediately before mining passes from a higher to a lower grade of ore. The transition, once accomplished, raises extraction costs and lowers resource rentals so that once again the former dominates in determining product prices. Thus, if there is a series of plateaus each of constant resource quality, there may be some sort of failure of expectations of the type described somewhat before the exhaustion of each grade. The greater the difference between the various ore qualities, the greater the danger of serious failures of anticipation. If there is a continuous gradation of ore quality, then abrupt changes of trend (along the optimal path) are unlikely until the lowest grade has been reached.

Uncertainty and the inadequacy of risk-pooling arrangements

Now consider primary uncertainty, i.e. uncertainty relating to factors external to the decision-making system. Clearly, no market mechanism, or indeed any other decision mechanism, can ensure that actions taken are appropriate to the external events that in fact occur. The most that can be looked for is that they are appropriate to the best current estimates of the possibilities of such events.

The problem is best approached through an example. Consider the sinking of an exploratory oil bore-hole; the outcome depends, first on the chance of finding oil, which is as low as 1 in 100 in many areas, and, second, on the size and quality of any find. The expected net present value (N.P.V.) of the project may be found as:

$$X = E \text{ (N.P.V.)} = \sum_i \pi_i x_i,$$

where π_i is the probability of the ith outcome and x_i the associated N.P.V. In the absence of risk a standard investment criterion is N.P.V. > 0. For risk-neutral firms this generalises to E (N.P.V.) > 0. However, most firms (and individuals) are highly risk-averse and impose stricter criteria on risky projects. Risk aversion may also be expressed, though not very satisfactorily, in terms of rate-of-return criteria. The criterion that the internal rate of return is greater than the appropriate discount rate (i) is generally equivalent to N.P.V. > 0 and hence applicable to risk-free projects. For risky projects a frequently used criterion is that the internal rate of return should exceed $i + a$, where a, known as the risk premium, depends on the riskiness of the project.

One consequence is that if the oil industry were split up into a large number of companies each bearing its own risks (and each risk-averse), very much less exploratory drilling would be undertaken than if the industry were under single ownership or the risks associated with individual drillings otherwise pooled.

The scope for risk-pooling is in fact very much greater than this example suggests. The risks associated with drilling for oil may be pooled with risks on quite different operations, and risks are particularly reduced if projects, the outcomes of which are negatively correlated, are undertaken. This indeed provides a major impetus to company diversification.

Risks may also be pooled across companies or across individuals and special risk-pooling or *insurance* markets have arisen to exploit these possibilities. Policy-holders pay a net premium (i.e. net of the expected receipts from claims) to transfer their risks to an insurance company. The company reduces these risks by pooling them with other risks. In a perfect insurance market the net premium will equal the administrative costs of the company plus the burden of any residual risk.

Unfortunately there are many risks which can be insured against only at very high premiums, or occasionally, not at all. One difficulty is that the 'outcome' must be defined in such a way that it is, as far as possible, independent of the actions of the policy-holder. If not, the outcome is as much a matter of choice as of risk and is said to be subject to 'moral hazard'. For example, profitability depends partly on the firm's own behaviour. It was assumed in drawing up the policy that the firm's behaviour is optimal; but the insurance company has no way of judging this, and hence the policy will almost certainly be geared not to profitability *per se* but to certain specific determinants of profitability. Since it will be impossible to specify these (complete with associated probability distributions), it will be impossible to transfer all or even most of the risks associated with a project to an insurance company. Another problem is that some risks may be unique or otherwise difficult to assess or may affect most policy-holders in a similar way, thus minimising the advantages of pooling (for example consider a major oil company seeking insurance against a technical breakthrough in the development of solar power). The gains from pooling in such cases are outweighed by the costs of devising and administering the policy.

Some writers (for example Arrow and Lind, 1970) take the line that if *all economic activity* is considered together, the over-all risk is negligible. Thus, if all decisions were taken by one central body, so that risks were automatically pooled, it would be appropriate for the central body to ignore risks altogether in project evaluation. The same outcome could be achieved under decentralised decision-making if risk-pooling arrangements, particularly insurance markets, were 'perfect'. The imperfections in these arrangements mean that, quite inappropriately from society's viewpoint, risk is an important consideration in the evaluation of individual projects. It should also be clear that these imperfections stem largely from administrative costs and fundamental difficulties in isolating and evaluating elements of risk and hence are largely irremediable.

The consequence of these imperfections is a preference for low-risk over high-risk projects. Projects in the high-risk categories include much research and innovation, prospecting for new resource fields outside established areas and, in general, projects with a long pay-off. Indeed, this last is explicit in the addition of a 'risk premium' to the discount rate.

While social risk is substantially less than private risk (giving rise to the biases indicated) it is unlikely to be zero. First, as several writers have indicated, since redistributive mechanisms are very imperfect, not only the aggregate outcome but also the distribution of gains and losses among individuals must be considered. Second, and more relevant here, risk-pooling requires a large measure of independence of projects. The possibility that all (or most) projects are similarly affected by a particular external event constitutes a social risk.

It is not difficult to think of major social risks: Will there be a breakthrough in fuel technology, for example the successful development of nuclear fusion or solar power? Will there be global climatic changes resulting from, for example, overheating or felling of tropical rain forests? Can loss of soil fertility through over-intensive agriculture be halted, through new agricultural techniques or more effective population control? And so on. The answers to these questions will clearly have a major effect on the net present value of any project with a distant pay-off. Nor is it reasonable to suppose that the over-all effect on all projects considered together will be zero. For example, a gloomy outcome, involving a drop in future living standards, could raise the value of distant benefits from all projects. On the other hand, an even gloomier outcome – unavoidable Doom in fifty years – reduces to zero all benefits accruing after this date. In both cases pay-offs are not independent – *all* projects are similarly affected.

The issue is further complicated by the influence of current activity on these outcomes and thus must be viewed in conjunction with the inadequacy of futures and resource markets.

Ownership uncertainty

A very special but common case of uncertainty arises when a resource is vested in sole ownership but the owners fear expropriation by the state. Clearly, there is no social risk involved (except in so far as expropriation involves a loss in efficiency, as occurred with several of the Middle-East oil takeovers, for example) but the private risk may be substantial. Ownership uncertainty will tend to make the owner advance his plans for extraction. Fear that the state may at some later date introduce harsher taxation of resource extraction will produce a similar response.

The discount rate

It has been shown (p. 50) that resource depletion is very sensitive to the discount rate. The higher the rate, the less the incentive to conserve resources for later use. It is widely suggested that discount rates generally used in the private sector (usually assumed to be 10 per cent in real terms on low-risk projects) are too high, for such heavy discounting appears to give very little weight to future benefits.

It must first be emphasised that the point applies to *all* decisions with an inter-temporal dimension, not just resource depletion, but also, for example, investment. Indeed, one of the points frequently made by advocates of growth (for example Ramsey, 1928; Tobin, 1964; Phelps, 1965) is that over-high discount rates are a source of under-investment and hence insufficient growth.

This point will seem very paradoxical to many conservationists, to whom investment is seen as the root cause of increasing resource use. Such a view in fact depends on an implicit assumption that physical capital and resoure use are complements in the production process. This is no doubt partly true, but they are also substitutes. In effect resources can be converted into physical capital, thus economising on resource use later on. Such a process can be beneficial to future generations and indeed could be a necessary condition of survival. Models have been constructed embodying these ideas (for example Dasgupta and Heal, 1975: see Chapter 4) and it is easy to demonstrate that in certain circumstances increased concern for the future can indeed raise the rate of capital accumulation.

In fact capital is far from homogeneous, and the contribution to future resource-saving depends crucially on the form of investment. Types of investment which will immediately be recognised by conservationists as benefiting future generations include energy-saving equipment, anti-pollution devices, environmental colleges (in which the principles of conservation are taught) and research into solar energy and better birth control. The discount rate automatically makes these distinctions. It automatically discourages the conversion of resources into consumtion goods, at the same time encouraging those forms of provision for the future which are most beneficial. It discourages investment which involves a heavy use of resources in its construction or use, but encourages investment (such as those enumerated) which

lead to a saving of resources. It provides little encouragement to investments with a relatively short-term pay-off, but great encouragement to
those with a long-term pay-off. Its effect on resource use is equally
discriminating. The depletion of some resources may in fact increase if,
for example, this is critical to the development of some important
resource-saving project or if exhaustion is not much of a problem, say
because of a renewable substitute. On the other hand, where conserving
a resource is critical to future welfare, then lowering the discount rate
will bring this about.

A consequence of this is that the *pattern* of investment and resource
use is dependent on the discount rate. The current mix of investment
projects has been selected on the basis of a high discount rate and is
quite possibly harmful to the long-term future. A reinforcing feature is
that the tax system provides the strongest incentive to investment in
manufacturing industry — which is likely to be particularly resource-
intensive — while providing no comparable incentives to refrain from
disinvestment in resources. Thus conservationists should not be misled
by present *patterns* of investment into thinking that investment *per se*
is necessarily the enemy of the distant future. At the same time
advocates of growth should take note that investment, if wrongly
structured, need not be of long-term benefit.

Discussion of 'the discount rate' may seem somewhat theoretical in
view of the wide range of interest rates actually observed. Perfect
inter-temporal allocation requires a uniform interest rate and the
existence of multiple rates appears to constitute a serious form of
market failure. A distinction should be made between returns to investment and returns to saving. There is considerable variation both within
and between these two broad groups.

Consider first the variation in returns to investment. Looked at *ex
post* this variation stems partly from the fact that many investments are
super-marginal, partly from divergences between expectations and outcomes — for it is the expected return that is related to the interest rate.
The expected rate is very difficult to determine and has attracted
surprisingly little research. Other crucial factors are risk and the cost of
borrowing. Typically the return demanded from a risky project is substantially in excess of that demanded from a safe project. This is
obviously the case if risk is handled by a risk premium but is generally
also the outcome of a more sophisticated appraisal. Variations in the
cost of borrowing are also largely related to risk as perceived by the
lender of the funds, but this may represent less the inherent riskiness of
the project as the reputation (or absence of reputation) of the

borrower. As discussed previously, it is quite likely that private allowance for risk is excessive from a social point of view. However, the 10 per cent p. a. rate quoted above is supposed to be the rate on a marginal 'low-risk' (equals zero-risk?) project. This is frequently referred to as the *opportunity cost of capital*, and is the rate used in the United Kingdom for the evaluation of government projects (the *test discount rate*). Most other developed countries use a similar rate. In view of the scanty evidence this figure is little morè than an informed guess, and in particular it is open to question whether this rate has been purged of all elements of risk and inflation.

Savers also encounter great variability in rates of return. This partly reflects the ease with which the savings can be turned into cash, and partly, once again, reflects risk. But more important than such variations is the low return on savings compared with the supposed 10 per cent p. a. return on investment. Rates of return on safe savings are typically 1 or 2 per cent in real terms. Sometimes, particularly at times of rapid inflation it seems, they are in fact negative.

This sizeable difference may be partly due to costs of operating money markets, possibly partly also to monopoly profits, but perhaps the major reason is taxation – of company profits, of property income (at very high rates for the richest, who do the most saving) and of capital gains. Since the tax base is in each case calculated in nominal terms, real taxation is highest at times of rapid inflation, when it may indeed substantially exceed 100 per cent.

Thus simplifying, there are two interest rates, *the opportunity cost of capital*, of perhaps around 10 per cent, and the *return on savings*, which is, perhaps, about 2 per cent. The difference is largely accounted for by tax. The tax falls on private provision for the future – which is thereby discouraged – though this impact could be offset by using the tax revenue to finance investment.

However, quite as important as the over-all level of investment is the *pattern* of provision for the future, i.e. the structure of investment – and of resource depletion. These, it was suggested above, depend crucially on the discount rate. Use of a 10 per cent rate will encourage projects with a short pay-off, and encourage the use of resources where exhaustion will pose problems only in the distant future. Adoption of this rate for project evaluation in the public sector will compound this bias.

Given the taxes (and they have a strong distribution justification), the public sector faces a characteristically difficult second-best situation. Clearly, a correct allocation of investment resources between the private and the public sector requires that both use the same discount rate. In so far as public-sector investment uses resources that would otherwise have been used in the private sector, use of a lower rate would draw funds from a superior to an inferior use. This is the case, which has so far officially prevailed, for using the *opportunity cost of capital*. On the other hand, if resources used are drawn from consumption, then the *return to saving* is more appropriate. In practice it is likely that public investment is at the expense partly of private investment and partly of consumption. A considerably more elaborate procedure is then required (see Marglin, 1967). However, since so much investment and resource depletion is in private hands, an improvement in the criteria, if confined to the public component, would make but a modest contribution to the problem.

However, this divergence between returns to savings and to investment is not the only source of insufficient provision for the future. Some would argue that even the return on savings is too high (and might be considerably higher were it not for the tax). Table 5.2 illustrates.

Even at a 2 per cent rate of discount (which is much lower than all but the more extreme conservationists would advocate), benefits accruing now are given 7.2 times the weight of benefits accuring 100 years hence.

Table 5.2   The effect of discounting

discount rate (% p. a.)	discount factor $(1 + i)^t$		
	10 years	100 years	200 years
0	1	1	1
1	1. 1	2.7	7. 2
2	1. 2	7.2	5. 2
5	1. 6	136	17400
10	2. 6	13800	6.6×10^8

This could be because members of the current generation do not care about future generations, but there are a number of other possible reasons, illustrated in Figure 5.1 (we abstract from population change — this complication is left to the energetic reader (or see Lecomber, 1974):

(i) *Lack of concern for the future*. In Figure 5.1(a) the production frontier FF' is symmetric to the 45° line, and the high discount rate stems from the asymmetries in the II' curve. The current generation attaches more weight to its own utility than to that of the future generation. This is arguably amoral, a point to which we return later. Note in this case that future consumption is less than present consumption, which is indeed what the Pessimists foresee.

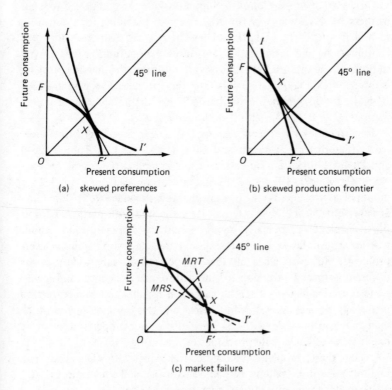

Figure 5.1   Inter-temporal choice

(ii) *Greater future riches*. In Figure 5.1(b), however, II' is symmetric to the 45° line, indicating complete absence of bias in the weight the present generation attaches to the future generation's welfare *vis-à-vis* its own. But FF' is skewed, indicating prospective technological change and the advantages of roundabout production (i.e. via investment). At the optimal point X the discount rate again exceeds unity, but this time future consumption is greater than present consumption. In other words, the current generation discounts the future generations' consumption mainly because, even at this high discount rate, the future generation is expected to be richer. Thus there are both diminishing-utility-of-consumption and equity-between-generations reasons for applying a high discount rate. If both *FF'* and *II'* are skewed (not illustrated), then it is not clear whether or not future consumption will be greater or less than present consumption.

(iii) *Market imperfections*. Suppose there are imperfections in markets for investment or for other ways of providing for the future, such that $MRS = (1 + i) MRT$. Then there is less-than-optimal future consumption and correspondingly more-than-optimal present consumption. The interest rate, the private return on the marginal project, is low at MRS. Figure 5.1(c) illustrates this for the special case in which *II'* and *FF'* are symmetric to the 45° line. In the absence of imperfections, $C_0 = C_1$, $i = 0$. With these imperfections $C_0 > C_1$, $i > 0$.

Imperfections have been discussed in an Optimistic growth framework, (ignoring environment and natural resources) by Tobin (1964) and Phelps (1965). I have reviewed and extended these analyses elsewhere (Lecomber, 1974 and 1975). Some examples from a long list are monopolistic elements in capital markets, inadequate risk-pooling arrangements, favourable externalities associated with particular forms of investment, particularly research and development and labour training, and unfavourable externalities connected with common-access problems. However, since all these imperfections vary widely across different forms of provision for the future, macro analysis and macro policies are inadequate. Each imperfection requires separate correction in the appropriate market. Nevertheless, and this is something on which many Optimists agree with the Pessimists, such imperfections are a major cause of inadequate provision for the future.

Again these problems could be combined with (i) and/or (ii). Optimists see these failings combined with (ii), and thus expect C_1/C_0 to be greater than unity but less than it ought to be.

(iv) *Social uncertainty*. Suppose an element of uncertainty over whether the world will exist in, say, 100 years time, due to some *uncontrollable* climatic change. If C_1 is the level of consumption, assuming the world to exist, then clearly some discounting of C_1 to allow for the counter-case is appropriate.

Endogenous risk of Doom can have the same effect but evaluation is rather different. All or even just some individual decision-makers perceiving a certain risk of Doom lower the weight attached to benefits beyond that date and this induces a rise in the discount rate. This leads to more rapid resource depletion, lower investment, and so on, thus increasing the risk of Doom. It is possible for there to be two stable equilibria — one with a low discount rate and sustainable, the other with a high discount rate entailing Doom. The uncertainty surrounding key technological developments (for example new energy sources) is more difficult. In general a higher discount rate will be more appropriate (and will materialise given suitably perfect markets) on optimistic assumptions than on pessimistic ones. One would expect therefore that the greater the probability attached by decision-makers to the optimistic outcome, the higher the discount rate will be. Broadly this is true but there are important exceptions. However, analysis is difficult and will not be attempted here (cf. Arrow, 1970; Haveman, 1977).

The proper response to high discount rate depends therefore on its origins. A future-biased production frontier (ii) provides a perfectly valid reason for according a low weight to the future — though it must be borne in mind that it is the production frontier perceived by decision-makers that determines the discount rate and these perceptions may be biased (see pp. 89—92). Likewise Doom-risk (iv) justifies a high rate, provided it is exogenous; on the other hand, endogenous Doom-risk is a form of market failure and a possible cause of serious concern. Other forms of market failure (iii) are important sources of a high overall discount rate but such factors are specific to particular forms of provision for the future and should be dealt with as far as possible at a microeconomic level.

Finally, there is the possibility (i) that the present generation accords inadequate weight not merely to future marginal *consumption* (*that* could be justified by (ii)) but to future *utility*. But if the present generation does not care much for future generations ('The future has never done anything for me!'), what then? Some writers (for example Pigou, 1924) point out rightly that future generations cannot take part in current decisions and argue that it is the duty of the government to act as custodians of their interests. However, the government is also responsible to the current generation. It is open to debate how far the government should act in opposition to the wishes of the people. Moreover, in a democracy scope for such action is strictly limited. A sharp drop in consumption to conserve resources for future generations (or indeed to aid the Third World) would surely cause electoral defeat. Thus if the current generation does not care, there is little, short of dictatorship, that can be done.

However, it has been suggested that the current generation are really less selfish than their behaviour implies. One idea (see, for example, Marglin, 1963) is that the market encourages selfishness and that greater altruism is expressed in the ballot-box or in answer to opinion surveys. Without wishing to deny that the context in which decisions are taken may sometimes be important, any general bias of this sort seems unlikely.

To elucidate this point it should be explained a little more carefully how market provision for future generations operates. Individual saving does not necessarily benefit future generations; the saving may be for the individual's own old age, in which case it will be balanced by later dissaving. The individual's provision for future generations is represented by his lifetime savings, or equivalently by his donations to them in the form of bequests, gifts *inter vivos*, donations to charities with long-term objectives, and so on. That individuals do make such donations indicates a measure of concern even if it is, arguably, insufficient. Moreover, to suppose that political behaviour is generally altruistic, or indeed any more altruistic than atomistic behaviour (which includes gifts of money and time), would be naive (see, for example, Downs, 1957).

However, a more specific reason why individuals, coming together in a political context, might wish to increase the aggregate level of bequests has been put forward by Sen (1961) and Marglin (1963). It is known as the 'isolation paradox'. The idea is that each individual acts selfishly in deciding his own bequests; however, he views the bequests of others more objectively and thinks these should be increased. Indeed, in order to secure such an increase he is willing to pay in kind — to increase his own bequests. To put the matter more formally, suppose each individual's relative marginal valuations are as follows: own consumption 1; contemporaries' consumtion β; own heirs' consumption γ; and other future generations a. The individual's isolated bequest will be such that:

$$\gamma k = 1, \tag{1}$$

where k is the marginal rate of transformation between current and future consumption. But each individual will willingly enter into a contract whereby each bequeaths an additional unit provided:

$$k[\gamma + (N-1)a] > (N-1)\beta, \tag{2}$$

where N is the number of individuals. Substituting (1) in (2) gives the condition:

$$\frac{\gamma}{a} > \frac{1}{\beta}$$

Sen considers that 'my egotism [will] not extend as much to my heirs *vis-à-vis* your heirs $[\gamma/a]$ as it applies to me personally *vis-à-vis* you $[1/\beta]$'. Hence such a contract appears attractive.

An extraordinary feature of this argument is that the direction (though not the magnitude) of the 'isolation bias' is apparently independent of the relative affluence of successive generations. In fact all the contributors to the controversy assume that future generations would be more affluent than the present generation. If so, why should we wish to enter into a contract to increase gifts from the poor to the rich (Tullock, 1964)? More basically, why are individual isolated bequests so generous?

One point is that Sen's basic reasoning is not as convincing as it at first seems. Suppose we care greatly for our own descendants (high γ) and for some or all of our contemporaries (high β) but care little for future generations in general, because they seem too distant to warrant our concern (very low a).[6] These assumptions, which seem not implausible, would yield $\beta a > \gamma$, i.e. the opposite condition to that given in (3). Isolation serves to inflate the general level of bequests above the optimum level. This both provides an explanation of why they are so high and also indicates that they should be reduced.

There are other reasons why bequests might be too high:

(i) they may be unintended by-products of saving for oneself; and
(ii) they may be subject to strong 'relative bequest effects'.

An individual may wish to set his heir up in the same relative position to which his upbringing has accustomed him. Moreover, a bequest may provide satisfaction to the giver (impressing friends, or the feeling that he is doing his duty), and such satisfaction is likely to be relative to the general level of bequests. Such considerations would tend to push up the level of bequests and a contract to reduce them would be beneficial.

These ideas are somewhat speculative and no attempt has been made at quantification. Nevertheless they provide a possible explanation of why a generation which is optimistic about future growth should be so generous in its bequests, and at the same time indicate that a reduction in bequests would better accord with individual preferences.

However, on *pessimistic* assumptions the original suggestion that bequests[7] are too low seems more plausible; indeed in such circumstances our counter-arguments are seen to have much less force. It is hoped that generalised concern for other future generations (*a*) will be greatly increased by their prospective poverty; unintended bequests become a smaller fraction of the whole; relative effects become less important relative to absolute effects at low income levels. So it is much more likely that bequests are too low. This in turn will mean that the discount rate is too high.

To summarise this long discussion of the discount rate:

(i) on optimistic assumptions high interest rates are not necessarily inconsistent with equal regard for the interests of present and future generations;

(ii) nevertheless a variety of important inter-temporal biases (including risk, the tax system and the isolation paradox) have been suggested, even by Optimists — some of these are greatly strengthened on a Pessimist view;

(iii) in these circumstances choice of the public-sector discount rate is complex and represents a third-best approach — the first-best policy is to attack specific distortions directly, the second-best policy to attempt to lower interest rates across the board;

(iv) other possible causes of insufficient provision for the future are mistaken optimism and selfishness on the part of the current generation — here education and persuasion are the appropriate remedies, otherwise it is not clear how far the government can or should act in opposition to the views and preference of its electorate.

Government-induced biases

Taxation can have a strong effect on resource use, and indeed the deliberate use of taxes for this purpose will be examined in the next chapter. As it is taxation is generally used more as an instrument for abstracting purchasing power from the private sector in relation to ability to pay, and allocation effects are largely incidental.

A special levy on resource industry profits (over and above normal profits tax), such as the Petroleum Revenue Tax levied on North Sea oil, makes marginal ventures unprofitable and leads to the early abandonment of others. Taxes on extraction have a similar effect, and in addition induce companies to delay extraction, since by so doing they postpone the payment of taxes and hence, at positive discount rates, reduce the net present value of total tax payments.

On the other hand, several writers (for example Herfindahl and Kneese, 1974; Brannon, 1975) have noted the frequently over-generous tax treatment of capital expenditure. Such concessions have the opposite effect of attracting capital into resource industries, thereby increasing exploitation in all periods.

Government-owned resource industries may be prevented from pursuing optimal price policies by injunctions to break even. The break-even price is average cost, excluding user cost and generally worked out on an historical-cost basis. The optimum price is of course marginal cost (higher than average cost in the typical rising-cost case), including user cost and worked out on a (usually higher because of inflation) replacement-cost basis. Inappropriate pricing policies in the private sector may be generated by prices and incomes policy and by the general fear that high profits may provoke nationalisation.

In the last section it was noted how taxation is a major influence on interest rates, which are themselves crucial determinants of allocation over time.

Finally, the government's normal commitments to provide infra-structure and regional support can constitute major externalities. Frequently resource exploitation occurs in remote areas, necessitiating an influx of population. New houses, schools, roads, medical facilities and other infrastructure will be required, and typically much of this is automatically provided by the government. It is true that the people concerned would have needed these facilities anyway, but under-utilised capacity may exist in other parts of the country, and costs are likely to be particularly high in remote regions.

If the resource is non-renewable, then further costs are likely to be encountered when exploitation is abandoned and, as in the coal-mining districts of South Wales and Durham, the government is left to cope with the problems of a depressed region. These costs, too, are an important externality. Such problems can occur in other industries but are particularly likely where natural resources are concerned, because of the dependence on a particular locality where the resources happen to be. Often, apart from particular resources, the locality is, because of its remoteness, climate or terrain, unsuited to economic activity (for example narrow Welsh mining valleys, desert oil fields, Alaskan north slope, north-east Scotland).

Population increase

Population is a major determinant of resource use, especially in poor countries. It will be argued (i) that child-bearing decisions are subject to large external costs, and (ii) that, without population control, adequate control of resource use is probably impossible.

Consider first a poor peasant economy. Subsistence needs grow with population increase: cultivation is intensified and extended to unsuitable land subject to erosion, trees are felled for firewood and then, as these run short, dung is used as a fuel instead of a fertiliser. At first sight these problems may appear to be associated with common access to land and other resources and remediable by establishing a system of property rights or otherwise restricting access. But, in the face of expanding population, effective control over resource use may entail mass starvation, and may thus be rejected as inhumane (and difficult to enforce). If so, and if new people are assumed to have automatic access to the means of subsistence, then population increase must be seen as the fundamental (common-access) problem.

In richer countries, though the link between population size and resource is considerably weaker, rather similar arguments apply. Let us set up the family's decision problem rather formally. Suppose, in the simplest case, contraceptives to be perfect, available at zero cost and not subject to religious or other taboos. This makes exposition much clearer without materially affecting the conclusions.[8] Each couple then faces a simple choice of how many children to have. Presumably they weigh up the costs and benefits; these will include the joys of child-bearing, as well as possible support in old age, the time and money costs of bringing up children, losses in freedom, and so on. Under these circumstances it is a reasonable assumption that a child will be conceived only when it is felt that the private benefits exceed the private costs. However, there are some important divergencies between private and social costs.[9]

(i) economies of scale and agglomeration (these, the only external benefits of child-bearing, are thought to be important in a few sparsely populated regions, especially in South America – here population is growing rapidly and economies of scale must soon be exhausted);

(ii) exploitation of common-access resources, including pollution, congestion, and so on;

(iii) consumption of marketed resources, if these are supplied below the full marginal social cost (as some of the other arguments imply);

(iv) 'positional' reasons for having children, for example 'status' (these clearly depend on societal norms and a reduction in everyone's family size would reduce correspondingly the number of children required to acquire any given status, or, more radically, if the social disadvantages of child-bearing were more widely appreciated, large numbers of children might cease to carry any status value);

(v) tax concessions and state benefits related to child-bearing or family size (for example in Britain, family and child allowances, family income supplement, maternity allowance, additional supplementary benefits, rent and rate rebates, and so on);

(vi) provision of state-financed or aided services, for example council houses, schools, medical facilities.

The last two factors are quantitatively important in countries with more developed institutions. For example, in Britain child subsidies ((v) and (vi) together) raise real income by about 15 per cent per child for an average family and very much more for a poor family.[10]

Similar factors can operate at group level, i.e. there may be divergencies between *group* costs and benefits and *global* costs and benefits as follows:

(i) enhancement of the group's political or miltary power (this may operate at national level or at the level of some ethnic or religious group within a nation seaking to increase its voting strength);

(ii) possible annexation of resources belonging to others (thus often in history, groups have acquired land and other resources through strength — here population enhances military strength ((i) above) and at the same time a *de jure* private resource becomes common-access through the possibility of seizure);

(iii) enhancement of claims for international aid, often allocated according to need.

These factors may influence the policies of the group. In particular some groups and nations, apparently motivated chiefly by (i), are aggressively pro-natalist (see Stycos, 1971). Again (iii) is particularly worthy of note. The needs of families, in this case a group or nation of families, is met, not by the families themselves, but by wider communities.

These subsidies to families and groups have an obvious and powerful humanitarian justification, but it must be recognised that they substantially reduce the incentive not to have children. Such subsidies amount to a substantial sharing of the community's resources. Each new individual has needs which are conceived as giving him a right to access to those resources. Essentially a common-access problem is created.

The quantitative significance of such financial influences on child-bearing are widely denied but this is in the face of considerable accumulating evidence (see, for example, Ben Porath, 1974). The critics are on better ground in stressing the importance of other influences on child-bearing, especially education and other outlets (especially employ-ment) for women. Influencing these factors provides a possible escape from the conflict between population policy and the satisfaction of need. To some extent these factors are conformable to the economist's model – the provision of a substitute (work) may be expected to reduce demand for children. But to a considerable extent they imply mallea-bility of tastes, the further ramifications of which are considered next.

Endogenous wants, relative income effects and the costs of economic growth

So far resource use has been presented largely in terms of consumption now versus consumption later. Environmental side-effects have been stressed, but otherwise it has been taken for granted that increases in consumption *per se* are beneficial; the conventional economist would say that they move the consumer on to a higher indifference curve and expand the area of choice. But recently the presumed association between living standards and well-being has come under increasing attack (see Mishan, 1967 and 1977; Scitovsky, 1976; Hirsch, 1976). These criticisms may be grouped under three heads, namely want creation, relative income effects and social side-effects.

It is a commonplace (see Veblen, 1899; Galbraith, 1958; Easterlin, 1974; Hirsch, 1976) that the process of satisfying wants creates new wants. Want creation occurs partly spontaneously through knowledge of new possibilities, emulation of neighbours, changes in social habits, partly through advsertising. These processes are so evident that no one but an economist attempting to preserve his paradigm would think of denying them.

A standard *reductio ad absurdum* riposte is that not only the commercial fripperies of life (which some of the social critics appear to have in mind) but also the best aspects of our culture (for example art and music, which presumably these social critics value) are created by socio-economic-cultural processes (see Hayek, 1963; Beckerman, 1974). However, this riposte is even more damaging to the conventional wisdom. Not only is it admitted that tastes are indeed malleable, but in addition it is being suggested that there are 'good wants' and 'less good wants'. On both counts the claim of consumer preferences as an arbiter of value breaks down entirely.

An alternative riposte is that the individual can and should allow for want creation. For example, in considering smoking or taking drugs, he should take into account addictive effects. On this view want creation is a problem only in so far as consumers are ignorant, myopic or otherwise 'irrational'. Doubtless consumers are all of these but it is widely maintained that the government's response should generally be confined to providing information and possibly propaganda. Only in extreme cases (bans on drugs, tobacco duty, and compulsory seat belts) is stronger action desirable. The reason for this abhorrence of intervention was discussed earlier (p. 83), namely that poor as the consumer-preference criterion is, it is virtually impossible to devise a better one. However, this does not settle the question, for it is easily shown that irrationality is not the only problem, and even if it were the impact of want creation on resource depletion is, or may be, sufficiently serious to justify intervention. Want creation is, as we have seen, partly a result of the individual's own actions, but it also results from advertisements and other forms of promotional activity (which therefore constitute a producer–consumer externality)[11] and purchasing decisions and behaviour of others (which constitute a consumer–consumer externality). The realisation that externalities are involved is important because it suggests possible remedies which do not override consumer preferences (see Chapter 6).

The seriousness of the problem depends largely on the view taken of future human prospects. Resource depletion permits more current consumption at the expense of less future consumption. Want creation inflates both, and on an optimistic view there is no reason to think that a revised appraisal would lead to very different results – it is simply a matter of present fripperies versus future fripperies.[12]

However, on a pessimistic view the cost of present fripperies is a disastrous drop in living standards, perhaps even Doom. Formally externalities and irrationality are serious distortions in rich countries toady but only minor distortions at the basic living standards of tomorrow. As a result inter-temporal choice is seriously distorted. These arguments are reinforced by the painful effect of a *drop* in living standards *per se*. High living standards are addictive, generating certain habits, life-styles, accumulation of capital and expectations which are difficult to adjust in conditions of scarcity (see Chapters 7 and 9). Of course, this problem stems partly from ignorance or irrationality, for individual Pessimists can protect themselves by adopting simple life-styles today.

Over all the results of want creation are surely so serious, on a Pessimistic view, as to justify intervention.

Next, it is suggested that welfare is partly dependent on relative income, so that an increase in everyone's income may have little effect on aggregate welfare (see Hirsch, 1976). This view is supported by evidence of dependence of *consumptions* on relative income (Duesenberry, 1949). This 'relative income effect' is usually discussed in terms of envy, which invites its dismissal as an unworthy emotion to be disregarded in any welfare appraisal (see Beckerman, 1971). Such dismissal is questionable on two grounds: first, there is surely little merit in creating the mere potential for happiness if, for whatever reason, most people are incapable of realising that potential; and second, much more than envy is involved, for example the rich may despise or taunt the poor or leave them out of their social arrangements; indeed, even without malice activity is geared to the norm so that, for example, those too poor to own a car will suffer the decline in public transport as car ownership increases; those without television may find themselves left out of the conversation. Many activities are competitive (for example securing a job, gaining promotion, winning a sporting contest) and much expenditure may be devoted to gaining a competitive advantage over rivals. One man's success is another man's failure and there may be no social gain (for further examples see Scitovsky, 1976; Hirsch, 1976). The relative income effect is closely related to the want-creation process. Formally it involves a consumer—consumer externality.

Space precludes adequate discussion of other side-effects of growth, which are very varied. They include, for example, the alienating effects of modern production methods, the effect of mobility on community values (cf. Hirschman, 1970), the impacts of rapid change and the interactions between materialism and the pursuit of economic gain. The reader is referred to the works of Mishan (1967, 1977) and, for the counter-view, Beckerman (1974). Possibly the most worrying aspect of these controversies is that such potentially crucial social processes have received so little systematic investigation.

5.4 Summary
The aim of this chapter was to investigate the implications of market failure for resource use. Could the direction, if not the magnitude, of any bias be determined?

Several distortions were identified in resource industries. Two of these, informational externalities associated with exploration and (probably) monopoly, result in a *downward* bias (i.e. too little production). But the rest, other externality and common-access problems, ownership uncertainty and various government-induced biases, involve *upward* bias. In general the latter would appear to dominate and in many cases (for example fisheries, U.S. oil) the net bias is large.

In addition resource use is part of a wider problem of inter-temporal choice. Here several further biases were detected — absence of adequate futures markets and insurance markets, various influences on the discount rate including taxation, myopia and generational selfishness, population externalities, want creation, relative income effects and other social costs of economic growth. In general there is a clear and possibly strong bias towards excessive population growth and towards early consumption. This bias is not especially controversial, and in particular the bias to early consumption (though not all the supporting arguments) is part of the conventional wisdom of pro-growth economists. In general this bias will involve excessive resource depletion.

This analysis can lend strong support to the Pessimists. It is easy to see how market failures can lead to substantial overuse of resources and a general neglect of the future. The biases are in fact particularly strong when (as the Pessimist believes) the human prospect is dismal. Then biases associated with the absence of futures markets, endogenous Doom-risk, the discount rate, want creation and relative income effects are particularly serious. Moreover, the effects of excessive depletion (for example through common-access problems, government-induced biases, population) cannot — on a Pessimistic view — be mitigated by technical advance.

However, these arguments will not convince the Optimist, for on an optimistic view the net bias, though probably unchanged in direction, is relatively weak.

Thus the analysis, while lending most support to the Pessimist position, is inconclusive. Its main value is to expose the nature of various resource problems, thus indicating possible directions of policy. This is the subject of the next chapter.

6 RESOURCE POLICIES

The analysis of the last chapter suggests certain policies to influence, and more specifically to reduce, resource depletion. The first (relatively uncontroversial) set of policies aims at specific sources of market failure in the resource industries themselves; these are considered in Sections 6.1 and 6.2. By themselves, however, such measures constitute a rather modest conservation programme which would hardly satisfy the resource Pessimist. Accordingly, three supplementary groups of policies will be considered: these are zero economic growth (Z.E.G.) and similar policies (Section 6.3), correction of specific distortions outside the resource sector (Section 6.4) and various *ad hoc* measures geared specifically to reducing resource depletion (Section 6.5).

6.1 Common access and externalities
The diagnosis of such problems is generally agreed (Sections 3.1, 3.2 and 5.3) but this does not mean that adequate controls are easy to devise. First, the distortion must not only be detected, it must also be *measured*, for only then can the appropriate modification to the decision environment be devised. For example, optimal regulation of a common-access mining operation requires knowledge of the cost function (often very complex and subject to change as technology advances) and of price movements. Optimal regulation of a biological resource requires similar information, as well as knowledge of the natural growth function. In some cases (for example exploration) there are offsetting distortions, so that even the direction of the net bias is disputed (but see p. 86).

Second, it is difficult to devise an operational control strategy. In some ways the most straightforward solution is to change ownership rights — to establish single ownership. Sometimes (for example common grazing) the resource could be divided into a number of singly owned pieces, though this might be technically inefficient (for example fences would be required). In other cases (for example marine fisheries) such division is infeasible.[1] Notice also that the establishment of single ownership in no way removes the problem of assessing user cost. This is simply transferred to each owner so that no externality is involved. It could be that a central regulatory authority would be better able to estimate user cost, in which case one of the methods mentioned below might be preferable.

The relative merits of other methods, general regulations, individually negotiated regulations, taxation, saleable licences to exploit, are the subject of much dispute, particularly in the context of pollution (see Ashby, 1972: see also p. 136). Whatever method is adopted, however, there is one important general principle, namely that the controls should operate as directly as possible on the source of the distortion. For example, control of shooting should ideally relate to the number of birds shot, rather than, say, the type of gun. Besides this, there are problems of heterogenity, for example should distinctions be made between different sizes and varieties of bird, different times and places? Often there is no body with adequate powers of regulation, so that any control required has to be negotiated between affected parties —this gives rise to conflicts of interest. Finally, whatever regime is adopted it is obviously essential that it be adhered to and this normally entails some efficient system of policing and appropriate penalties to law-breakers. Consider three specific examples:

(i) *The common oil field*
In the United States and elsewhere many oil fields lie under the property of more than one land-owner. If each owner has unrestricted right to extract oil, then, as demonstrated in Chapter 3, both the number of bore-holes and the rate of extraction will be socially excessive. The cost of depletion is shared among all with rights to extraction and is predominantly external to individual extractors.

In principle the simplest solution is 'field unitisation', i.e. the establishment of single ownership. This will not remove the complex problem of determining depletion cost, but will at least remove the externality. Since the over-all value of the field is increased by single ownership, it should be possible for one extractor to buy out the others. While such takeovers have occurred, small producers persist in the United States. This may be attributed variously to financial constraints, the desire of the small man to stay in business even where a sell-out would be more profitable and government encouragements of the small producer, discussed further below. The government could encourage or even enforce field unitisation, and some states have instigated appropriate programmes (see McDonald, 1971). However, an exaggerated belief in the virtues of competition have tended to discourage such initiatives. In fact since there are a large number of fields in the United States quite apart from a world market in oil, unitisation of individual fields would not create monopoly power except to a limited extent locally. Instead state governments have attempted to restrict depletion by direct controls, known as 'pro-rationing'. The provisions are complex and variable across jurisdictions, but the salient features are quotas for individual bore-holes, with exemption for high-cost 'stripper' wells – on distribution grounds. This limits extraction, but somewhat arbitrarily and at considerable cost in efficiency. First, it discriminates perversely between high-cost and low-cost wells, and second, since quotas are per well, it encourages an excessive number of wells, and frequently under-utilisation of each. Wunderlich (1967) quotes a case where the quotas were fixed at about one-third of the 'efficient productive capacity' of the wells, implying *inter alia* that the same rate of extraction of oil could have been secured for about one-third of the capital costs. The system is widely condemned.

A preferable way of restricting production would be a depletion or 'severance' tax levied per unit of output extracted. In principle this should be set to equal the depletion cost. Severance taxes are widely used but are mainly seen as a means of raising revenue from an affluent source, rather than a means of internalising the depletion cost. Hence no attempt is made to vary severance taxes in accordance with the cost functions and ownership structures associated with particular fields.

An alternative method (cf. Dales, 1968) is to issue extraction licences each permitting, say, the extraction of one barrel of oil per day. Then, by controlling the number of licences, the authority has exact control over the extraction rate (something which is not achieved under the tax system). If the licences are transferable between wells and are also marketable, then the conditions of the market are restored. Access to the resource in the form of licences is restored to transferable private ownership. The number of licences can be varied to equate the price to an estimate of the depletion cost. If the two diverge, then the authority can intervene on the market, buying back licences or selling new ones. Of course, depletion cost cannot be estimated at all exactly, but if the authority has *no* idea of this it has no basis for *any* policy of depletion control.

(ii) *The fishery*
As demonstrated in Chapter 3, above a certain level of fishing, but well below maximum sustainable yield, depletion externalities begin to occur.

A particular difficulty is lack of any effective authority over the use of the High Seas. It is not in the interests of any one country to reduce its catch unilaterally, while international agreement seems extraordinarily difficult to reach. One reaction is unilateral extension of fishing limits; the first attempts to do this (for example by Iceland) were strongly resisted, but the resistance was largely unsuccessful and other countries followed suit. Countries with long coast-lines and distant from other countries gained most. This established conditions nearer private ownership over larger parts of the sea. But common-access problems remained: first, since fish do not respect national fishing limits, fishing in one area imposes external costs via its effects on the stock in another area; second, establishment of a national fishing zone provides only the potentiality of national control and in no case is this efficiently exercised.

Quotas are often used to restrict the catch. However, difficulties arise in setting the quotas initially and in adjusting them in the light of changing circumstances. If mounting inefficiency is to be avoided, a mechanism is required for changing market shares and new entry. A simple procedure (cf. Dales, 1968) is that the fishing rights be marketable.

More frequently control is exercised indirectly via restrictions on the extent or techniques of fishing, and thus fishing may be limited to certain times or places, or there may be restrictions on the type or size of boat or equipment. These controls tend to be ineffective even in their immediate purpose of restricting catches, for only some of the factors influencing catches are controlled, and operators can react by varying others. For example, if the fishing season is reduced, operators can fish for longer hours or increase the size of their fleets. Thus the restrictions need continual modification, and the lags in this process frequently mean that damaging depletion has occurred in the meanwhile. Second, the controls tend to mean that any given size of catch is taken in a very inefficient way, for example short fishing seasons involve the inefficiency of boats and men lying idle for the rest of the year. Crutchfield and Pontecorvo (1969) sum up the situation thus: 'Existing national and international agreements . . . "solve" the problem [of overfishing] by a reduction in productivity of the inputs in an almost endless variety of ways, with an equally wide range of explanations for each.' The inefficiencies are enormous. In one (typical) case, 50 per cent of the gear was found to be redundant; in another, quoted by Pontecorvo (1967), 'no less than 90 per cent of the gross earnings go to redundant inputs'. One may draw the following general conclusion. In conditions of potentially excessive fishing fish stocks are a scarce resource, capable of earning an economic rent. In single ownership this rent would accrue to the owner in the form of the discounted net profits on the fish caught.

Under common access additional entry will occur so long as a positive net profit is obtainable. Assuming all operators are equally efficient, none will earn net profits and thus the rent to the fishery is entirely dissipated. (If some operators are more efficient than others, then they will earn profits but these should be regarded as returns to their abnormal efficiency not to the fish stocks.) Regulations of the type described which prevent overfishing without restricting access also reduce the surplus to zero, for otherwise there would be further entry. This does not necessarily mean that there is no virtue in such restrictions, which may at least preserve fish stocks. This may have some advantage, if, for example, stocks have other values, such as beauty or scientific interest, or if more satisfactory controls can be devised at some later date.

Licences on catch would maintain the rent, which would accrue to the operators, or the government, or to both, according to the exact conditions of issue. Taxes on catch would likewise maintain the rent, appropriating it for public use.

However, this view of regulations, characteristic of some of the fisheries literature, is somewhat one-sided. Some kinds of regulations (even including some of those on which Pontecorvo pours such scorn) have a place even in an optimal regime. The issues are somewhat obscured by the expository model in which fish are homogeneous and the sole aim of policy is to reduce the total catch. In fact, of course, fish vary in species and in age, and it is clearly desirable to avoid catching young fish because the ratio of the weight of the catch to the effect on future stocks in particularly unfavourable (see p. 43). For a similar reason it may be desirable to reduce catches in the breeding season. This is the origin of some of the restrictions – for example on size of mesh, on closed seasons, and fishing in spawning areas. Such limitations would be adopted voluntarily in fisheries in private ownership. This is not to say that all restrictions on these factors can be justified in this way. As the detailed investigations (for example Crutchfield and Pontecorvo, 1969) show, closed seasons and mesh-size restrictions frequently far exceed those that would be adopted in single-ownership regimes and are intended primarily as general restrictions on catch. As such they suffer from the objections discussed above.

One might also justify, at least in the short term, measures which, while apparently inefficient, preserve employment. Fishing is often (though by no means always) carried out from remote ports where little alternative employment is available. Declining manpower in fishing often involves unemployment in the short run. In the long run this could be cured by migration or possibly by new industries. But the latter might be hopelessly economic or environmentally damaging while the former would aggravate regional imbalance. Such arguments are often used to justify hill-farming, forestry and other activities in remote regions. In such circumstances the rejection of labour-saving fishing methods, even if more efficient on conventional grounds, may be justified. Formally fishing techniques should be re-evaluated using a low or zero shadow price for labour.

(iii) *Amenity costs of quarrying*

The final example concerns resources which though in private ownership give rise to externalities. The amenity effects of quarrying are varied, including visual effects, noise and vibration as well as congestion and noise from quarry traffic. Some are related to the rate of mining, others more to the existence and state of the mine.

At a technical level these problems may be ameliorated in a variety of ways: (i) choice of site; (ii) choice of techniques of extraction and transport; (iii) adaptation of the environment, for example widening roads, suitable siting of houses; and (iv) reducing the rate of quarrying.

In the United Kingdom quarrying is governed by planning controls. Establishment, extension or a major change of operation of a quarry requires a *planning consent*, except that quarries given consents before the 1947 Town and Country Planning Act can automatically continue quarrying the remainder of the deposits and revocation of this general permission would entail compensation. These consents are crucial in determining which sites are chosen. Additionally, since conditions can be attached to consents, they may be used to influence the choice of technique. For example, limits can be placed on the explosives used, and special techniques stipulated to reduce dust; it may be insisted that the hillside facade be largely retained with quarrying taking place behind, or that a belt of trees be planted to mask the site. Conditions can also be made relating to reclamation after quarrying has ceased, though there is some danger that, meanwhile, the company will go bankrupt. Roads may be widened or new roads built, though the cost will generally be borne not by quarry-owners but out of public funds. There is provision to include conditions on the rate of quarrying, but this is rarely invoked and only then if over-rapid quarrying in a particular locality would cause severe local problems, of road congestion for example.

No attempt is made to influence the over-all rate of quarrying, though this may be marginally retarded by additional costs imposed on the quarry-owners in the conditions attached to the consents. Various public planning documents on the subject (see Verney, 1976) refer to the needs for stone and other quarry products and consider how this might be met. Some of them express concern at the near exhaustion of favourable deposits, for example sand and gravel in south-east England.

The general presumption of these documents and of the planning system is that there are given needs for stone, etc. which must somehow be met. Planning controls can affect the choice of site and can reduce the environmental costs associated with quarrying at any particular site, but it is a reasonable presumption that eventually all sites will be quarried unless dramatically unsuitable (for example under Central London or in a particularly outstanding beauty spot). What happens when this time approaches is not entirely clear — presumably then at last a serious search is made for substitute materials and for means of curbing demand.

However, this approach represents a serious oversimplification of the issues. First, the 'needs approach' to supply ignores the important distinction between 'needs' and 'demands' and the dependence of the latter on price (this is a familiar criticism levied against numerous examples of 'needs-orientated' planning of, for example, housing, manpower and public utilities). Doubtless some uses of stone have a high social priority — homes for the overcrowded or the homeless spring to mind. But stone is also used for homes for the rich, including second homes, and for road-building, uses which cannot be accorded such overriding priority. Decisions on the use of stone should be made in the light of costs; uses considered to have sufficient social priority could still be met. In addition the use of stone could be reduced by substitution of other materials, including various wastes. The costs of stone include not only manpower and capital but environmental damage. There is no more reason for neglecting the last than the first two.

This brings us to the second point. The division between land suitable and land unsuitable for quarrying is artificial. Rather, there is fairly continuous variation in environmental suitability, just as there is a variation in conventional unit costs of extraction. A cost of quarrying very suitable land is that earlier recourse must be had to less suitable land. This cost may be referred to as the 'external depletion cost'.

In summary, demand for stone is not absolute and may be presumed sensitive to price. At the same time price fails to include the environmental costs of quarrying, including the external depletion cost. Hence use, and hence depletion, is to some extent excessive. The planning mechanisms, while valuable, do not meet this problem. What is required in addition is some mechanism for reducing the extraction of stone.

Once again the obvious mechanism is a tax. This could be a tax levied in relationship to the external costs associated with *particular* quarries. In principle this would obviate the need for the present system of planning controls. The expectation is that, as quarrying moved to progressively less environmentally suitable sites, the tax and hence the price would rise automatically and act as an incentive to conservation, following the general theory presented in Chapter 3. However, such a tax would need to be individually tailored to particular methods of working in particular quarries and would be very cumbersome.

An alternative would be to levy a uniform tax to retard the rate of quarrying (formally this would be the external cost of the *marginal* unit of extraction, including depletion cost) and retain the present system to control the choice of site and techniques.

While the formal validity of this line of argument is clear enough, the quantitative importance of the issue could be questioned. It depends on four factors:

(a) *the price elasticity of demand* (clearly, the method requires some cutback in demand in response to a price rise).

(b) *evaluation of amenity costs* (these include items which are very resistant to systematic evaluation).

(c) *future mining techniques, etc.* (improvements which reduce the environmental cost of mining would reduce depletion cost); and

(d) *the discount rate* (as demonstrated in Chapter 3, this is crucial to the evaluation of future events on which depletion costs depend).

6.2 Private resources
Government-induced bias
While there are problems in the exact definition of tax neutrality, there is widespread agreement that in most countries many extractive industries receive substantial government favours in the form of tax concessions as well as supporting expenditure (see Chapter 5). Clearly these should be removed.

A major obstacle is powerful vested interests, for example the oil lobby in the United States (see Anderson *et al.*, 1977). A common argument is the overriding need to secure domestic supplies for various immediate purposes. For example, in the United States the importance of encouraging supply is urged to reduce dependence on insecure OPEC oil. National security is indeed a possible external benefit of current extraction, but it is important to realise the conflict between present and future supplies and hence between present and future security.

Conceivably the future security problem may be reduced to minor proportions by technical advances or improved relations with the Arabs, but one suspects that the scarcity argument is accompanied by myopia — solve the current problem and hope that future problems will vanish. It has also been pointed out (for example by Nordhaus, 1974) that security could be achieved at lower cost in other ways, perhaps by reducing demand and certainly by stockpiling oil.

Another difficulty is that *transition* to a neutral system can involve inequity and unwanted allocational effects (Vickrey, 1967). For example, a reduction in tax concessions would reduce the value of mineral rights and of shares in mining companies. Although windfall gains and losses frequently occur, it is sometimes held that government measures with strong direct effects of this sort should be avoided. The allocational effects stem from the anticipation of higher taxes in the period in which they are being planned and piloted through the legislature. In principle this would tend to accelerate depletion, though this effect would be moderated by the short-run inflexibility of supply.

In the case of nationalised resource industries there is little excuse for failing to charge marginal extraction cost (including user cost). The resultant profit may be dissipated by a two-part tariff (with the first part negative) or transferred to the exchequer by means of a tax.

The difficulty with government supporting expenditures (see p. 105) is that they follow normal criteria, ostensibly conferring no particular favours on resource industries. Unfortunately, however, the cost of satisfying such criteria in remote areas is often abnormally high. However, there are precedents for passing on to the consumer abnormal costs of providing standard services (for example water and sewerage connections) and these should be invoked.

The reduction of uncertainty

Many of the market failures discussed in Chapter 5 stem from the vast uncertainty surrounding developments in the longer term. Moreover, other market failures are serious if prospects are poor, but not otherwise. Hence reduction of uncertainty, for example by systematic long-range forecasting, would appear very valuable. Such an exercise could also be supported on the general ground that knowledge is a predominantly public good.

A first step is to take an inventory of resources. This is by no means a novel idea. There have been several such inventories, especially in the United States, in response to pessimistic views of future prospects (for example U.S. Dept. of Interior, annually; World Energy Conference,

1974). Generally these have revealed adequate supplies of most re-sources for the 'foreseeable' future, perhaps for about fifty years. Pessimists have criticised such surveys for failure to take account of growth in demand and for their short time horizons. Clearly, fifty years' survival is not an appealing prospect to most of us.

Unfortunately such surveys can tell us very little about resource prospects, even if their scope were very greatly expanded. The diffi-culties, basically those encountered in our assessment of prospects in Chapter 2, are the following:

(i) *Ricardian scarcity*. 'Ultimately recoverable' resources depend on the costs one is prepared to incur in recovery. The survey could be designed to yield a *supply curve* for each resource. However, this would not cater for the full complexity of the cost function, for, as we have seen (p. 15), extraction costs may depend on such factors as the rate of extraction, the quantity previously extracted, while the order of ex-traction and the proximity to markets may also be relevant.

(ii) *Other limitations on supply*. Exploitation of some resources (for example minerals under major cities, very low-grade ores) would involve heavy environmental costs. Some such resources are excluded from consideration as not feasible to exploit but otherwise environmental costs are ignored. Such black-and-white treatment is inadequate; feasibility is a matter of degree.

(iii) *The influence of demand*. The adequacy of any given resource supply depends on demand, which must therefore also be forecast. Price changes will induce economy and substitutions, thus diminishing the use of some resources while possibly increasing the use of others. In any behavioural or optimising model of resource use the interaction of supply and demand as functions of price must play a central role. Demand will also depend on growth in population and income per head as well as tastes. These depend on a variety of economic and social factors (including resource prices) and prediction would not be easy.

(iv) *Technical progress*. This is the most important, uncertain and controversial factor of all. In the past it has dramatically reduced ex-traction costs and brought about substitutions of materials and products. In some cases materials may be introduced which had not previously been regarded as resources at all. Optimists see technical progress continuing, driving resource scarcity ever further into the distance (see p. 17). Pessimists doubt whether this can be relied upon and point also to the adverse side-effects (often externalities) which new technologies frequently involve. The crucial importance of technology is discussed in relation to energy in Chapter 8. Thus in assessing prospects for resources some view must be taken of future technical developments.

This brief review indicates the complexity and uncertainty of any assessment of resource prospects and suggests two questions:

(1) Is an inventory of resources worth constructing in view of the limited contribution which such knowledge could make to the over-all assessment of resource prospects?

(2) Are more elaborate models, attempting to incorporate some of the other factors, particularly the interaction of supply and demand, population growth and technical progress, worth while?

The first question turns out to lack adequate precision. Inventories can and have been constructed, based on company data on 'known' reserves supplemented by geological data. Minor improvements can and are being made to such data. The scope for further improvements is virtually unlimited. For example, in assessing the quantity of oil in an uncharted area one could rely on general geological information or one could sink one, a hundred or ten thousand test bore-holes, or one could even begin to extract oil to improve one's estimate of extraction costs. Clearly, costs of such an exercise are a major consideration and diminishing returns are soon to be expected. The question is how far along the path it is worth going. Without a detailed study of costs and benefits (which could vary from one resource to another) this question can be answered only in the most general terms.

The important thing is to be very clear about the role of such an inventory. 'Known' reserves at current extraction costs provide a lower limit of resource availability. The estimate of the supply function, though it could be too high, will in general be biased downwards by its failure to make adequate allowance for technical change. This means that such estimates are of limited value in looking further ahead than about fifty years. They are of most use when the picture they tell is gloomy, indicating the possibility of imminent changes in trend of resource prices and consumption, for it is then that naive extrapolation is likely to mislead.

This suggests that if a preliminary survey indicates the high probability of a particular resource being in adequate supply to meet prospective demands for the next few decades, without significant increase in cost, then further refinement is unnecessary. A simple addition of company estimates of known reserves is frequently sufficient to guarantee this. If, on the other hand, the survey indicates an imminent shortage of some resource, then, depending on the importance of the resource and on survey costs, it may be worth extending the survey in an attempt to confirm or deny this initial finding.

This concentration on the short term does not mean (as is sometimes stated) that longer-run scarcity is irrelevant to current decisions. On the contrary, if on 'current trends' key resources are in fact to run out in, say, a hundred years, then (except at a very high *utility* discount rate) rather stringent conservation measures are needed now – and would indeed be stimulated by the higher current level of resource prices which correct anticipations would generate. It would also be appropriate to increase the efforts devoted to population control and resource-saving technology. Hence it would be useful to assess the likelihood of a resource crisis beyond the next few decades. But, unfortunately, the mere compilation of an inventory of resources can make very little contribution to such an assessment.

It must be emphasised that a government survey which indicates specific locations for resources acts as a subsidy to the finding of resources and hence may accelerate their use. This will not of course worry the Optimist. One might argue more generally that public information-gathering is justified partly by the lack of adequate futures and insurance markets, partly by the public-goods nature of information; in the new post-survey state of information, the market guarantees the optimal rate of depletion, and it is unimportant whether or not this is in excess of what would have prevailed in the absence of the survey. However, in the face of other market imperfections (and there are many) such an argument carries little conviction. If, as Pessimists think, there are tendencies to over-exploitation, then subsidising companies' search for resources could well exacerbate them. Thus it is arguable, from the Pessimistic viewpoint, that if the surveys are at all detailed, any gain from additional information is outweighed by the impetus given to depletion.

The importance of looking beyond the next few decades has been stressed; but to form an adequate longer-term assessment, allowance must somehow be made for technical change and for the interplay of various economic and social forces. Some models embodying these complications have recently been developed (see Meadows *et al.*, 1972; Nordhaus, 1973a). In general it may be said that the models are much too broad and much too dependent on essentially arbitrary assumptions about population growth, technical change and the capacity of the environment to absorb wastes. They do little more than confirm, in a formal way, the wide area of uncertainty.

These models could be greatly improved by further work. One can easily list some of the main improvements required: (i) much more detail, for example on resource types, commodity groups, pollutants, income groups, geographical areas; (ii) more careful modelling of adjustment mechanisms, especially via prices; (iii) more explicit treatment of policy variables; (iv) deeper empirical investigation of all the relationships included; and (v) a detailed investigation of prospective technical developments. The cost of acquiring this information and the scale of the resultant model would be prodigious. (These difficulties have been expressed in terms of a formal model, but would arise equally in more informal methods of assessment.)

After all this has been done it may be doubted whether the area of uncertainty has been reduced significantly, and therefore how much guidance the model would provide to current decision-making. Thus while, in a general way, consideration of the distant future should be a major factor in current decision-making, there is no virtue in heavy expenditure on a detailed assessment of distant possibilities if the picture obtained is too blurred to be of much practical use.

Without elaborate modelling it is possible to see some of the main long-term dangers and indeed devise some policies to minimise them. For example, it is evidently *conceivable* that important resources *could* run short within 100 years and that technology *could* fail to find adequate substitutes. In general the appropriate policy response is (i) to increase general provision for future generations on account of their possible need, and (ii) to encourage the conservation of resources which seem likely to be critical. This second item must be viewed widely — it involves, for example, discouraging dependence on such resources and stimulating research into resource-saving technologies. Potentially a detailed assessment would throw light on the trade-off between present sacrifice and the reduction in the risk of future catastrophe and on the optimal mix of capital (man-made capital, know-how, natural resources — and which types) to leave to future generations, but in practice, as suggested above, the light shed is likely to be minimal. Also crucial to the decision of how much to sacrifice is the degree of risk aversion and the rate of utility discount. These are crucial ingredients of any decisions, and ones which the model cannot illumine (though it can investigate the implications of any *given* judgements in any desired degree of detail).

It would be wrong to condemn all long-term assessment. It is the grandiose comprehensive models, which approach the question in a very general way, not geared to specific current decisions, which are likely to yield minimal information at prodigious cost. More limited investigations of important sub-problems, of which the outstanding example is energy, could be valuable.

6.3   Z.E.G., Z.E.D. and the stationary state

These moves to eliminate or reduce market imperfections and gratuitous tax distortions in resource industries would be valuable, and would in some cases reduce depletion very substantially. However, in other cases the effects would be slight and Pessimists would probably consider the degree of conservation achieved inadequate to prevent a serious risk of catastrophe. Indeed the market-failure approach to environmental and resource problems has been likened to protecting beach-chairs from the incoming tide by building a barricade around each! Such critics call for across-the-board measures, such as zero economic growth (Z.E.G.) or zero environmental degradation (Z.E.D.).

Zero economic growth (Z.E.G.).

The call for Z.E.G. is usually expressed vaguely without any accompanying programme for its attainment. In fact economic growth is normally defined in terms of G.N.P. — and aggregate of the numerous individual types of production, each measured by value added. Hence there are an infinite number of ways of varying the structure of G.N.P. within any given total.

One possibility is to freeze not only the present total but also the present structure. However, this is neither feasible nor desirable. Indeed an immediate freeze would be ludicrous. To take one example, the present scale of production in investment-goods industries is related to the over-all rate of growth of production. A halt in the latter indicates a *drop* in the former. In this context freezing investment at its current level would bring about an increase in unused capacity, and with it a totally unproductive depletion of resources.

Moreover, even the present scale and pattern of output is giving rise to serious environmental problems. Many of these — depletion of minerals and fuels, erosion, deforestation, persistent pollution — are of a cumulative nature, so that to accept current activity is to accept a continued deterioration in the environment in these respects. It is probably essential that certain forms of production, especially certain techniques of production, be progressively *curtailed*. Indeed some of the more damaging activities *are* being curtailed as a market response to incipient scarcity or through public action (for example on pollution) so that a freeze would be a retrograde step indeed. By the same token it is equally vital that other activities (for example research into birth control, pollution control, installation of energy-saving plant) be increased. So the idea of freezing economic activity must be rejected as being a recipe for catastrophe.

But if variations are to be allowed, some up, some down, it is difficult to see how constraining the over-all change in some aggregative index such as G.N.P. to zero is either desirable or feasible.

Zero environmental degradation (including resource depletion) (Z.E.D.)
This is the main object of Z.E.G;. and it seems worth investigating whether it stands up as a policy in its own right. Now, immediate elimination of environmental degradation (including resource depletion), even were it feasible, is plainly undesirable. For one thing in many cases the only purpose of conserving a resource is to exploit it later — to exploit it never is pointless; if this is accepted, then the best time to exploit some resources may be now. Second, as emphasised by Barnett and Morse (1963) (see p. 95), much resource use is essentially *conversion* into other forms of capital: equipment, human skills and knowledge. Such conversion may be beneficial to future generations or even essential to survival. Third, even where resources are devoted to consumption, this may be a necessary condition of a reduction in the birth rate. Fourth, the immediate cessation of depletion of fossil fuels or minerals is surely a recipe for immediate Doom.

The case for maintaining stocks of renewable resources is perhaps stronger but even this is not always desirable or even feasible, particularly in the light of the inevitably vast population increases of the next few decades. Some use of D.D.T., some heavy metal pollution, some rise in global temperature, running down of some fish stocks, felling of some forests, may be essential to avoid mass starvation in the short term, particularly in the absence of altogether infeasible changes in distribution. At the same time some stocks are currently being increased. To require that on balance the *net* degradation of the environment be halted is perhaps a reasonable long-term objective in general terms, but unless some method can be devised for adding up the gains and losses it is difficult to see how it could be made operational.

Environmentalists have rightly stressed the interconnectedness of everything and the inadequacies of a partial approach. A simple and expositionally useful response is a macro analysis, dealing in such generalities as G.N.P. and 'environmental quality'. But this approach, too, can be misleading. There is not one environmental problem but many, interconnected but distinct, and there is really no alternative to a selective disaggregated approach. Ideally what is required is a fully articulated 'general-equilibrium' model in which all the interconnections are spelt out. In practice this is not feasible and, as with the more limited 'second-best' problems of conventional economics, there is no alternative to a piecemeal approach, in which, however, the possibility of more distant ramifications is kept constantly in view.

The stationary state

The more careful writers stress that Z.E.G. and Z.E.D. are long-term objectives and part of the wider objective of the *stationary state*. Daly (1971), a leading advocate, defines the stationary state as 'an economy in which the total population and the total stock of physical wealth are maintained constant at some desired levels by a "minimal" rate of maintenance of throughput (i.e. by birth and death rates which are equal at the lowest feasible level and by physical production and consumption which are equal at the lowest feasible level)'. He contends that the stationary-state economy is a 'physical necessity'.

In fact it is difficult to see why consumption should be held at the lowest feasible level, as long as stationarity is really being maintained. Moreover, changes in technology or tastes may indicate changes in activity. Changes could even be continuous, leading to continual growth (as in the model on p. 35). Even if continued change leads to Doom, this may be desired (Daly describes the post-Doom state as stationary, but this is quibbling). Georgescu-Roegen (1971) emphasises the inevitable loss of entropy, concluding that strict stationarity is impossible.

Meadows *et al*'s (1972) view of the stationary state is more flexible: 'Population and capital are the only qualities that need be constant in the equilibrium state. Any human activity that does not require a large flow of irreplaceable resources or produces severe environmental degradation might continue to grow indefinitely.' But here, too, there are difficulties. Many activities each requiring a small flow of irreplaceable resources could together involve serious resource depletion, and far from being allowed to grow will need to be cut back if equilibrium is to be preserved. It is perhaps significant that Meadows's computed 'equilibrium state' involved the continued depletion of resources leading to Doom within three centuries.

However, the greatest limitation of the concept of the stationary state is that, by itself, it provides little positive guidance to current action. Which of a wide variety of possible (almost) stationary states should we aim for? Should we seek to attain stationarity next year or next century?

But it would be wrong to conclude on this unsympathetic note. The stationary-state idea should be seen as a reaction to 'growthmania', the unquestioning assumption that 'growth' in G.N.P., or even 'progress', is beneficial and can be maintained (see Beckerman, 1974). Daly and others emphasise, perhaps in an oversimplified way, the long-term constraints within which the economy must operate and the dangers of failing to recognise such constraints early enough to make appropriate adaptations. They also emphasise that it may be insufficient to confine our attention narrowly to resource sectors.

'Don't grow!' and 'don't change!', like 'grow!' and 'change!', serve well as rallying cries but are scarcely adequate as guides to action. Difficult as it may be, each facet of our complex society must be considered on its merits. Here it is well to recall that 'growth' is supported by a variety of serious market biases discussed in the last chapter. A useful approach, which has received surprisingly little attention from the anti-growth school, is the elimination or reduction of these general biases.

6.4 Pervasive distortions
The discount rate and the tax system
It has been shown (Chapter 5) how the high level of pre-tax interest rates encourages rapid depletion and generally discourages provision for the future. At the same time these high rates are partly a reflection of current opinions and preferences. The latter reduce the scope, and arguably the justification, for depressing interest rates.

One possibility would be a cheap-money policy, i.e. a reduction in government borrowing matched by an increase in taxation. The immediate effect is a decrease in the demand for loanable funds, which tends to depress interest rates. However, there are other ramifications and the over-all impact is controversial (see Houghton, 1970). A useful approach is to examine *saving*. Assuming no change in government expenditure, the change increases public saving, and over-all saving will be increased provided there is not a matching reduction in private saving. It might be thought that the increased tax commitment would be met partly out of saving, partly out of consumption or that individuals may even increase savings in an attempt to offset the apparent reduction in wealth. However, in fact this reduction is largely illusory, for it is matched by a reduction in the national debt and hence in the tax burden in the future. The change in financing may be looked at as 'forced saving' by the government on behalf of individuals, and a rational response would be an equivalent reduction in voluntary (private) saving. Hence if individuals take account of future tax burdens, then any decrease in the demand for loanable funds engineered in this way will be exactly matched by a decrease in supply from reduced private saving, and interest rates will remain unchanged. However, it may reasonably be argued that such reasoning implies an improbable degree of sophistication among the public at large. Of course, the monetary–fiscal mix may be constrained by other considerations, for example price stability or the balance of payments.

Another approach, more closely related to an identified distortion, would be to reduce taxation of saving. Returns on savings are currently taxed at 50 per cent in standard tax brackets and at rates approaching 100 per cent in the highest tax brackets. It was shown that the effective rates are much higher in times of inflation and that real tax rates could substantially exceed 100 per cent.

A useful reform would be to calculate returns in real terms, and this should extend also to taxation of capital gains, company profits and the proposed tax on wealth. It might be said that inflation has had the by-product of increasing the tax burden on the wealthy and that this reform would eliminate this useful effect. However, the effect is largely accidental and if it is desired to increase redistribution this should surely by done by explicit legislation. Moreover, the redistribution effect acts somewhat erratically, having greatest impact on assets earning taxable capital gains or income. This enormous increase in the level of tax liability, and its variation across different assets, greatly increases the incentive to look for means of tax avoidance. This (i) reduces any redistributive impact, (ii) discriminates strongly in favour of those who are less scrupulous over the morality of tax avoidance, (iii) creates large gratuitous distortions in asset markets, and (iv) increases the proportion of national effort devoted to finding and plugging avenues to tax avoidance and evasion. These difficulties are encountered to some extent in any attempt at strongly progressive taxation but are aggravated by the gratuitously discriminatory nature of this particular system of tax.

A second reform would be to remove the surcharges on 'unearned' income. One could go further and eliminate the tax on saving altogether by changing the taxation base from income to expenditure, as advocated by Kaldor (1955).[2] There appears to be little practical difficulty in operating such a scheme, though there would be very substantial transitional problems (see Meade *et al.*, 1978). Since expenditure is an inelastic function of income, an expenditure tax levied at the same rates as income tax would be less progressive, but this could easily be rectified by modifying the rates. However, an expenditure tax would bear less severely on unspent wealth. On the assumption that wealth *per se* only confers utility through spending, this is perhaps appropriate. But of course this assumption may not be accepted: wealth provides also various non-marketed services; some of the more straightforward of these, for example the housing services provided to the owner-occupier, could be taxed by imputation, but others, for example the power that wealth is alleged to confer, would be difficult to tax except by taxing wealth or its accumulation (saving).

Another useful reform would be to base taxation of bequests or gifts on the cumulative amount *received* by particular individuals (rather than on the amounts given). This would better serve the redistributive intentions of such taxes and would reduce the deterrent to saving in many cases.

Endogenous wants

Want creation both aggravates resource depletion and reduces the benefits of the associated increases in consumption. While want creation is partly a spontaneous process, it is clearly powerfully aggravated by advertising. This could be curbed. The most extreme suggestion is a complete ban on all or most forms of advertising. An alternative and, as we shall see, preferable approach would be an advertising tax, as proposed by Corden (1963) and others.[3] The chief objections to such curbs are that advertising revenue is essential to the press and other media, that it plays a central role in the competitive market process, that it has an important informatory function and that in practice it is not easy to devise a satisfactory definition of what is to be curbed.

The first contention is undeniable; advertising revenue accounts for over 50 per cent of press revenue — without it prices would rise sharply, putting newspapers beyond the means of all but the richest of the public and placing in jeopardy the continued existence of many or all papers, thus reducing the variety of views conveyed to the public. This reduction in press activity would, it is argued, place democracy in jeopardy. Of course, the newspaper is no longer the predominant medium of communication, but many of the alternatives such as weekly journals and television are heavily supported by advertising, which also bolsters entertainments (cinema, sports) as well as public transport and local authorities. However, concentrating on the press, there are two strong counter-arguments — namely the danger that advertising itself may influence editorial policy and the possibility of finding alternative forms of finance. Deliberate attempts by advertisers to influence editorial policy are unlikely in view of the strong tradition of freedom of the press; rather, the danger is that the importance of advertising makes it essential to maintain a readership with a large potential for buying the kind of products advertised. This forces editors to publish 'appealing' material, leading to an obsession with sex, crime and violence with, arguably, a pernicious effect on public behaviour (see Bronfenbrenner, 1971). Of course, this can be defended as 'giving the public what it wants', a kind of 'reader sovereignty'; and the alternative image of 'enlightened' editors giving the public what they ought to have can be condemned as undemocratic and elitist. However, the issue should not be exaggerated: even under the current system editors have considerable discretion, while under alternative systems of support a high readership is still likely to be among the aims of newspaper proprietors. The alternative to support by advertisers is support by the government. Such a suggestion tends to raise fears of official censorship but these could surely be avoided if the subsidies were automatically available to all-comers. There would be no *resource* cost from this change in source of finance, though there would be a cost to the exchequer. This is one advantage of an advertising *tax*, namely that it would provide the finance for the subsidies.

One of the roles claimed for advertising in a capitalist economy is to create demand. Without it, it is alleged, profits and jobs would be endangered. But if wants were not created artificially, there would be less concern with rising incomes, hence less industrial conflict and less inflation; it would be easier to find resources to satisfy public and social needs and to enhance the environment, while leisure time could be increased and resources saved. All these are inhibited by constant pressures to increase private spending. The change would involve some transfer of jobs from the private to the public sector, but to regret that would surely be to confuse ends with means. Arguably there are a wide range of goods and services which are best supplied by the private sector, but there seems little to be said for artificially expanding these simply to promote private enterprise. Lipton (1968a) suggests that the consumption of heavily advertised goods be discouraged, but the virtue of this is doubtful; once the wants have been created, failure to satisfy them is seen as a deprivation and is resisted. Hence, for example, the present government (1978), even though professing socialism, finds it necessary to encourage the private sector. The only way out of these difficulties is to intervene earlier in the process to discourage want creation.

It is also claimed that advertising plays an important part in sustaining competition (see Harris and Seldon, 1959). For example it may facilitate the entry of new firms, thus creating potential and sometimes actual competition. But it can also be used as a weapon to discourage entry. Some studies have been performed on the influence of advertising on competition (see Cowling *et al.*, 1975) but the results are conflicting. In any case they largely miss the point. The major effect of advertising is to stimulate 'product differentiation', an effect which is not picked up in measures of concentration. The search for means to differentiate one's product may sometimes lead to significant innovation, but the differentiation is usually trivial and the alleged addition to consumer choice of little significance. Product differentiation and the associated phenomenon of brand loyalty constitute important entry barriers.

Perfect knowledge is a standard condition for the perfect market. Advertising is often defended as supplying information. However, the informative content of many advertisements is very low and what information is provided is often confined to trivial or irrelevent features of the product. Very clearly the primary aim of the advertiser is to persuade the consumer to buy the product and this is not generally done very effectively by a full catalogue of information about the product (see Packard, 1957, or any manual on marketing), Notwithstanding this, some advertisements (for example 'small ads', trade catalogues and even some displays) do retail important and useful information which one would certainly not with to suppress. Some of the discussions make a distinction between informative and persuasive advertising; conceptually this is unsatisfactory since information relates to the content of an advertisement and persuasion more to its manner of presentation, and most advertisements are both in varying degrees. There is a corresponding difficulty in distinguishing a category of 'primary informative' advertisement to be singled out for special treatment.

A rather similar problem of definition surrounds other promotional activities. Clearly, the objections to advertising apply also to promotional coffee mornings, door-to-door salesmen, some of the activities of commercial salesmen, packaging, gift offers and competitions and to the sponsorship of sports events, university chairs or medical research. If such activities were unrestricted, not only would an important form of want creation be unaffected but firms would redirect their activities from conventional advertising to these forms of salesmanship, which could be more pernicious. On the other hand, some of the activities listed (for example packaging, visiting by commercial salesmen) are, despite their strong promotional overlay, basically functional in origin, while in others (for example sponsorship of medical research) advertisement is intermingled with an exercise in public concern. However, it is difficult to find much virtue in a promotional coffee morning. Hence the boundary, which should almost certainly be drawn wider than conventional advertising, would not be easy to draw and there would be anomalies.

The 'boundary problem' is a serious one, but it is important to realise that it applies to *any* form of tax or regulation. It would be most serious if (as at the moment seems likely) firms were unconvinced of the virtues of the curbs and sought every available means to exploit the anomalies. It should also be stressed that the boundary problem would be more acute under a ban than under a tax, which would at least permit (though it would penalise) activities on the 'wrong' side of the boundary.

Population increase

In the last chapter it was suggested that a major factor in the population problem is a divergence between the social and private costs of child-bearing, which in advanced countries is greatly aggravated by various forms of child subsidies. An obvious remedy is the removal of these subsidies. However, children, once born, have needs, and the removal of such subsidies (unless entirely effective in eliminating large families) would cause serious deprivation not only to the parents, who at least had some choice, but to the children, who had none.[4] However, care should be taken to ensure that subsidies do not exceed needs. This is particularly important in the case of young children. In view of myopia and discounting, a divergence between subsidies and the needs of older children are less likely to affect child-bearing decisions. A divergence is particularly likely if there are a large number of different benefits under different legislation and disbursed by different agencies, so that it is difficult to keep track of the combined impact. It may also occur where substantial in-kind benefits, notably council houses, are in short supply and allocated according to need; an additional child can then crucially affect eligibility. A system of economic rents, with a sliding scale of rebates related to need, would be greatly preferable in this respect. It is also important that the subsidies should benefit the children rather than the parents, and in this respect appropriate in-kind grants, for example free education, medical treatment, welfare foods, are preferable to cash grants.

The system of issuing marketable child coupons (which one would have to purchase if one wanted a child, or presumably if one accidentally found oneself pregnant), though in some ways very attractive, in that it would allow the government to control the birth rate exactly, would be open to the same distributional objection. The poor might have large families despite their poverty and the need to purchase coupons would increase their poverty and cause deprivation. Subsidising small families involves the same problem, since the subsidies can only come from larger families.[5]

In this respect, indeed, a *ban* on large families is to be preferred as, assuming effective enforcement, it avoids this distribution problem. *Ex post* punishment of those breaking the ban would be unthinkable, especially with imperfect contraception: the only feasible method would be compulsory sterilisation of certain categories of family, for example those with more than, say, three children. This 'solution' to the population problem is certainly not attractive, and is advocated only by extreme Pessimists. If the choice is between compulsory sterilisation and mass starvation (as indeed it already is in some parts of some less-developed countries), then to proclaim in lofty moral tones that compulsion is an infringement of human rights is perhaps a little simple-minded.

Turning to more appealing methods, the most widely advocated relate to birth control. First, barriers to the production, sale and use of birth control could be eliminated. Second, there could be government subsidies to contraception, and perhaps abortions, clinics, domiciliary advice and research into birth control. In this way we could move nearer to what the United Nations' Declaration of Human Rights has described as the 'basic human right' of parents to choose the size of their family.

There is perhaps little the social scientist can say concerning the various religious and moral objections that have been raised to birth control except to beg the objectors to ponder afresh the dire consequences of rapid population growth. On the question of 'basic human rights' the United Nations' declaration, though perhaps useful as propaganda at the present time, is extravagant and ultimately absurd. It is one thing to assert a basic human right to the *use* of contraceptives, quite another to assert that they should be *subsidised*, or more generally that one should have a basic human right to choose family size *without reference to cost*. Strictly, though this is underplayed, the assertion implies the right to have as many as well as as few children as desired, and further that the decision be not constrained by cost. As we saw, the costs of bearing and rearing children are often largely borne by the state, but this is justified on distributional grounds not in terms of the right to choose family size. Likewise, limitation of family size, though socially desirable at the present time, cannot be defended as an absolute human right. In fact there is no limit to the subsidies that could be provided to promote contraceptive knowledge and research, and the degree to which this right can be approximated (it can never be reached) must be purchased at a cost. The extent to which it is appropriate to subsidise contraception must in fact be a matter of social judgement, of weighing up priorities, not of overriding human rights. It could indeed be argued that if parents were made to bear the full costs of child-bearing and -rearing they should also be made to bear the full costs of contraception. In this way their decisions would be made in the light of the relevant costs together with their personal preferences (see p. 106). It is the difficulties surrounding the removal of the large divergences between the private and social costs of child-bearing that provide the main justification for subsidies to birth control. However, simply to provide free contraceptives is not sufficient, even in advanced countries — it is necessary also to provide clinics which are situated conveniently (especially in poorer areas) and which are open at convenient times. Women, especially less educated ones, are often embarrassed to seek birth control themselves and initiatives by staff in maternity hospitals or through domiciliary family-planning services have a vital role in encouraging the cost of effective birth control (see Bone, 1973). In less-developed countries the need to overcome ignorance and prejudice is even more crucial.

However, studies of intentions on family size (see, for example, Ehrlich and Ehrlich, 1970) show that even if 'unwanted' pregnancies were to be completely eliminated by universal use of effective birth control, population growth would continue to be rapid. Family planning is not enough. Family-size intentions vary widely between countires, being highest in the less-developed countries, and typically falling rapidly with development. This may suggest that increased consumption in less-developed countries could play a useful role in resource conservation despite the initially adverse effect. On the other hand, certain specific features of development appear to be crucial, particularly urbanisation, education (especially of women), job opportunities for women, decreases in child mortality and social-security benefits for the old (see Hawthorn, 1970). In order to reduce population growth it is encouragement of these specific changes, rather than an indiscriminate programme of development, that would appear to be required.

Appraisal

These policies reach out far beyond the resource sector. They are *radical* in the true sense that they aim at the roots of the problem. They strike at processes that are deep-seated in the socio-economic systems of capitalist and collectivist countries alike. This brief review indicates not only how much could be done to reduce these important market failures, but also the severe difficulties involved. These arise not only from generational selfishness (an obstacle to *any* measure for protecting the future) but also from heavy enforcement costs, both in conventional economic terms and in the form of infringements on personal liberty; for example, while it is relatively easy to discourage advertising, it is more difficult to influence some other forms of sales promotion and virtually impossible to eliminate want generation arising naturally from social contacts. In two important cases effective measures have adverse distributional implications: it is impossible to tax wealth (inherited or not) without inhibiting saving and raising the discount rate; while the needs of large families cannot be met without encouraging child bearing.

Hence serious distortions are likely to remain, leading *inter alia* to excessive resource depletion. This provides a possible (second-best) justification for policies aimed directly at reducing resource depletion.

6.5   Policies to reduce resource depletion

Subsidies to specific resource-saving activities

This appears to strike directly at 'wasteful' practices (for example failure to insulate or to recycle) and is by far the most popular proposal. Such subsidies have been employed on a very modest scale by government. The issue will be discussed in relation to recycling, where subsidies are particularly often recommended (insulation is discussed further in Chapter 9). The first point to realise is that recycling is not a panacea for resource problems: where recycling is relatively cheap it is already extensively practised; thus substantial increases in recycling are generally costly and 100 per cent recycling quite infeasible (see Pearce and Walter, 1977). In some cases recycling can be more expensive *even in terms of resources*. For example, collection and processing can use more energy than extraction (and possibly also add to problems of pollution and road congestion). Thus a saving of metal is traded for increased energy consumption. Depending on relative scarcities, this is not necessarily a gain. In other cases, while there may be a net saving in resources, there will be heavy labour costs, a factor which should be given some weight. Thus recycling does not merit unlimited or indiscriminate encouragement.

Another difficulty is that recycling is but one way of reducing consumption of virgin materials. Alternatives include product substitution and increased durability. Sometimes these alternatives may be in direct conflict. For example, recycling subsidies might stimulate design changes which facilitate recycling but at the same time make the product less durable. In any event the government will have to decide how much to stimulate recycling, how much durability, how much product substitution. This is at best a very complex exercise in cost—benefit analysis. It is probable that certain means of resource saving (for example lower consumption of resource-using manufactures, balanced by higher consumption of services) will be neglected altogether.

Some commentators (for example Page, 1976; Pearce and Walter, 1977) have suggested that recycling subsidies could make little contribution to reducing extraction, the recycled metals simply being added to the current level of extraction, facilitating an increase in consumption. One could indeed regard recycling as a link in the chain of activities involving resource extraction – processing–consumption–recycling–consumption–and so on – and thus complementary to extraction. To subsidise recycling is to subsidise the whole sequence and thus cheapen resource-intensive products relative to others, for example services. Depending on the relevant price elasticities, consumption of resource-intensive products could increase so substantially that extraction actually increases.

A final difficulty is that subsidies, far from being costless, involve a substantial burden on the exchequer and thus on society. Taxes must be raised (unpopular and often resulting in evasion, avoidance and damage to incentives) or public expenditure curtailed.

Advocates of recycling subsidies sometimes use a 'second-best' argument, invoking the favourable tax treatment of competing virgin materials, price discrimination by transport undertakings, unwarranted discrimination in product-quality regulations and the absence of adequate pollution controls. These distortions are particularly important in the United States (Page, 1976). However, all are best tackled at source.

Regulations
Such regulations as currently exist tend to favour virgin resources. This

discrimination could be reversed to favour recycling and re-use, or limits could be placed on the rate of extraction from particular mines. The major objection to this approach is that it involves centralised bureaucratic decisions as to precisely what activities are to be regulated and to what extent. Regulations tend to be set arbitrarily, and achieve their objects (if at all) at considerable cost in inefficiency (for example regulation in the United States; see p. 113)

However, regulations may be the best way of tackling specific forms of market failure. For example, the demise of the returnable bottle is partly, perhaps mainly, attributable to a lack of standardisation, which means that each bottle must be returned to the original maker. The forces of competition do not promote standardisation; rather, they promote various forms of product differentiation, including individual bottle types. The appropriate response to this market failure is a law (or perhaps an incentive) requiring the use of standard bottles. Another candidate is product durability. It could be argued that throw-away products are taking into account time preference, changing tastes, a desire for flexibility and relative costs, and that consumers often prefer short-life products. Some of these involve market failure, but only as part of much wider problems such as endogenous wants, thus requiring ideally much wider solutions. However, an alternative view is that lack of durability represents a lack of knowledge on the part of the consumer. He can see that the less-durable product is cheaper but he does not know with any certainty that the other product is more durable, that spares will continue to be available, and so on. This lack of knowledge is a clear case of market failure biasing decisions in favour of short-lived products, and incidentally giving rise to excessive pollution and resource use. Legislation (or perhaps incentives) to promote durability, or specific aspects of design which ensure durability as well as to continued servicing and provision of spares, would be useful.

Taxes on resource depletion

As a general means of reducing depletion, particularly of non-renewable[6] resources, taxes have obvious advantages. They impinge on a small number of producers and hence (unlike, for example V.A.T.) are cheap to collect. They provide an equal stimulus to *all* forms of resource saving, for example input or product substitution, increased durability and recycling. There is thus no need for the government to work out which resource-saving activities should be encouraged or by how much, no danger that certain methods may be overlooked or difficult to subsidise, no danger that the encouragement of certain activities will be counter-productive. It is left to the market to decide how far, at the new prices, each resource-saving activity should be taken.

However, such taxes are not greatly liked, especially outside the economics profession, and such resource taxes as are employed are generally seen in terms of revenue or distribution (for example oil petrol taxes, and the Petroleum Revenue Tax). Subsidies to approved methods of resource saving are usually preferred by the government and by the public at large, despite the strong disadvantages indicated above. The objections to taxes, real and imagined, are therefore worth examining in some detail.

First, taxes are unpopular because they are seen to raise prices, while subsidies reduce them. Here, however, appearances are misleading. There is a real cost in saving resources whatever means are employed. If a lower level of resources is combined with the same quantities of labour and capital (in the longer term the capital stock may also be lower), then output will generally be lower. This reduction is an inescapable result of cutting back on resource use but will be less if an efficient method (such as resource taxes) rather than an inefficient method (such as recycling subsidies) is used. In addition there is a transfer payment, between the resource-using sectors and the government. If a subsidy is used, then there is a reduction in the costs of resource products, but this is counterbalanced by the loss in revenue to the government, which involves a reduction in government expenditure or in private expenditure following a rise in other taxes. If the latter method of financing the subsidies is used, then there will be a further loss in efficiency through the distorting effects of most taxes. If, on the contrary, resource taxes are levied, then the prices of resource products rise, but there is a corresponding increase in government revenue, which may be used to increase public expenditure or cut back on other (allocatively inefficient) taxes. Thus the notion that subsidies reduce costs while taxes increase them is a partial and misleading one derived from focusing attention exclusively on the resource-using sectors.

The related notion that taxes, but not subsidies, result in unemployment or inflation is also bolstered by a neglect of the impact on exchequer finance. A *sharp* cutback in resource use does carry serious dangers of both inflation and unemployment, associated with the large structural shifts in production involved away from resource-intensive activities. These dangers and the ways in which they may be met will be discussed at length in the next chapter. However, the salient point at the moment is that these dangers are largely independent of the choice of subsidies or taxes to achieve resource saving.

A further objection, for a country like the United Kingdom which exports predominantly resource-intensive manufactures, is that the balance of payments would suffer from a tax on the inputs to these industries. Here much depends on whether resource-saving policies are adopted globally or confined to the home country. If globally, then increases in the prices of U.K. manufactures would be matched (approximately) by increases in competitors' prices. Demand and hence exports would still fall somewhat, but prices would rise and, assuming the revenue to be collected by the exporting government, the balance of payments could even improve. However, if a resource tax were applied unilaterally by the United Kingdom, then there could be a serious deterioration in the balance of payments. But again it should be emphasised that the tax generates revenue which could be used to reduce industrial costs, for example by a reduction in V.A.T. or corporation tax. While the costs of resource-intensive industries still rise relative to the costs of other industries, the rise will be less than the resource tax and may be further reduced by the adoption of resource-saving technologies. The effect on adverse competitiveness can be virtually eliminated by means of an export rebate and an import equalisation tax in relation to the estimated resource content of the product. Effectively this would mean that the resource content of home *consumption* rather than home production was being taxed. This seems not inappropriate. There might be difficulties in estimating the resource content and hence the appropriate rebate or levy and such provisions might conflict with certain international agreements. However, these provisions parallel existing provisions in respect of V.A.T., they have the same logic and present much the same administrative difficulties. If they conflict with the letter of international agreements, they do not conflict with the spirit; over all the provisions, taxes plus rebates and equalisation levies, do not improve the competitive position of U.K. industry, they merely prevent a deterioration. International agreement is surely possible.[7]

Probably the most serious difficulty with resource taxes is to decide which resources to tax and at what rate. In principle, of course, the tax should represent the difference between perceived private cost and true social cost. But this is difficult to determine, depending on a correct view of future discoveries, substitution possibilities and technical change. Moreover, taxation of, say, copper will encourage the substitution of aluminium, thereby increasing its scarcity and affecting the appropriate tax to be levied on the latter resource. Thus in principle the optimum taxes on various resources are interrelated. Clearly, these optima are a matter of judgement, as evidenced by the opinion of many economists that the optimum levels are frequently low or even negative (see p. 88).

But, again, the important thing to realise is that these difficulties, though made more obvious by the use of resource taxes, are inherent in any programme of resource saving. For example, the appropriate level of recycling subsidy is equally dependent on how far the price of virgin metal falls below the true social cost. But it depends also, which resource taxes do not, on the relative merits of *alternative ways* of reducing the consumption of virgin metal. Hence the determination of the optimum recycling subsidy involves all the difficulties of the determination of the optimum resource tax plus some additional ones.

Finally, it is suggested that since resource-intensive goods mostly have an income elasticity of less than unity, resource taxes would be regressive. However, with the possible exception of energy taxes, the degree of regressivity is slight. Any adverse impact on the poor may be met by explicit redistributive measures, and here it should be noted that expenditure on social services is limited by a tight budget constraint which is alleviated by the revenue from the taxes (see Lecomber and Fisher, 1978).

6.6 Conclusions

'Excessive' resource use has been traced to (i) failure of preferences to take 'due' account of the welfare of successor generations, and (ii) failure of market mechanisms to reflect these preferences. The first is barely soluble in a democracy, and accordingly this chapter has been directed to the second.

The general theme was that resource policies should be directed as closely as possible to specific sources of market failure, noting, however, that some of the most important of these pervade the whole economy and hence require equally pervasive policies. The inefficiency of a more arbitrary approach was repeatedly illustrated. Where direct remedies are not available, a second-best policy (such as resource taxes) is generally to be preferred to a third-best policy (such as recycling subsidies). Resource taxes, while discriminating, inappropriately, between resource saving and other means of providing for the future, at least achieves parity between various methods of resource saving which recycling subsidies do not.

The discussion has been brief and general; it has not been possible to give more than an indication of the difficulties that surround particular controls and the consequent need for a flexible approach.

7   PROBLEMS OF REDUCING RESOURCE USE

At the present time growth is supported by accelerating depletion of most resources. It is evident that this pattern of development is not sustainable indefinitely. Optimists place their faith in further technical advance both to extend the resource base and to support growth even when cumulative depletion finally forces a reduction in resource use. It was suggested in Chapter 2 that while such an outcome was possible, it was unwise to base current actions on the assumption that appropriate technologies will always emerge at the right time to counteract effects of the declining resource base. Any faltering in technical advance could spell disaster, as could unexpected side-effects or failure to cope effectively with the social ramifications. It is in this context, and bearing in mind the difficulties of a sudden cutback in resource use, that it might be prudent to begin curbing resource depletion now. This chapter is directed to an examination of the problems that this entails and how these may be minimised by suitable policies.

7.1   Images of a low-resource society

Conservationists by no means agree amongst themselves as to the desirable shape of a future society. These disagreements, as will be shown, derive partly from differing perceptions of what is feasible either technically or in terms of behaviour (for example, what degree of altruism can be expected from mankind?), partly from differing value judgements. The next few pages sketch some of the main points of controversy.

Technology
Conservationists generally stress the baleful role that technology has played in human development. It has facilitated material advance but largely at the expense of more extensive resource depletion and environmental degradation. Optimists suggest that this is the fault not of technology as such but of the crude, ignorant and short-sighted manner in which it has often been applied. All that is necessary is to modify the direction of technology to take fuller account of environmental and social implications and resource constraints. The effect on growth of this more sophisticated approach may be minimal (see

Chapter 2). Conservationists are more cautious and believe that growth should be curbed in case the hoped-for advance in technology fails to materialise; but this does not necessarily mean they shun technology. Schumacher (1973), for example, writes: 'Man cannot live without science and technology any more than he can live against nature.' Chapman (1975), while highly critical of nuclear power, advocates vigorous development of solar heating, more economical cars and the hydrolysis of straw, all in the interests of conserving fossil fuels. Gouch and Eastlund (1971) look to fusion technologies to facilitate recycling in the steady state. The *Blueprint for Survival* (Goldsmith, 1976), while rejecting persistent pesticides, advocates integrated biological pest control as well as research into material substitutions, the development of rapid mass transit and alternative technologies generally. Nearly all conservationists advocate contraceptive technology.

That such advanced technologies could be an important aid to conservation is obvious, but there are also dangers – in fact much the same dangers as are involved in technology for growth. First, new technology tends to entail change – in behaviour, in attitudes and social arrangements, and in manpower requirements, tending to involve structural unemployment and other social problems ultimately destructive of the fabric of society (see Mishan, 1977). Second, there is the serious danger of unforeseen side-effects (see World Health Organisation, 1976). For example, the uncritical espousal of integrated pest control by Goldsmith (1976), following in the distinguished footsteps of Rachel Carson (1962) and the Ehrlichs (1970), is surprising, as the technique appears to involve very similar dangers to the now discredited control by persistent chemicals. The introduction of foreign predators, like that of foreign chemicals, modifies the ecosystem – as indeed it is designed to do. But ecosystems are complex and poorly understood and hence the full implications are unpredictable. Past introductions of foreign plants and animals – not for biological control, of which we have as yet little experience – have caused considerable damage (for example the water hyacinth, grey squirrels and the dutch elm beetle in the United Kingdom). This is not to say that biological control should never be used – the benefits must be weighed against the risks of adverse long-term effects – only that the general preference over chemical means of control so frequenty displayed remains to be justified. Again, the risks of fusion power (for example its possible contribution to global overheating) do not immediately vanish because the technology is to be used for recycling.

At the other extreme there are conservationists who would avoid as far as possible new or even existing advanced technologies. This view stems partly from the considerations just discussed, partly from a willingness or even a desire to return to a simple life-style, discussed below (see, for example, Ellul, 1965). In fact the direction one can travel along this road is severely limited by the size of the present and prospective future population, which cannot be maintained even at subsistence (let alone the standards to which a significant proportion have become accustomed) without the use of quite sophisticated technology. Further technical advance is, as the more thoughtful conservationists such as Schumacher (1973) recognise, probably essential to survival. However, while both extremes are easy targets of attack, the *degree* of caution appropriate in considering new technologies is likely to remain controversial.

Scale

Closely associated with the issue of technology is that of scale. A characteristic feature of modern technology is its massive scale, which appears in so many cases to promote efficiency. Some of the technologies advocated by conservationists, for example district heating and public transport, involve large-scale centralised organisation.

However, many conservationists are deeply suspicious of scale. Schumacher (1973) writes in his well-known book *Small is Beautiful:*

> We must look for a revolution in technology to give us innovations and machines which will reverse the destructive trends now threatening us all . . . . We need machines and equipment which are (i) cheap enough so that they are accessible to virtually everyone (ii) suitable for small-scale application (iii) compatible with man's need for creativity.

Work is seen as a potentially creative experience, not simply a sacrifice of leisure and a means to securing consumption goods (see also Mishan, 1967). Smallness of scale is important in facilitating greater identification with the product of one's labours. In addition small groups can generally work harmoniously together, subject to informal influences of one member on another. In large groups the 'public-good' problem emerges: each man's contribution accrues largely to other members of the group, for which, the group being large and impersonal, he feels no sympathy (Olson, 1965: cf. the problem of the common-access resource, p. 85). Hence artificial incentives, such as piece rates, have to be imposed. Often these fail: perhaps they are considered unfair or can be evaded, and they will need to be reset whenever external conditions change. Such problems have led to the abandonment of piece rates in many work-places (see Brown, 1962) and have contributed to the well-known frictions in the British motor industry. Recent studies have shown that the incidence of strikes increases with plant size (see Shorey, 1976).

Now it may be argued that such difficulties, since they impinge on the firm's profits, will be taken into account in decisions on plant size and that the continued existence of large plants is adequate testimony that these acknowledged disadvantages are outweighed by traditional economies of scale. However, the latter are obvious, quantifiable and immediate; the latter are uncertain and delayed. Moreover, decisions on plant size are often taken on engineering criteria by people largely ignorant of industrial psychology, and who (in line with modern theories of the firm) attach importance to expanding their empires.

Besides, many of the disadvantages of scale are felt outside the work-place; for example, strikes can have widespread ramifications through related industries. Plausibly, though less certainly, the boredom of tedious work in an alienated environment may breed an instrumentalist attitude to work: the worker is likely to become excessively pre-occupied with take-home pay as the only justification for his daily boredom. This would both aggravate inflation and generate resistance to policies, such as public-goods provision and conservation, which reduce take-home pay; moreover, it could breed materialism, selfishness and violence. These are all costs external to the firm.

Finally, an economy of large firms is inflexible and vulnerable to adverse circumstances. Consider, for example, the immense difficulties involved in running down the British motor industry. The work-force is concentrated in a relatively small number of large plants, and alternative work in these areas would be hard to find on the scale required. Hence closure of the plants would cause massive unemployment. As a result the government is likely to shore up the industry with massive subsidies, and in the event of full or partial closure the redundant workers will receive unemployment benefit. In this way a large proportion of the risks associated with large firms are borne by the government.

Similar arguments may be advanced in favour of small settlements. Thus Schumacher (1973) writes:

> I think it is fairly safe to say that the upper limit of what is desirable for the size of the city is probably something of the order of half a

million inhabitants. It is quite clear that above such a size nothing is added to the virtue of a city. In places like London . . . the millions do not add to the city's real value but merely create *enormous* problems and produce human degradation.

Blueprint for Survival (Goldsmith, 1976) calls for settlements of 100,000. These matters are controversial (see Richardson, 1973; Gilbert, 1976); in particular it is not clear whether problems observed in cities (for example crime, suicides) are caused by cities or rather whether cities attract problems that would otherwise have occurred somewhere else. The evidence is inconclusive.

One particular advantage of small settlements could be a reduction in travel. Large cities are characterised by large commuter flows involving heavy consumption of energy and metals. Smaller communities would drastically reduce the need for motorised travel, since jobs, shops, schools and other facilities could mostly be within walking or cycling distance. On the other hand, the smaller the community, the less able it will be to supply its own needs. Thus the gain from reduced travel within the settlement must be weighed against the additional need for transport between communities.

Traditional arguments in favour of large cities are economies of scale and agglomeration − i.e. the advantages of close proximity of related firms. If individual firms need to be large to secure economies of scale and related firms need to be close together to secure economies of agglomeration, then large cities are the inevitable result. Some of these economies have particular relevance to conservation. Ambient temperatures are higher in large cities, thus reducing heating needs; moreover, district heating is viable only in dense settlements. On the other hand, in some spheres, for example transport and waste disposal, including sewage, while there are economies of scale (so that, for example, underground railways are viable only in large cities), these are probably outweighed by the greater problems created by large areas of high population density.

Means of social control
Excessive resource depletion has been associated with market failure, perhaps combined with ignorance, irrationality and indifference to the fate of future generations. A common reaction is to invoke a greatly increased role for government in remedying these effects, especially market failure. Such intervention could take a variety of forms and conservationists are as divided as others over the preferred method.

Some advocate fiscal assistance of the invisible hand; others prefer regulations. Others believe the market mechanism not only involves inequality but encourages selfishness and materialism, major enemies of conservation; this group, despite the lessons of Eastern Europe, looks to greater collective ownership and control. Another group sees conservation as a matter of individual behaviour, partly instinctual, partly motivated by conscious concern for successor generations, rather than something that is imposed by 'the government'. Some indeed see not only market institutions but also political and even educational ones as hostile to conservation and seek to minimise the role of government by breaking up society into small, largely self-sufficient, groups, each small enough to be governed without much formal apparatus; severe difficulties would appear to be involved in achieving and maintaining such communities and in controlling important inter-group externalities (including overt hostility). Unless the 'right values' are dominant in all groups, some rather strong form of central control would be needed. Each view has distinctive implications, for technology and scale for example. Thus, clearly, the last view implies small-scale activities, while the collectivist view favours large-scale technologies such as district heating and public transport (for a variety of views, see Kneese, 1976; Page, 1976; Kapp, 1973; Ophuls, 1977; Edel, 1973; Illich, 1971).

Distribution

Conservationists (again like everyone else) are equally divided in their views on distribution. Equality can conflict with conservation just as it can conflict with any other allocational goal (for example growth). Some see the allocational problem as so serious that, if necessary, equality must be sacrificed (the conflict is especially critical with respect to population policies: see p. 133). But others suggest that inequality breeds conflict and is thus inimical to the co-operative effort required to achieve adequate conservation (see Meadows *et al.*, 1972; Conservation Society, 1973).

Population

One of the fiercest controversies among conservationists concerns population. Some advocate stabilising world population at two or three times the current level, while others insist on an absolute decline. However, both groups agree that ideally the current population is too large, differences arising because of the draconian measures (such as discontinuing subsidies to children or compulsory sterilisation) that would be necessary to effect a decline. Some reject such measures as a monstrous infringement of human rights; others consider them preferable to severe overpopulation and in particular to 'natural' control by pestilence, famine and war. And in this connection there is considerable difference of opinion over whether a threefold increase in population would significantly reduce the quality of life (for example by straining the environment, by involving crowding and necessitating more stringent government controls and greater resort to new technology). An extreme view is that the carrying capacity of the land is insufficient to maintain the current population, let alone one three times as large. There is also some doubt as to whether, in the absence of such measures, population could be stabilised even at this level (for a variety of views on population, see Ehrlich and Ehrlich, 1970; Commoner, 1971; Meadows *et al.*, 1972; Goldsmith, 1976).

7.2 Problems of low-resource society

This section is concerned with problems that arise or are alleged to arise in a society operating at a low level of resource use. The next main section concerns the problems of moving to such a mode of operation.

Unemployment: a non-problem

The argument is clearest in connection with the stationary state. If productivity (P) is rising (and surely there will always be improvements) while output (Y) is held constant, then as a matter of simple arithmetic employment ($L = Y/P$) must fall. A common response to this argument (for example Meadows *et al.*, 1972) is that unemployment may be avoided by work-sharing and a welcome increase in leisure, perhaps by longer education, earlier retirement and even by more encouragement to 'voluntary unemployment on the dole'. Some of these might be beneficial in their own right, but it is not difficult to see problems. Leisure should be enjoyable and a source of personal enrichment if properly used, but it can too easily involve mere idleness, boredom, violence, vandalism and abuse of the environment. In so far as it is enforced (for example by compulsory work-sharing or early retirement) it may be a source of personal misery and resentment. These problems are perhaps soluble but not necessarily easily.

A more fundamental reason for rejecting this argument is that there is no overruling need to hold Y constant. If it is recognised that the aim is to preserve resources, then a problem arises only if the ratio of resource use (R) to output (Y) is fixed. In that case it is impossible to raise Y without raising R. But while this is a simplification appearing in some models, it is scarcely realistic. If a productivity increase allows a given Y to be produced with less L and the same R,[1] full employment may be restored simply by varying the proportions in which L and R are used in producing particular products, or by varying the mix of products. In this way the original levels of R and L may be combined to produce a larger Y. (One output which may be increased is indeed the labour-intensive commodity, leisure.)

Living standards

Constraining resource consumption may be expected to lower both the level and the rate of growth of living standards in the medium term (but cf. Section 7.3, p. 157). Of course, the objective of these measures is to procure a higher-than-otherwise level of consumption in the longer term.

According to the conventional view less consumption is an un-ambiguous disadvantage. However, there are many (for example Schumacher, 1973; Mishan, 1967) who question whether, above a certain level, additional consumption brings happiness and suggest, moreover, that obsessive striving after higher consumption is conducive to unhappiness. Some support for this view is provided by Easterlin (1974), who finds 'avowed' happiness uncorrelated with consumption levels and negatively correlated with growth. These findings he rationalises mainly in terms of rising expectations. Thus, *once appropriate revisions had been made* to expectations, there seems no reason to suppose that people would be conscious of deprivation in the low-resource society.

Distribution

It is often maintained (for example Beckerman, 1974) that growth fosters equality and that reducing resource consumption would endanger this process. The connections between growth and distri-bution are complex, working through socio-political as well as economic channels and doubtless vary widely. However, to cite one counter-example, major innovations and change necessary to facilitate growth have often created unemployment and misery. Here, as else-where, the actions of the government are crucial.

This leads to the suggestion that government action to promote equality is easier in a growing economy than in a static one, for living standards of the poor may then be raised without actually depressing those of the rich. While this is clearly true arithmetically, it does not follow that governments will necessarily follow more egalitarian policies in a growing economy. This is especially the case when it is considered that the rate of growth is not something that is given exogenously (to the extent that it is, the growth debate is sterile), it is something that is, to some extent, *chosen.* And there is a major conflict between income redistribution and growth such that governments espousing growth will be forced to neglect distribution. A highly compressed wage scale, highly progressive taxation and a high level of welfare benefits are damaging to incentives, for example they discourage working long hours, at unpleasant tasks in inconvenient places or at all, they discourage training and saving and encourage emigration. This contention is often resisted but there is accumulating evidence (for example Institute for Fiscal Studies, 1976) that these effects are quantitatively important. Moreover, a growth-orientated strategy will frequently involve encouraging change (thereby endangering employment) and activity in the most favourable locations to the neglect of regional problems. In agrarian countries efficiencies can be increased most easily by consolidation of land holdings and by concentrating resources in large units. Where this has been done distribution has suffered (see Lipton, 1968b; Smith, 1975).

Advocates of the stationary state (for example Meadows *et al.*, 1972; Daly, 1971) often stress the importance of an equitable sharing of material sacrifices, but consider it a positive advantage that 'the problem of relative shares can no longer be put off by appeals to growth . . . the stationary state would make fewer demands on our environmental resource but much greater demands on our moral resources' (Meadows *et al.*, 1972). Such writers welcome this challenge — clearly the distributional problem has not been solved, though it may have been alleviated, by growth and is a constant source of friction. If the stationary state could force us to solve it once and for all, this would be a great gain, at least if the 'solution' were considered acceptable. However, others fear that the result would be a disastrous conflict. It is widely considered that the recent heightened conflict over distribution has been aggravated by the slowing-down of economic growth. But there, as in other matters, it is important to distinguish between a slow or zero rate of growth and a falling one. In the latter case real-income growth falls short of expectations, thus giving rise to dissatisfaction; the mutually inconsistent attempts of all to realise their expectations generate inflation and conflict. The transition to a stationary state or a low-resource economy could involve similar problems, to be discussed in the next main section. But once the low-resource economy is firmly established, expectations will adjust, thus removing a major source of conflict.

It is worth noting that despite a very unequal distribution of income, the relatively stationary states of the pre-industrial revolution era were characterised by little conflict over distribution. This could be explained partly by the distribution of power, but it is also the case that the various classes accepted their position in society. Arguably, change, mobility and constant increases in the national cake to fight about have been important in fanning the distributional struggle. If (which may be doubted) this process is reversible, then a low-resource economy of the future once established could also be characterised by reduced conflict over distribution. Whether this is to be welcomed depends partly on whether a 'satisfactory' distribution has been achieved in the transitional phase, and partly on how one views distribution. The orthodox view is that inequality is bad (even if the poorer groups are happy in their poverty) and that considerable conflict is desirable in the interest of reducing this inequality. But should we not be concerned with the distribution of *welfare* rather than income? And if so, how are we to compare a society in which the poor are content in accepting their poverty with one in which conflict has lessened their material poverty but shattered their contentment? Those who pride themselves on their progressive thought will shudder that such a question should ever be mooted, but it is one that demands an answer (cf. Mishan, 1977).

Finally (to return to less philosophical matters), it is sometimes suggested that the specific policies required to secure lower resource use and lower environmental impact are distributionally damaging. This issue was considered at appropriate points in Chapter 6. It was concluded that, with the possible exception of population policies, no serious conflict is involved.

Age structure
A slowly growing or constant population would be an important aid to low resource use. Such a population would have a markedly different age structure from present-day populations, being more biased towards older age groups. It is sometimes suggested wrongly that such a structure involves a high dependency ratio. In fact the high proportion of old people is generally outweighed by the low proportion of children. Other problems are discussed by Ayres and Kneese (1971).

7.3 Problems of transition
Unemployment
The nature of the unemployment danger seems to be unduly mis-

understood. It is often suggested that slowing down growth will lead to unemployment, as happens in cyclical downswings. Attention may also be drawn to jobs lost in motor-vehicle assembly, construction and other industries particularly affected by conservation. Conservationists often respond (inappropriately) by advocating work-sharing, etc., as discussed above (p. 148).

An *indiscriminate* cutback in output (as in downswings) would indeed involve unemployment. But this is a very poor recipe for re-source conservation (cf. p. 125). It is true that some activities (for example car manufacture) would be cutback drastically, but others (for example pollution control) would be expanded; extraction would be cutback but recycling and repair work increased, while agricultural practices would be modified to employ more labout. The over-all impact on the labour force is in fact not clear from this catalogue, but more general considerations indicate that a general surplus of labour need not be a problem. The reason is simply that whatever the effect of any chosen set of conservation measures on Keynesian (demand-deficient) unemployment, it can be neutralised by a general stimulus (or the reverse) to aggregate demand. The net long-term effect would be to alter the *structure* of employment without altering the *total*. It is in fact only on the unrealistic assumption that resources and labour are entirely complementary in the productive process that a cutback in resource use entails a cutback in employment. Indeed, the problem is rather the reverse: reducing one of the inputs to production, i.e. re-sources, reduces output — there will be a shortage of labour supply rather than demand. (Some of the reactions of an impoverished labour force are likely to be increased overtime, moonlighting and housewives working, hence making conservation more difficult.)

While resource conservation need not lead to general (Keynesian) un-employment, *structural* unemployment is likely to pose a very serious problem. Consider, specifically, car workers no longer needed in a society that minimises travel. In the long run there will be jobs for them, in the recycling or repair trades, in pollution-control research or on the land, Some may be able to find work in more closely related trades, perhaps in making buses, but generally large changes in job content will be required entailing retraining and adaptation. It is often claimed that repair jobs or work on the land are intrinsically more satisfying and rewarding than work on an assembly-line but it must be remembered that much of the present labour force is conditioned to the latter. There has in fact been considerable experience of trying to retrain those with obsolete skills, all indicating great difficulties, especially with older men. It will be possible to find some of these workers jobs locally but for most it will entail a move, for car factories are concentrated in certain locations, especially in the West Midlands. This is a familiar-enough situation: coal, textiles and shipbuilding were similarly concentrated and their decline left the regions concerned economically and socially depressed and unattractive to new firms. In this case there are additional reasons why substitute employment could not be concentrated in these areas. Most of the industries expanded by conservation would need to be dispersed; obviously agriculture must be situated in the country and, being land-intensive, must be thinly spread – limited agricultural work could be found near the towns previously specialising in car production. Repairing, distribution and various services must, by their nature, be spread roughly in proportion to the population, so that again only a small proportion could be in, say, Dagenham or Coventry. Thus many car-workers would need to move to another part of Britain, a high proportion of them to the country. Again, past experience emphasises the difficulties of such moves, the resistance (many prefer to stay unemployed in the region they know), the difficulties of life in a new area (for example how would car-workers adapt to a 'quiet' country life?), the social problems of new estates, especially where movement is enforced and/or on a large scale (Young and Willmott, 1957). Leaving aside the social and human problems, the sheer logistics of moving thousands of car-workers, providing houses and social infrastructure, are formidable. In short, it is very clear that if car production is cut back suddenly, early redeployment in desirable industries would be quite impossible and massive structural unemployment must result.

Location

Resource conservation affects location in two major ways. One, via changes in industrial mix and the structure of the workforce, has already been discussed. The other relates to the heavy demands for energy and materials from the transport sector. These could be reduced in two (partially conflicting) ways. The first involves location activities to favour the resource-saving bulk modes: for example, people would be housed densely to facilitate travel by bus and even train, and facilities would be clustered at (possibly newly opened) railheads. The second involves a reduction in transport achieved by shortening the distances between jobs (and shops and other facilities) and houses and by firms selling a much higher proportion of their produce locally. This shift – towards greater local self-sufficiency – has important implications quite apart from the direct savings of resources through reductions in transport. On the one hand, scale economies may be lost, involving in some cases the abandonment of resource-saving technologies such as district heating. On the other hand, smallness of scale involves other advantages which to some extent are of overriding importance (see p. 144).

The main obstacle to engineering smooth locational shifts is to overcome the rigidities and complex interdependencies in the existing structure. Thus buildings and transport links last decades or centuries, while individuals have developed particular skills and attitudes in the context of their existing environment. It is difficult to change one piece of the fabric without creating dislocations elsewhere. In a decentralised decision-making system individual responses to policy may be wholly different from those intended. Three examples must suffice to illustrate these difficulties:

(i) *The Green Belt*. One reaction to the establishment of a Green Belt around a city is the development of commuter suburbs beyond the Green Belt. This may in some ways be preferable to continuous city development but it has severe social disadvantages, including an adverse effect on commuting distances. In this case higher transport prices would greatly alleviate the problems.

(ii) *Industrial sites*. Resources are generally saved by the transfer of freight from road to rail. This would be facilitated by siting new industrial estates near railheads — possibly new railheads on the edges of towns. However, firms setting up on these sites might, despite their proximity to rail, continue to use the roads. Given this behaviour such sites are generally inferior to sites with favourable access to motorways. Again, much of the problem stems from inadequate road pricing.

(iii) *Decentralisation*. Consider the problem of reorganising a city to reduce commuting distances. For simplicity it is assumed that work-places are concentrated at the city centre while the rest of the city is given over to housing, together with schools and other facilities (see Figure 7.1). In theory commuting distances could be reduced by relocating a proportion of work-places at U, V, W, X, Y, Z, replacing the released land in the C.B.D. by housing. Clearly, the physical obstacles to such a simple exchange may be considerable. However, there may sometimes be derelict suburban sites suitable for work-places; or possibly work-places could be sited on suburban parks and new parks created out of derelict land elsewhere. In the absence of derelict land or old housing ripe for demolition the new work-places might have to be situated beyond the current urban boundary, which would have the disadvantage of eating into the Green Belt and into agricultural land. However, to explore other difficulties let us set aside these considerable physical obstacles.

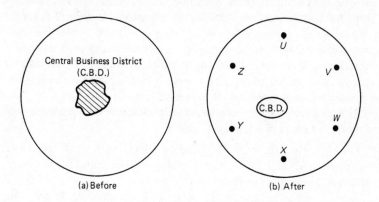

Figure 7.1   Decentralisation of work-places in a city

Consider an office which decentralises from the C.B.D. to X. Formerly its employees were drawn from all over the city. The object of the decentralisation is that employees should be drawn locally from the environs of X. Those living near Z, say, should work for another office that has relocated there. So, to reduce commuting distances, these people will need to change either job or home. But a change of job involves a break with colleagues and work routines and perhaps loss of seniority and a non-transferable pension, while moving house involves a break with neighbours and a change of school. Some may prefer to remain as they are. But to the extent they do this, commuting distances are actually lengthened, and moreover involve awkward cross-town trips, for previously journeys were along radial routes which, if congested, were at least designed for this pattern of travel. Flows were concentrated, thus facilitating public transport, generally the dominant mode in large towns. The new transport pattern is liable to involve longer criss-crossing journeys, much less concentrated and therefore much less suitable to public transport. All the problems of commuting, including energy consumption, are thus increased.

In principle this is a transitional problem. In the longer term appropriate moves are more likely. People may anyway wish to move house when their children leave home and take the opportunity to move nearer their work. People may later become dissatisfied with their present employers and move to a job nearer home. And of course the new generation starts relatively uncommitted both to employers and neighbourhood. So in the long term decentralisation on this pattern may be successful. However, even that is not certain, for in the meanwhile public transport will have lost patronage and hence will probably have been reduced in scale, families facing cross-town journeys to work and poorer-quality public transport may have acquired a car (or a second car). Thus the problems of transition may aggravate the familiar vicious circle of declining public transport and increased car ownership, a process which is very difficult to reverse.

This example has been treated at length because it illustrates so well a number of issues of wider significance:

(a) life-styles (for example those associated with work and home neighbourhood) and facilities (for example radial transport) are inter-related and geared to the status quo;

(b) it is important to consider all these aspects together in designing any reform — action on one front (for example work-places better distributed among residential areas) is likely to conflict with other aspects of existing life-styles (for example transport facilities, work and neigherbourhood ties);

(c) the problems can sometimes be avoided by compulsion (for example making transport prohibitively expensive) but even so there are severe welfare losses associated with the enforced changes to be considered; otherwise

(d) allowance must be made for perverse reactions (for example commuting times increasing through a failure to move or change jobs), which may endanger the objects of the policy in the short term and possibly in the long term as well.

The resource costs of change
Paradoxically an abrupt transition to a low-resource economy could be very expensive even in resource terms. Substantial movements of population are required, involving the building of new houses plus new or extended facilities, schools, shops, roads, sewers, and so on. Moreover, the new pattern of industry, while ultimately more labour-intensive, requires 'tooling up' — a process which involves substantial use of energy and materials. Agricultural workers require tools, re-cycling requires building and machinery, and only in a few cases will it be possible to adapt existing buildings and machinery to meet new purposes. These new buildings will also take land; in the long term it may be possible to return the land vacated by disused buildings (for

example car factories) to agriculture, but certainly this could not be done quickly. In short, a low-resource economy involves a substantial modification of the nation's capital stock. This, in turn, involves a considerable cost, not only in conventional terms, but more especially (since capital formation is typically very resource-intensive) in terms of resources.

Here, again, these costs are reduced by a slower transition. Buildings and machinery deteriorate, especially the current generation – not built for durability. The older they are, the less the real cost of scrapping them. To take the extreme case, when an asset is due for scrapping, replacement costs must anyway be incurred, and replacing them by quite different assets (for example extraction plant replaced by recycling plant) involves no additional cost.

Human skills may be considered analogously. Typically a change in the occupational mix involves premature 'scrapping' of existing skills and the cost of an investment in new skills. However, existing skills are inevitably scrapped as the workers embodying those skills reach retirement age. Hence a programme of transfer relying on natural wastage avoids premature scrapping of existing human capital and minimises training costs.

In practice the wastage of physical and human capital, while it can be reduced substantially, can never be eliminated by a slow transition, due to the interrelationships discussed earlier and the consequent need to synchronise the transition process. For example, not all related items of capital (buildings, machinery, workers) will reach the end of their natural lives simultaneously and some will have to be scrapped prematurely if the transition is ever to be achieved.

Slower growth in material living standards
At first sight it would seem that saving resources for the future must result in lower consumption today (or if the cutback is phased over a number of years, a lower-than-otherwise growth in consumption). In fact this is not necessarily the case.

A *pure* conservation policy may be defined as one which simply involves trading present for future consumption. Such a policy might be to vary the discount rate – for example by an adjustment of the balance of fiscal and monetary policy. However, most conservation policies also affect efficiency.

Consider next a policy to internalise an *instantaneous* externality. If the externality impinges on firms (for example congestion on lorry routes), the policy will increase output. Typically (through market adjustments) the benefits will be spread between time periods, so that both present and future consumption are increased. (If the externality impinges on individuals, the benefit is not picked up in G.N.P., etc., but it may be expected that both present and future *welfare* will increase.) Clearly, this kind of measure, though perhaps appropriately described as 'environmental', is not properly a conservation measure.

Common-access resources, typified by the fishery, also involve an externality problem but here the damage impinges mainly on the future. Fishing is excessive, and it is also inefficient. A tax on the catch not only reduces fishing, thus benefiting the future, but also increases over-all efficiency. Current consumption of fish may well be reduced but the resources (labour and capital as well as natural resources) freed may be devoted to producing other goods. There is no general presumption that current over-all consumption will be reduced by such a measure. A large number of conservation measures, in fact all those designed to deal with specific sources of market failure (other than general inter-temporal bias), fall into this class, for example taxes on persistent pollution, standardisation of containers, encouragement to product durability, and even pollution taxes (which apart from their main purpose tend to discourage throughput of virgin resources).

On the other hand, other conservation measures, while helping the future, may involve a reduction in efficiency. For example, recycling subsidies not only involve an arbitrary encouragement to *one specific form* of resource conservation but also necessitate raising (generally) distorting taxes to finance them. Future-orientated policies which are arbitrarily restricted to conserving particular natural resources likewise involve an efficiency loss. Such policies must increase the current sacrifice needed to secure any given level of future gain.

Whether or not 'welfare' rises it is the impact on consumption that is likely to be most widely noticed and give rise to resistant behaviour. First, the drop in consumption is likely to be politically unpopular, and since in a democracy the population is sovereign the government cannot force a strong conservation policy on an unwilling electorate. Even in dictatorships the power of government to enforce unpopular measures is limited by the possibilities of riots and uprisings. Second, people are likely to take economic and industrial action in defence of living standards. The immediate manifestation of scarcity created by restrictions on resource use is rising prices. A probable response of the work-force is to seek higher wages. If met, this could trigger off a fierce inflation. The government could attempt to prevent this either by a non-expansionary monetary policy or by prices and incomes control.

The former would lead to unemployment (over and above the structural unemployment discussed above), while the latter would probably provoke industrial action, involving a further loss of output, and indeed experience suggests that it would not long be effective in keeping down inflation.

In conclusion, a programme to cutback consumption *severely* to benefit the future stands little chance of success if this is in opposition to the preferences of the people.

7.4 Policies
Gradualism
Sudden unexpected changes inevitably cause hardship to those who, through their equipment, home, habits or job, are committed to the status quo. Alleviations to the transitional problems of change are liable to inhibit the change. Thus subsidies to declining industries may inhibit their decline and are widely opposed for this reason (see Pryke and Dodgson, 1975). Of course, some slowing in the rate of decline is justified by the costs of change; but a balance must be struck, and there is a danger that once granted subsidies are not removed, or not until they become too burdensome to the exchequer, when they are removed very qucikly, creating just those problems of rapid adjustment which it was the aim of the subsidies to avoid. (One might cite the coal and rail industries in the early 1960s and in all probability the car and steel industries of the late 1970s.) In the same way a sharp rise in energy prices, such as that experienced recently, involves hardship, both directly by those with high energy consumption and indirectly via effects on employment. The imposition of a large energy tax would have a similar effect. However, this might be moderated considerably, if the tax were levied initially at a low level rising to, say, 100 per cent over twenty years *according to a previously announced programme*. This would allow individuals to make appropriate adjustments at convenient times. For example, new entrants to the labour force would train for jobs in low-energy industries, those moving house would seek houses near to their jobs and to various facilities and they would prefer houses with high standards of insulation and perhaps solar heating; these preferences would put commercial pressures on builders to supply houses with these characteristics and would provide some encouragement for houses and facilities to be provided in appropriate localities. Again, energy-intensive firms might be able to modify their processes to cut down on energy use. But such modifications might require replacement of equipment and perhaps research and development. Immediate

price increases could lead to bankruptcy and unemployment before the necessary changes could be introduced.

Of course, not everyone would be making critical decisions within twenty years, and a young man with a good job in the town and a beautiful home far away in the country would inevitably suffer, as would one who had undertaken a long training for a job in an energy-intensive industry. But at least he would be provided with a longish period to work out his preferred response before he was penalised too heavily by the higher prices. Of course, the transitional time could be made even longer, but only at the expense of a slower reduction in energy use. One consequence is the importance of anticipating the need for conservation sufficiently far in advance that a slow transition is possible.

Objections have been raised to announcing tax changes in advance but these seem largely misplaced. There is a strong tradition of Budget secrecy, though this is partly directed against leaks, which can operate unfairly. It is sometimes suggested that announcement of increases (decreases) in indirect taxes will bring forward (retard) spending. The results are mildly undesirable, but it should be remembered that *guesses* as to the Budget content also affect spending, and the effect, though more erratic, is not necessarily less pernicious.

In the case of resource taxes there might be some tendency to bring forward purchases of storable resources and resource-intensive commodities. Two rather different kinds of problems arise. First, people and firms would tend to buy such commodities just before, rather than just after, tax rises, and this would give rise to fluctuations in purchases. This phenomenon already occurs with, for example, seasonal tariffs for coal and could be undesirable if it causes a peaking problem in deliveries. The effect could be minimised either by raising taxes frequently by small amounts or by timing the increases to coincide with periods of low demand. The second problem is that purchases might be made many years in advance of need; this could be undesirable on four counts: (i) it increases storage costs – the most economical way of storing resources is (generally) in the ground, but expectations of tax increases encourage storage after the point of tax; (ii) there may in some cases be a risk of deterioration in storage; (iii) mining and all other activities before the point of tax are brought forward, which at any positive discount rate increases the net present value of their cost; and (iv) in so far as bringing forward purchases reduces the tax burden, there will be less reduction in resource use. These effects are minimised by either effecting the required increase in a very short period, which gives little time for those involved to devise suitable arrangements for storage, etc., or conversely affecting it over a long period, in which case the advantages of bringing forward purchase on a large scale would be small enough to be outweighed by storage costs. Specifically, if resource tax rises were scheduled to raise prices by an additional 3 per cent p.a. (over what they would otherwise have been),[2] the incentive to store would be modest; and yet this would be sufficient to raise the tax rate to 100 per cent in twenty-four years and 300 per cent in forty-eight years.

A further objection is that the government should not make a commitment to policy so far in advance. One aspect of this is that taxes are used for short-term demand management. In the normal course of events resource taxes, once introduced, would be subject to variations with this in mind. Against this it could be argued that there are many other instruments for influencing demand, including income tax and monetary policy, and that a rigid commitment on the level of resource taxes does not materially reduce flexibility. Alternatively, it would be possible to allow short-term variations from the announced trend in resource taxes. The trend would be a kind of base-line from which changes would be made, in the same way that 'no change in tax rate' currently provides a base-line. Provided the deviations from trend were not too great there could be little damage to the objects of the policy. It could be stipulated in advance that resource tax rates might be varied in the interests of demand management but that deviations from the announced trend would never exceed, say, 15 per cent.

A more serious difficulty is that circumstances might change, rendering the announced trend inappropriate. For example, a major breakthrough in harnessing solar energy might render unnecessary careful conservation of fossil fuels; or, with no change in the objective situation, a new government might come to power, holding different priorities or taking a different view of future possibilities. This is especially likely with detailed policies (such as road pricing) which are aimed only partly at conservation. On the one hand, it would clearly be undesirable to preclude changes in policy in such circumstances. On the other hand, the very purpose of announcing tax changes far in advance is to provide an element of certainty to facilitate smooth adjustment and prevent the hardships associated with sudden unexpected changes. These advantages are greatly reduced if it is thought that the programme is likely to be substantially modified later.

However, this is a characteristic dilemma and is by no means unique to this kind of scheme. For example, in the 1950s the Conservative

Government relaxed rent controls, partly with the object of increasing the supply of rented accommodation; the failure of this policy was, perhaps, largely due to the expectation (justified by events) that a later Labour Government would introduce further controls. Again, a Green Belt around a city provides a reasonable certainty about planning decisions, and more generally that the area will retain its rural character and individual plans can be made accordingly. But the system somewhat ties the hands of local planners, and it is arguable that some areas within a designated Green Belt are more suitable for development than some areas outside and that each planning application should be taken on its merits. In practice the local planners do exercise a limited discretion in considering planning applications; more crucially the boundaries of the Green Belt are revised periodically. This detracts considerably from the certainty that the Green Belt was intended to provide but at the same time allows a valuable element of flexibility in face of changing circumstances (or social theories). Maximum certainty would be achieved by freezing the Green Belt, maximum flexibility by abandoning the concept altogether. The present system is a compromise between the irreconcilable aims of certainty and flexibility.

In devising a resource tax programme it would be equally essential to strike a satisfactory balance between certainty and flexibility. To make no advance commitment would be too great a sacrifice to flexibility, to insist on the commitment being fulfilled in all circumstances too great a sacrifice to certainty. The required compromise is a recognition of the value of certainty and (as with the Green Belt) a corresponding reluctance to depart from the programme in the absence of a very compelling justification.

Aids to mobility

A strong conservationist policy entails large changes in the structure of industry and in the geographical distribution of jobs and homes. Immobility (geographical and occupational) is a serious obstacle to such changes and the root cause of structural unemployment; but much can be done. First, remaining artificial barriers to mobility should be removed; prominent among these are non-transferability of some occupational pension schemes and the system of allocating council houses. Central to the latter is the so-called 'residence qualification', according to which priority is accorded partly according to length of residence in the district, so that those newly arrived may be precluded entirely. The recent Green Paper on housing (Department of the Environment, 1977) seeks to outlaw the residence qualification. A less obvious difficulty is that tenants whose financial circumstances have improved are allowed to remain but are ineligible for similar accommodation in another area. The solution (not mooted in the Green Paper) is to eliminate the advantage of living in a council house *per se*, i.e. to charge an economic rent and provide housing subsidies (if at all) according to financial circumstances. An 'economic rent' is not (as interpreted by so many local authorities) that which covers historic costs but that which the house would command on the open market. In view of inflation the latter exceeds the former by a substantial margin (depending on the age of the housing stock in the area) and those authorities that base their rents on historic cost provide a very substantial subsidy to tenants. Charging an economic rent would eliminate the waiting-list and hence the incentive to cling to an existing tenancy (see Pennance and Gray, 1968).

Positive aids to mobility could be justified as providing assistance to 'unfortunate' people trapped in the wrong localities or jobs (example: rehousing subsidies, used in Sweden) or countering specific externalities (example: retraining subsidies). But there is some danger in indisccriminate subsidies to movement which is perhaps not to be encouraged.[3] Assistance should, as far as possible, be confined to assisting desirable movements. Such a principle indeed already underlies investment incentives which are confined to depressed areas. Similarly, government retraining schemes should concentrate on skills required in a low-resource society.

Public forecasting

Gradualism would reduce but not eliminate problems of adjustment. Past structural problems have sometimes been the result of sudden external changes but equally often they emerged gradually and should have been easy to anticipate. One difficulty is that the full implications of external events and policies are not always obvious. This would certainly be the case with resource taxes. It would of course be relatively easy to predict the impact on the prices of the resources themselves but more difficult to predict the impact on other aspects of the economy. For example, an energy tax would tend to raise the relative prices of goods with a high energy content; however, the price rise, and more particularly the impact on output and employment, would also depend on the elasticity of demand. Complements to energy-intensive products (for example cars) would be adversely affected, unless, as with buses, the complementarity effect operates more strongly on a rival good. Incomes will be affected, and hence income elasticities will also be relevant. Changes in transport costs will influence the most suitable places for houses and work-places, and hence will lead to changes in the geographical pattern of demand. Thus the ramifications of a large energy tax are complex and not easy to predict.

Predictions are of course made by private firms and agencies, but private forecasting activity is distorted by the public-goods nature of information. The social benefit of publishing a forecast is considerable, but the private benefit is zero or even negative (in view of the help given to rivals). As a result private forecasts are not generally published. Thus some of the more obvious lines of enquiry will be the subject of numerous unco-ordinated investigations; others will not be pursued at all because the private benefits to any *single* investigation exceed the costs. Long-range forecasts, which are particularly relevant to resource problems, are rarely undertaken. Small firms and individuals lacking the resources for sophisticated work will rely on trend extrapolations and hunch.

One of the most important users of forecasts is the government itself. The public-goods argument suggests that the government should publish its forecasts, and moreover extend its forecasting activities beyond items required for its own purposes (for a review of various objections to these ideas, see Lecomber, 1970).

Also, other decision-makers could be asked to predict their actions and successively revise their predictions (or 'plans') in the light of the implications demonstrated in the national prediction. This procedure is known as 'indicative planning', though for various reasons (see Lecomber, 1970) the actual attempts at such planning in the United Kingdom and France have not followed this model at all closely. The major difficulty is that firms have too much incentive to attempt to influence the forecast plan and hence perhaps their own tax—subsidy treatment by misrepresenting their intentions. If, as was certainly the case in the U.K. National Plan, industrialists are asked not for the intentions of their firms but for their forecasts of the behaviour of the industries, it is probably better for expert advice to be derived from disinterested parties, perhaps within the Civil Service.

The case for such an exercise depends on the public benefits of forecasting, and is, in a sense, independent of whether or not conservation policies are adopted. Nevertheless the value of a sophisticated forecasting exercise is greatest when naive extrapolative methods are mostly likely to fail, namely following marked shifts in the direction of external events or policy.

7.5 Concluding comments

Apart from a probable drop in material living standards, the main problems of reducing resource use are problems of *change*. The amount of change depends to a considerable extent on the particular low-resource society in view. If, for example, it is intended to establish a nearly stationary state of small largely self-sufficient communities, then substantial changes are involved (this is somewhat ironic, since one of the objectives of such a society is a reduction in the amount of change). If, however, the main object is simply a moderate and not too rapid reduction in resource use, then the changes need be no greater than those accepted without question in the interests of growth. It should also be borne in mind that since consumption of most resources is rising there may be opportunities for combining curbs on resource use with reductions in the amount of change.[4]

Finally, it should again be emphasised that the object of cutting resource use now is to avoid being forced to cut back later if, for example, technology should falter. Such a forced cutback would be unexpected and from a higher initial level. However serious the problems of a slow transition now, the problems of a larger more rapid transition later would be infinitely worse.

8 ENERGY, A CASE STUDY:
(I) SUPPLY

8.1 Supply and demand – a preliminary view

We begin by juxtaposing resource limits and exponential growth in the manner of the Pessimists. This exercise has the limited purpose of indicating how long current growth rates (in energy consumption) can continue without major extensions of supply. This paves the way for an examination of the possibilities both of extending supply and of curbing demand.

In Table 8.1 three estimates are given of 'relatively conventional' resource supplies. The first is relatively pessimistic, relating to 'proved and probable' resources; these are known with reasonable certainty and are economic to work at current prices and technology. The second is relatively optimistic and includes resources estimated from general geological data as well as resources (known or estimated) that at current prices and technology are somewhat sub-economic. Information on sub-economic resources is, not surprisingly, poor, and treatment not consistent between energy sources. Very low-quality resources (for example sea-water as a source of uranium) are not included. The third set are those used by Nordhaus (1973b) in the study discussed in the next section.

Also, in Table 8.1 growth rates are given for three periods. The difference between the over-all growth rates in the first two periods is not significant and depends on the choice of end years. The third period exhibits a slower growth rate (even more marked at the end of this period), which is attributable to the oil crisis. In extrapolating demand we have used the 1960–70 growth rates. This is not because we consider underlying trends unaffected by the oil crisis: the long-term effect may have been considerable, but it is not reflected adequately in short-term trends. The oil crisis precipitated a sudden increase in energy prices, and the problems of short-term adjustment, adding to existing problems of global inflation, led to a deep depression. Thus energy trends were subjected to both a price effect and an income effect. The latter was only partly the result of higher energy prices, and its impact was exaggerated by the suddenness of the crisis. Energy prices are now (1978) falling back relative to the general price level, and there are signs of a recovery in economic activity; it may well be that energy consumption will resume earlier trends. At any rate new trends have not yet established themselves. The long-run significance of the oil crisis lies in the jolt it gave to the world. It was widely (if falsely) interpreted as heralding long-run scarcity, and at the same time increased awareness of the problems this would bring. This stimulated a wide variety of energy studies, including research into alternative energy sources and possibilities of conservation. It is this research that could ultimately transform long-term trends. Rather than attempt to allow for such developments by modifying the underlying trends, we prefer to examine these possibilities explicitly.

Table 8.1 World energy resources (10^{21} Joules) and exhaustion dates on various assumptions

	(1) Reserves proved + probable	(2) Resource base	(3) Nordhaus[c] resource estimates	(4) Consumption 1975	(5)	(6)	(7)	Hypothetical resource lives[a] using cols		
					Growth rates (% p.a.) 1952–60 1960–70 1970–5			(1)	(2)	(3)
Coal	6.0	830	57.1	0.07	3.6	0.9	1.8			
Natural gas	5.5	40	5.9	0.05	7.8	8.2	3.9			
Crude Petroleum	4.8	50	7.5	0.11	7.7	8.7	3.8	17	43	20
Tar sands	1.2	10	–	–	–	–	–			
Shale oil	4.6	1500	23.4	–	–	–	–			
Uranium-235 (for 'burners')	0.8	1430[c]	1429	0.001	–	14.0	12.7			
Uranium-238 (for 'breeders')	48.0[d]	85200[d]	205935		–	–	–			
Thorium	0	1400	–							
All sources of oil[b]	16.6	2390	88.0	0.18	5.0	4.1	–	38	157	75
All excluding Uranium-238 and thorium	22.9	3860	1521	0.24	5.4	5.0	3.2	36	139	117
Total non-renewable	70.9	90460	207456	0.24	5.4	5.0	3.2	57	201	218
Hydro-electric	0.04	0.04	–	0.005	7.1	4.3	–			

Notes: [a] Calculated by applying the 1960–70 growth rates (col. 6) to the 1975 consumption level. Hydro-electric energy supply is assumed to grow exponentially at 4.3 per cent p.a. until the limit is reached. [b] Crude petroleum, tar sands, shale oil and coal. Columns 4–7 relate to consumption of oil and coal. [c] From Nordhaus (1973b). [d] 60 times the corresponding uranium-235 figures (see, for example, World Energy Conference, 1974).

Exclusions: (i) wood and peat; (ii) some quantitatively unimportant sources, for example conventional geothermal energy; (iii) novel sources.

Sources: For reserves and resource base Ion (1976) except where otherwise stated; for consumption and growth rates *United Nations Statistical Yearbooks*.

The last three columns of Table 8.1 give hypothetical resource lives on the various supply assumptions. Such figures could be presented for each individual energy source. But as long as the various sources can be substituted one for another such dates are of little interest: as one source is exhausted, another takes over. Accordingly, we have concentrated on non-renewable energy as a whole. However, two subgroups are worthy of special attention. First, use of the massive resources of uranium-238 and thorium depends on the controversial fast-breeder reactor. In view of the problems and risks associated with a large-scale breeder programme (discussed below) it is worth investigating the implications of foregoing this particular technology. Second, there are certain fields (particularly road and air transport) where oil has no fully satisfactory substitutes. Hence even if energy supplies as a whole are adequate, shortage of oil could constitute a major problem. Correspondingly, resource lives are shown for crude petroleum and for the wider group of fuels from which oil can be derived.

It will be seen that current growth cannot be sustained for long on the basis of proved and probable reserves. Crude petroleum is in particularly short supply, though the growth of oil is significantly prolonged by recourse to tar sands, shale and coal. In all cases the resource base substantially exceeds proved and probable reserves, but the respite is not very impressive (to readers of the Pessimist literature or Chapter 2 of this book this will come as no surprise). Specifically, all listed energy sources last two centuries, or only 140 years if the fast-breeder reactor is rejected (again this small difference suggests that the crucial role of the breeder is sometimes exaggerated), while sources of oil are even more short-lived.

It would be possible to adopt even more optimistic resource figures, based on crustal abundance and assuming 100 per cent recovery rates. There are, for example, impressive quantities of uranium contained in sea-water and granite. Not surprisingly resource lives are comparatively insensitive to expansions in supply. For example, a millionfold expansion of total non-renewable energy extends the resource life by rather under 200 years. It is difficult to escape the conclusion that before long either radically different sources of supply or a slow down in the growth of consumption is inevitable.

8.2   An optimisation model
The supply side of the problem has been investigated systematically in a world model (see Nordhaus, 1973b). He describes his study as 'an investigation of the efficient [roughly, optimal] allocation of energy resources over time by determining the cheapest way of meeting a

[given] growth path of final demands for energy products with a given stock of energy resources and a given set of processes for converting resources into products.' After ensuring that the programme was feasible for a very long time period, the procedure was to find the optimal path for consuming scarce resources and the prices associated with this path. This study is instructive both for its success — in pinpointing certain key problems and indicating how they may best be met — and for its limitations. The model, the results and the limitations will be discussed in turn.

The model
Demands for fuel were broken down into five categories (electricity, industrial heating, residential heating, transport in which substitution for oil is difficult, and other transport) and by five regions of the non-Communist world. They were derived by a simple extrapolative procedure for given assumptions about economic growth. These are no-where clearly set out, the only explicit statement being that *per capita* income is assumed to grow at '2 per cent per annum [in] the United States and at higher rates [in] other countries'; assumptions about population growth are not given. However, it is clear that the demand assumptions represent a continuation of current trends. No allowance is made for sensitivity of energy demands to prices and, in view of the changes in price trends which emerge, this procedure may somewhat overestimate demand. (Nordhaus comments that 'price elasticities are quite low' and 'the problem already strains reasonable computational budgets'.)

With respect to *supplies*, resources are estimated for each primary fuel, broken down by grade and regions of origin (the latter is required because the model includes transport costs). These estimates, shown in column (3) of Table 8.1 will be seen to be reasonably conservative, except in the case of uranium-235 and, more especially, uranium-238. However, a doubling of reserves is quantitatively unimportant in the face of exponential growth, so that the results of the model would be little affected by taking a lower figure.

Next technologies are listed and costed. This list includes some technologies which are not fully operational (for example the breeder reactor and the electric car), though, as all are assumed to have high costs, none enters the optimum schedule until 2020, affording nearly fifty years for successful development. The costs assumed must be somewhat speculative, but sensitivity tests indicate that large (x 100) changes make little difference to the results. No account at all has been taken of more 'exotic' possibilities such as solar energy and nuclear fusion.

Apart from these specific technical developments the model incorporates labour-augmenting technical progress in both the energy sector and elsewhere. This assumption, characteristic of Optimists and criticised in Chapter 2, may in this context be relatively harmless in that it inflates demands for energy as well as supplies. On the other hand, it is critical to an assessment of the discount-rate assumption (see below). Of course, if technical progress were faster in the non-energy sector or if it exhibited an energy-using bias, the optimal programme would be affected. In view of rising energy prices the opposite biases are likely.

The objective is to minimise the discounted cost of fuel inputs. The discount rate used (the conventional 10 per cent) is discussed below.

In many ways Nordhaus has been careful to use conservative assumptions, and moreover sensitivity tests indicate that on a variety of issues (especially *re* technologies) 'anything but the most drastic pessimism didn't seem to matter much'.

The results

Virtually all the results quoted by Nordhaus — and hence here — relate to the United States. Fortunately this provides an adequate illustration of most of the important issues.

The optimal path is characterised by the progressive phasing out of fossil fuels and their replacement by fast-breeder electricity. This process of transition is marked by the increasingly high costs of fossil fuels, as royalties and extraction costs both rise — the latter due to the exhaustion of superior deposits. The progression varies markedly between sectors according to the comparative advantages of the various fuels in particular uses. In particular the changeover to nuclear fuel for electricity generation is completed in 2000 (burners initially, followed by breeders in 2020). However, oil persists for 'transport in which substitution is difficult' until 2120, when it is finally replaced by hydrogen and electricity both based on the breeder.

The case of oil is particularly interesting. This is both the scarcest fuel (in relation to prospective demand) and the most difficult to replace in key (i.e. transport) uses.[1] Using Nordhaus's reserve estimate, conventional crude petroleum may be expected to last twenty years (or forty-three years using Ion's (1976) estimate of the resource base). There are a number of ways of extending these supplies, two of which are distinguished in the Nordhaus model. First, oil can be derived from tar sands, shale oil, even coal. All the three sources are already in use on a minor scale. Cost estimates are given by Nordhaus and are reproduced together with alternative estimates by Lovins (1975) in Table 8.2. It will be seen that the costs, though far above those associated with most operational oil fields, are not prohibitive. Indeed, they lie below the costs of the worst conventional sources distinguished in the Nordhaus study and are mostly just economic at current (1978) world oil prices. The techniques involved are relatively new and the processing of the huge reserves of low-grade shales has been little investigated so that costs must be expected to fall. On the other hand, these alternative sources of oil involve environmental problems which may or may not be soluble through technical advance. If all sources of oil are taken together and related to demands for oil and coal, then supplies may be expected to last a further fifty-five years on Nordhaus's reserve estimates.

Table 8.2   Crude petroleum production costs ($/bl)*

Source	Lovins	Nordhaus
Persian Gulf	0.1–0.2	0.06 (drilled) 0.29 (undrilled)
Other land (excluding United States)	0.4–0.6	–
United States drilled undrilled	– 1.7–2.5	0.29 2.41–19.45
North Sea	0.9–2.0	–
Large Deep Sea	2.0–	–
Tar sands: Easier	2.0–6.0	–
Oil shales High grade Lower grade	3.0–4.5 –	5.58 11.59
Syncrude (oil from coal)	3.0–6.0	7.62

* Volumetric unit: 1 barrel (bl) = 34.97 gallons.

The second way of extending supplies is to replace oil by other fuels in selected uses. Use of oil for electricity generation is halted immediately for industrial heating in 2000 and for residential heating in

2010. This conserves oil for use in transport for a further 120 years. Transport accounts for nearly 50 per cent of oil use in the United States and about 30 per cent in the United Kingdom and elsewhere. All air transport, virtually all sea and road transport and a high proportion of rail transport use oil. Substitutes are difficult to find.

Nordhaus relies on two technical developments. The first is the electric car. Electric drive is already used for milk-floats and fork-lift trucks. The chief obstacle to more extended use is electrical storage. Conventionally the lead-acid battery is used, but this stores very little energy per unit of weight, especially if high speeds are required. For example, 1000 lb of batteries will fuel a car for some 40–50 miles at an average speed of 30 m.p.h. (see Pole, 1973). Such performance might be acceptable for cars and buses that are to be used exclusively for short journeys in towns. Cars could be provided (at a cost) with facilities for both electric and petrol drive, the latter to be used for longer or faster journeys. Some writers (for example Pole, 1973) consider the electric car to be feasible now and blame the motor industry for its conservatism and lack of imagination. But the official (U.K.) view is that 'the feasibility of electric road vehicles depends almost entirely on the successful development of suitable batteries' (see Department of Energy, 1976a). An alternative is the hydrogen-fuelled vehicle. Hydrogen is abundant but costly to produce (three times the current energy price per unit of electricity) and difficult to store, though these difficulties might be reduced by technical advance.

In the case of aircraft electric fuelling is not feasible in the absence of totally unforeseen developments. In particular the weight of lead-acid batteries is decisive. Here hydrogen has the advantage of a high energy/weight ratio and, while considerable research and development is still required, is a promising long-term prospect. If these problems can be overcome, hydrogen could also be used for road transport.

A further possibility not considered explicitly is modal switching. Tracked vehicles, i.e. trains, trolley-buses and trams, can be run off mains electricity. These 'bulk' modes of transport have been declining as the travelling public and freight have transferred to the more convenient and flexible 'individual' modes. Rapidly rising oil prices associated with incipient exhaustion may reverse these trends (especially in the absence of electric- or hydrogen-fuelled vehicles), though apparently at some welfare cost. All the empirical studies show modal choice to be insensitive to prices, at least in the short term (see Harrison, 1974). This means that only a very substantial price rise would generate a significant shift indicating a large welfare loss.

Arguably, however, the apparent preference for 'individual' modes is partly spurious, stemming from the failure to impose charges for the large external costs associated with road travel, especially in towns; imposition of such charges would reinforce the effects of rising oil prices, though price-insensitivity implies that the impact of correct pricing may be small. These possibilities are discussed further in Section 9.5 below. Similarly, air traffic could be switched to train or sea, though the additional time involved on long hauls would be considerable.

Prices. A particular focus of interest in the Nordhaus model is the behaviour of prices associated with the optimal path. The key results are shown in Table 8.3. First, notice the rapid rise in royalties (row 11). In principle (cf. Chapter 3) these should rise at 10 per cent p.a. (the discount rate used). In fact the rises are somewhat depressed by the inclusion of 'quasi-rents on direct costs'; these are significant for natural gas and oil.

Table 8.3   Energy prices in the Nordhaus model

		Oil ($/bl)		Natural gas ($/th. cu. ft.)	Coal ($/ton)		Electricity (c/kWh)
		Undrilled	High-grade shale		West coast	East coast	
(1) Actual price	1970		3.23	0.17	6.26		0.77[a]
(2) Shadow price	1970		1.20	0.21	11.91		0.68
(3) Shadow royalty	1970	0.00	0.02	0.16	0.01	0.07	—
(4) Shadow price	2000		3.19	0.64	13.34		1.03
(5) Shadow royalty	2000	0.63	0.37	0.59	0.21	1.23	—
(6) Actual price/ shadow price	1970		2.69	0.82	0.53		—
(7) Shadow royalty/ shadow price	1970	negligible	0.02	0.76	0.001	0.007	—
(8) Ditto	2000	0.20	0.12	0.92	0.02	0.09	—
(9) Actual price (% p.a.)	1950–70		−1.5[d]	2.5[c]	−1.3		−2.8[b]
(10) Shadow price (% p.a.)	1970–2000		3.3	3.8	0.3		1.4
(11) Shadow royalty (% p.a)	1970–2000		10	10	10		

Notes: [a] 1968. [b] 1968–70. [c] −0.7, decade 1960–70. [d] But price rose rapidly 1970–4.

General Notes: all prices are relative to general price level in year in question; all figures given relate to the United States (though model is multi-regional).

Source: Nordhaus (1973b) tables 6, 7, 8.

Royalties form a rather small share of product prices in all cases except natural gas (row 7), and the rise in product prices (= royalty plus cost of extraction, etc.) is markedly lower (row 10). These rises, though not dramatic, do in most cases represent a distinct change of trend (cf. row 9). The rises in the prices of oil and natural gas are particularly high, because 'with the exhaustion of petroleum resources the economy must turn to costlier processes – either shale oil or coal gasification and liquification'.

A comparison of rows 1 and 2 (summarised in the ratios given in row 6) shows no general tendency to underpricing. Nordhaus notes that 'natural gas appears to be the only fuel that is underpriced relative to future availability'. Several commentators have made a similar complaint that North Sea gas is underpriced. Coal is even more dramatically underpriced but, according to Nordhaus's calculations, this cannot be associated with a failure to allow for royalties, for these form an almost negligible proportion of the shadow price (row 7). Coal is in fact substantially underpriced, even relative to extraction costs, presumably to reflect the social costs of unemployment in the industry. The electricity price is almost right, while oil is substantially overpriced, even in 1970. ('A policy that aims at further increases in the long-run price of gasoline would be pushing in the wrong direction'.)

Thus the model, though indicating that energy prices should rise quite rapidly (relative to the price level as a whole) suggests neither that current prices are outrageously low nor that the world is heading for imminent disaster.

A critique

Nordhaus has attempted to adopt conservative assumptions. As noted, he has ignored the sensitivity of demand to price, and has assumed that, despite rising energy prices, technical progress is labour-augmenting (apart from certain specific developments, notably concerning hydrogen and the electric car). No account is taken of probable cost reductions in newer energy technologies, for example oil from shale or coal, or of improvements in recovery rates and conversion efficiency. Finally, a wide range of proven and possible energy sources (considered later) are ignored. However, four major doubts (two of which are discussed by Nordhaus) surround his optimistic conclusions:

(i) *The energy requirements of energy production.* There are two categories of requirements: one is allowed for adequately in the Nordhaus study; the other, which is likely to be of increasing importance, is not. The first is simply that primary energy (for example coal) is used to make secondary energy (for example electricity); Nordhaus allows for this dependence by working in terms of demands for primary energy. But in addition most energy processes, especially the newer ones, are very capital-intensive and the required capital very energy-intensive. Thus the core of a nuclear reactor requires 'loading' with uranium before production can begin – this entails the mining of uranium, which is likely to become increasingly energy-intensive as lower grades of ore are pressed into use; energy is expended now in building up the capacity to supply energy later; these energy demands are related not to the levels but to the rate of growth of energy supply. Thus a rapid build-up of nuclear capacity involves a high usage of current energy supplies. Studies, by Chapman (1975) for example, indicate that in a period in which the stock of nuclear power-stations is doubled every four years, only about half of the energy produced is available to the rest of the economy (i.e. after the energy demands of the power-station programme have been met). If the stock of nuclear power-stations is doubling every two years, then the demands of the building programme rise to more than 35 per cent of total national energy demands (for the United Kingdom), roughly double the output of the power-stations. Chapman points out that these considerations place a major constraint on the rapidity with which nuclear capacity can be installed.

The significance of all this for Nordhaus's model is that no *specific* allowance is made for the energy demands associated with the installation of energy-producing capacity. Since Nordhaus's solution indicates a very rapid build-up of nuclear and other capital-intensive energy techniques, involving heavy demands for energy, the general extrapolative methods used by Nordhaus probably lead to a serious underestimate of the demands implied by this kind of programme of supply.

(ii) *Environmental problems*. These are not ignored altogether; only those technologies are incorporated which satisfy environmental standards that are 'at least as strict as existing laws'. However (as Nordhaus admits), these may be 'inadequate to ensure a satisfactory environment. Stringent environmental constraints coupled with the inability to find technological solutions to them might very well mean drastically different results.'

By 2120 energy consumption will have grown 1000-fold assuming current rates of growth (possibly it will not, doubtless it should not, but demand cutbacks are not considered in the Nordhaus model). 'Existing laws' are obviously inadequate to maintain a satisfactory environment in the face of such growth and are entirely irrelevant. Stricter laws are clearly necessary – the question is whether corresponding 'technological solutions' will be forthcoming. This cannot be assumed.

The newer energy technologies are especially worrying. The more difficult sources of oil (for example Alaska, the Continental Shelf, the Deep Sea) are vulnerable to serious accidents (for example the leaks in the trans-Alaskan pipe-line and the Santa Barbara and Ekofisk blow-outs): very large quantities of oil can be disgorged; beaches ruined and sea-birds and fish killed; wider ecological effects have not been demonstrated but remain a worrying possibility. It should be emphasised both that the incidents referred to are relatively minor, and that the effects may be cumulative. Open-cast mining of coal and shale involves problems of land disturbance, air and water pollution and above all disposal of very large quantities of solid waste. In the case of shale a new technique of *in situ* retorting is being developed whereby conversion to oil is achieved without displacing the shale.

In view of the heavy reliance on electricity in the Nordhaus programme, the environmental effects of this fuel are especially important. At the consumer end, use of electricity avoids many of the problems, notably pollution, associated with fossil fuels. Unfortunately this gain is counter-balanced by problems at the generation stage. First, some 70 per cent of energy is dissipated as waste heat, giving rise to local pollution problems (as well as possible climatic effects considered below). Conversion efficiency is being increased steadily, and waste-heat emissions correspondingly reduced, but the scope for further improvements is limited by a theoretical limit to conversion efficiency of 68 per cent. A much-canvassed possibility is to harness the 'waste' heat for industrial or district heating, but (unless techniques of transporting heat can be vastly improved) this requires siting power-stations in industrial or residential areas; arguably such siting is feasible for conventional power-stations (though air pollution was often serious) but nuclear power-stations are invariably sited in remote areas on safety grounds.

Second, modern power-stations are large and unsightly installations, and it is becoming increasingly difficult to find suitable sites, especially when the heat-disposal problem is taken into account (see Flowers, 1976).

Third, and most notoriously, there is the problem of nuclear safety. The fission reaction produces highly dangerous radioactive wastes which, even in small quantities, are capable of producing illness, deformities, deaths and genetic mutations. Workers are exposed to these risks but evidence to date suggests they are no greater than in many other occupations (see Lave and Freeburg, 1974). The more serious problems involve the disposal of waste and the possibility of accident (see Flowers, 1976). The radioactivity of the waste decays, but very slowly over thousands of years. Currently in 1978 the most dangerous wastes are 'awating disposal'. Various promising techniques are being explored, for example conversion to a stable solid form and perhaps burial in old salt mines. While these solids are apparently stable, it is not entirely clear whether, over the many centuries involved, some leakage to the atmosphere might occur. The procedures for disposal of low-level wastes, for example dumping in the ocean deeps, are even less satisfactory, especially as the size of the industry grows. Nuclear power-stations have a life of only a few decades and the problems of decommissioning have yet to be faced. Accidents could occur in power-stations, for example through overheating: very careful precautions are taken to reduce these to proportions which would normally be considered negligible; however, it should be borne in mind that the effects of a major accident would be abnormally severe; accidents could also occur in the transport of nuclear material or in associated plant such as the proposed enrichment plant at Windscale. There are also various possibilities of sabotage; nuclear materials could be stolen by terrorists for the manufacture of bombs, or a nuclear station could be taken over by anarchists. Again, these are perhaps unlikely events but in view of the serious consequences they remain worrying. Finally, it may be wondered whether it will be possible to keep nuclear technology to the more stable nations of the world; even supposing that the United Kingdom could ensure adequate safety in its own nuclear programme, could the same be said of a developing country (see Johnson, 1977)? In summary, reliance on the fast breeder trades substantial benefits for a (possibly small) risk of a disaster of cataclysmic proportions. It is a risk that is widely rejected as unacceptable (see Kneese, 1977; Lovins, 1975).[2]

Finally, energy from non-renewable resources raises the temperature of the atmosphere. This can given rise to local problems. For example, the temperature in towns is already several degrees above that in rural areas; this could make it uncomfortably warm in hot climates, besides generating thermal inversions and hence petrochemical smog and possible whirlwinds.

Global effects are more uncertain but potentially more disastrous (see Nordhaus, 1977; Massachusetts Institute of Technology, 1970). Somewhat simplified calculations yield the following: at current rates of growth of energy consumption, energy release will reach 10^{25} joules (see p. 194) in the middle of the next century. This is approximately 1 per cent of the energy received from the sun, and sufficient to raise the global temperature (on average) by $0.7^\circ C$. This apparently rather small increase would, it is thought, be sufficient to melt the polar ice-caps, raising the sea-level by up to 300 feet, thus flooding many low-lying cities and farmland; paradoxically such a quantity of cold water, combined with the consequent cessation of energy release, could pre-cipitate a new ice age. A disturbing feature is that since water absorbs much more heat than ice, the melting process would be self-reinforcing; once the polar ice-caps began to melt, it would almost certainly be too late to prevent the catastrophe. There are many complicating features: first, the temperature increase would not be uniform; second, temperature increases could cause other climatic variations (for example in rainfall, wind currents, etc.) which affect temperature; third, burning fossil fuels has two other important effects — it releases carbon dioxide, which could lead to further increases in global tem-perature and dust which, by increasing cloud cover, could reduce it. With all these complications it is impossible to predict with any con-fidence what level of energy release would be required to melt the polar ice-caps. This greatly increases the danger of reaching the critical level at which diastrous and irrevocable climatic consequences are induced without much prior warning. Research on the determinants of the global climate is being undertaken, but on a rather modest scale, scarcely commensurate with the difficulty and importance of the problems. The extent of these risks and their proper evaluation are of course highly controversial. Certainly, many environmentalists consider them sufficiently alarming to make the programme spelt out by Nordhaus very unattractive.

(iii) *The discount rate*. This was found to play an important role in the theoretical models, and it is therefore not surprising that the results of the model are highly sensitive to a reduction in the rate. For example, Nordhaus reports that the (1970) royalty on undrilled petroleum, negligible at a 10 per cent rate, rises to 80c./bl at 5 per cent, $ 12/bl at 1 per cent and $ 20/bl at a zero rate. The impact on product prices is much less, partly because the capital costs associated with extraction are *reduced* by reductions in the discount rate. Nordhaus's finding that the outcome is insensitive to the costs of new technologies (such as the breeder) is almost certainly dependent on the use of a relatively high discount rate (10 per cent p.a.) which depresses the impact of future scarcity so heavily.

Nordhaus adopts a 10 per cent discount rate on the grounds that this is the rate used elsewhere in the economy. The latter is taken as *datum* — the possibility that a lower discount rate should be used economy-wide (which would have greatly complicated the model) is not considered. Given this constraint he presents the common but misleading argument that, were a lower discount rate to be used in the energy sector, welfare could be increased by converting energy resources to physical capital, which at the margin earns 10 per cent p.a. (As explained in Chapter 5, the objection to this argument is that only some of the additional energy used as a result of a high discount rate goes into investment — much of it will be consumed.) Curiously he suggests that his argument applies only if there is a 'feasible' (by which he means indefinitely sustainable) path; otherwise, the use of a high discount rate is 'definitely inappropriate', for 'resource exhaustion implies extinction'. Yet the same efficiency argument applies: if a lower discount rate is used, resources can be translated into physical capital, thus representing a clear efficiency gain and possibly, by saving resource use later, postponing extinction. In all cases it is a condition of efficiency that the same discount rate should be used in the energy sector as elsewhere. But if a 'wrong' rate is used for one, then it is not clear *a priori* what rate should be used for the other.

An important consideration (see Chapter 5) is the production trade-off between present and future consumption, and it is here that the optimistic assumptions embedded in the model are crucial. Specifically, Nordhaus assumes a continuation of trend growth sustained by continued technical progress and also that environmental standards can be maintained. He also considers, wrongly (see below), that breeder power is indefinitely sustainable. On such optimistic assumptions a 10 per cent discount rate may be acceptable. On more pessimistic assumptions (but even where actual extinction is not implied) its use is more questionable.

(iv) *Sustainability.* Nordhaus attaches great importance to sustainability: in the absence of an indefinitely sustainable path he considers this 'kind of analysis . . . very misleading'. Sustainability, he considers, is ensured by the existence of a *backstop technology*, which '(1) is capable of meeting the demand requirements and (2) has a virtually infinite resource base'. This technology is the breeder: 'Resources for automobiles operating on electricity generated by breeder reactors will last approximately 100 million years.' But this *ignores demand growth*. As shown in Table 8.1, Nordhaus's supplies (for all uses) last only 205 years at current rates of growth, i.e. just beyond the formal terminal date of Nordhaus's model (2170).[3] Thus indefinite sustainability of current trends depends on major technical developments in the energy field (the probability of which is assessed below) beyond those explicitly assumed by Nordhaus.

8.3   Alternative sources of supply
Non-renewable sources
Geothermal energy. Rather under 0.1 per cent of global energy supplies are currently obtained from geothermal resources. So far utilisation has been confined largely to electricity generated from naturally vented reservoirs of hot water or steam. It is estimated that such reservoirs contain $0.02.10^{21}$ J. The capacity of unvented reservoirs is much greater (8.10^{21} J to a depth of 3 km, 40.10^{21} J to 10 km.) and can be utilised by drilling. Additionally, hot rocks provide concentrated sources of heat which could in principle be tapped, for example by drilling holes fracturing the rock and circulating water. Richardson (1975) reports an estimate of 95,000 square miles of dry rock at $550°F$, 3.5 km below the surface in the western states of the United States. Hot granites in Durham and Cornwall are also under active investigation, and it has also been suggested that it might be possible, when North Sea oil is exhausted, to use the bore-holes to extract heat (see Department of Energy, 1976b). As a theoretical upper limit of geothermal resources it has been estimated that the top 10 km of the earth's crust contain $1.25.10^2$ J (see World Energy Conference, 1974). a magnitude comparable to estimated resources of uranium-238. However, most of this is dispersed, inaccessible or far removed from population centres. Electricity generation from relatively low temperature sources is not currently feasible, and transport of heat as such to centres of population would involve excessive heat losses. As it is 99 per cent of energy from existing installations is dissipated as waste heat. There has so far been little study of possible environmental side-effects, though problems of pollution and thermal waste are reported (see World Energy Conference, 1974).

Nuclear fusion. This is a much more important possibility, and is often accorded the role of a 'backstop technology'. The basic energy source is the hydrogen isotope deuterium, which is very abundant and in particular can be obtained from sea-water. The main technical problem, which is proving very intractible, is to control the fusion reaction, which is that employed in the hydrogen bomb. There are no radioactive wastes but problems of accidents, sabotage, blackmail and concentration of energy supply are comparable to those involved with nuclear fission. Decades of further work are required.

The fuel cell. This is a device for converting chemical energy to electrical energy. It comprises two electrodes (usually made out of platinum or other noble metals) and an electrolyte (an acid or alkali). A 'fuel' (which could be hydrogen, ammonia, natural gas or several other substances) is fed continuously to the anode and oxygen is fed to the cathode. The chemical reaction generates electricity. The fuel cell, first discovered in 1839, is operational and has impressive advantages: it is relatively efficient (40 per cent efficiency has been achieved, and in contrast to conventional electricity generation the maximum theoretical efficiency is 100 per cent), it is pollution-free and very flexible: a single cell generates a small current but large numbers of cells can be grouped together to form a large generator; it even has possibilities for vehicles, if problems of weight and dangers of explosion can be overcome. There are three major snags: (i) high cost; (ii) limited supplies, not so much of fuels as of noble metals for the electrodes; and (iii) contribution to climatic problems. Nevertheless the fuel cell would seem to merit more attention than it currently receives (see Aaronson, 1971).

These three technologies could make a major contribution to energy supplies. However, they share the inherent problems of non-renewable energy: not only are supplies ultimately limited, but (a probably more immediate constraint) utilisation increases the global temperature, giving rise to the climatic problems discussed above.

Renewable energy sources.
The sun provides a constant source of energy. This may be used directly, for example for heating water; the only effect on global temperature is via the temporary capture of the heat prior to its release as the water cools. Solar (and lunar) energy is also available indirectly after transformation into mechanical energy (winds, falling water, waves, tides) or chemical energy (plants, animals). These sources may also be tapped to provide electricity or heat, and here again there is only a temporary effect on global climate, as such energy is anyway soon dissipated to the atmosphere as heat.

Before running through the possibilities it is worth considering two problems that beset most renewable resources — namely they tend to be *dispersed* and *erratic*. As an example of dispersal, consider rivers as an energy source. All river-water is moving downward toward the sea, but slowly. This often suffices for small-scale local power, for example water-mills, but not for large-scale electricity generation. For the latter the energy content must be concentrated, typically by building up a head of water behind a dam. An additional problem is that many rivers are far removed from centres of population and energy transporation over large distances is generally uneconomic. This problem is even more acute with tidal and wave energy, most of which is dissipated in the open sea. An important aim must be to find means of converting energy into a form in which it can be transported at minumum cost.

Second, winds, waves, tides, stream flows and sunshine are all variable and unpredictable. This reduces their value as an energy source. There are three possible approaches to this problem. First, activities could be varied to accommodate varying supplies. A classic case is the use of the windmill to pump water into a reservoir; the precise timing of the pumping is immaterial. Hot baths and hot meals could be confined to times of high supply, or on windless or sunless days energy-intensive factories could be closed and the opportunity taken to service the machinery. The scope for this kind of action is probably rather limited, depending on the amount of inconvenience considered tolerable. Second, the erratic energy source could be used in conjunction with one which can be varied at will, for example nuclear electricity. However, such doubling up of capacity increases costs, especially as the nuclear installation would have to be large enough to cope with periods of minimum supply from the erratic source. Third, and most promising, some means may be found of storing the energy. The conventional hydro-electric dam is a simple example. In other cases storage may be more indirect. For example, the energy may be used to pump water into an upper reservoir, to be released for electricity generation as needed. Compression of gases could perform a similar role. A particularly interesting idea is that the energy (especially from tides or waves) could be used to separate hydrogen from sea-water. As mentioned earlier, hydrogen could be used as a fuel, especially for transport, or its isotope deuterium could be used in the fusion reaction.

It should be emphasised that renewable energy resources require construction, maintenance and replacement of equipment which in turn use energy and materials. In some cases (especially hydro-electricity, tidal power, centralised solar collection) these requirements are very substantial.

Hydro-electric power. Conventional hydro-electric power, obtained from falling water generally using dams, is the only significant renewable source currently tapped. It could in theory be expanded many times to supply at least the electrical component of current energy demands. There are often important additional benefits from flood control, navigation, water supply and recreation. However, most of the more promising sites are already used and others either involve serious land-use conflicts or are far removed from centres of population. Also, capital costs are high, reservoirs are liable to serious siltation and there is a danger of ecological, medical and social effects characteristically associated with large projects (see Farvar and Milton, 1973). In view of this last point, small-scale facilities merit reconsideration.

Tidal energy. Electricity is currently generated in the *Rance* estuary in France, while the *Severn* estuary in the United Kingdom is among the other sites under consideration (see Department of Energy, 1977a). But costs are high and the technology suffers from all the disadvantages of hydro-electric power. Tidal energy is very dispersed, most of it being dissipated in the open seas, and at most 2 per cent of the theoretical global supply of $0.1 \ 10^{21}$ J, is considered potentially recoverable.

Wave energy. This appears more promising and is being actively explored in the United Kingdom and elsewhere. The basic details of the technology are uncertain, and it is not clear whether the energy should be transmitted ashore as electricity, compressed air, water, or even hydrogen. The Department of Energy (1976a) has written: 'the cost is still in doubt . . . but it seems likely that wave-generated electricity would be somewhat more expensive than nuclear energy'. Notwithstanding this there are environmental hazards, for example coastal erosion, turbidity, effects on the marine ecology and interference with fishing and other inshore activities. The Department of Energy hopes that wave energy could contribute about 5 per cent of total U.K. energy supplies by 2025. It is interesting to note that this source of energy has received virtually no attention until the last few years and is not even mentioned in the World Energy Conference's (1974) comprehensive study.

Ocean thermal gradients. These were first used to generate electricity (in a small demonstration plant in 1929). But there has been little subsequent interest prior to the oil crisis and both the economic viability and possible environmental side-effects are highly uncertain. As with tidal energy, potential supplies are enormous, but only a small proportion is accessible.

Wind energy. This has long been used for sailing boats and windmills. The main contemporary use is small-scale water-pumping, but some electricity is also generated, for example in Norway, Australia and Uruguay. The recent rises in energy prices have stimulated more general interest, particularly in large-scale electricity generators. These are already economic under favourable conditions, but their widespread introduction depends on further technical advance and/or further rises in the prices of conventional fuels. If offshore sites were to be used in addition to windy inland sites, wind energy could contribute some 5 per cent of U.K. primary energy supplies (see Department of Energy, 1977d). Consideration has also been given to small-scale domestic applications, which take advantage of the geographical spread of supplies, but these are likely to be economic in the near future only in areas which are both windy and isolated so that more conventional energy sources are expensive. Although outputs from wind machines are generally highest in the winter when demand is highest, unpredictable fluctuations in supply present a serious obstacle. The development of more efficient energy stores is therefore crucial (see Ryle, 1977). There are no adverse environmental side effects apart from the noise and visual costs of modern generators and possible interference with shipping in the case of offshore installations.

Vegetable energy sources. Food is of course the most important energy source of all, but is a rather special case. Wood and dung are major fuels in many parts of the world, but both are low-density energy sources with valuable competing uses. Over-use has impaired the fertility of the land and precipitated erosion. However, the possibility of developing special fuel crops, with a high rate of intake of solar energy is being investigated. It would not generally be worth while to sacrifice good farmland to such crops, but poor land might be so used, though attention would have to be paid to the dangers of erosion. Specially grown marine organisms present another possibility, particularly in the tropics. Organic waste (for example straw and other farm wastes, kitchen and garden wastes and waste paper) represent another important possibility. Currently the disposal of such wastes frequently involves heavy financial or environmental costs. Direct burning is often not the best way to extract the energy from organic sources, both because of their characteristically high moisture content and because of their potential as high-grade fertilisers. Bacterial decomposition (as in sewage works or the familiar garden compost heap) can be used to generate both energy (in the forms of direct heat and gas) and fertiliser.

Alternative techniques which are being actively explored include pyrolysis and hydrolysis. Many of these techniques are already economic, especially when alternative means of waste disposal involve financial or social costs. However the potential to over-all energy supplies is small. Their main advantage is their potentiality as a locally available source. Thus Chapman (1975) considers that all energy needs on U.K. farms could be met by hydrolysis of straw. Similarly, a proportion of domestic energy needs can be met from household wastes (see Department of Energy, 1976a). *Inter alia*, this reduces the energy demands for transporting wastes and fuels.

Direct solar energy. Large-scale electricity generation from solar energy is probably ruled out by the vast collection areas required. Extraterrestial collection and transmission to the earth has been suggested as a futuristic possibility and cannot altogether be dismissed (see Commoner *et al.*, 1975). However, solar energy is a low-density source and advantage should be taken of this property by using it as a localised source of supply. Domestic solar heating is already economic in favourable circumstances and the potential contribution is very large indeed. However, energy storage is a major problem. The possibilities are considered more fully in Chapter 9.[4]

8.4 Conclusions

Energy supplies are governed by Ricardian rather than Malthusian scarcity. They will not suddenly 'run out', for even with existing technology there exists a spectrum of higher-cost sources including some that are renewable indefinitely. However, in the absence of sufficient advances in technology, recourse to successively higher-cost sources will put a (possibly strong) brake upon economic growth. Changes in the mix of energy supplies can involve transitional problems; in particular associated investment is often energy-intensive and involves long lead times. For example, solar heating is cheapest when installed in new housing, but only 0.4 per cent of the U.K. housing stock is replaced each year. This underlines the importance of anticipating future supply problems. However, the major dangers are probably environmental: that nuclear energy and coal may be preferred on account of their relatively low costs, giving rise to possible cataclysmic disasters of major nuclear accidents or global overheating.

9 ENERGY, A CASE STUDY:
(II) DEMAND

9.1 The scope for conservation: concepts
The continued expansion of supplies (beyond the next few decades) is hazardous and uncertain. The alternative is to cut back demand; such an alternative may be forced on an unwilling world, if hoped-for developments fail to materialise or if available methods of expanding supply prove too hazardous; if so, it may be preferable to anticipate such crisis by cutbacks today.

Energy policy must strike a balance between current sacrifices involved in cutting demand and risks associated with expanding supply. The latter include the risk of a more abrupt cutback at some future date. Rational appraisal involves a view on the scope for energy conservation – both now and in the future when technology has advanced and appetites expanded. How great are the sacrifices? How much difference does it make if the cutbacks are abrupt, rather than being phased over several decades?

While the emphasis is still on expansion of supply, the less painful methods of cutting demand are being actively explored at national and international levels and numerous studies have recently appeared (for example N.E.D.O., 1974; Central Policy Review Staff, 1974; Organisation for Economic Co-operation and Development, 1976). Investigation of larger cutbacks has been mainly confined to unofficial work (for example Ford Foundation, 1974; Chapman, 1975).

Here the United Kingdom will be used as an example. It may be taken as representative of developed countries, though in countries of greater affluence and/or cheaper energy (notably the United States) *per capita* energy consumption may be higher and relatively painless reductions easier to find. Some quantitative estimates will shortly be given, but first it is important to clarify some conceptual problems involved in answering the apparently straightforward question 'What is the scope for conservation?'

Leak-plugging and belt-tightening: the sacrifice curve
First, the scope for conservation clearly depends on the level of sacrifice one is prepared to tolerate. This idea is represented graphically in the *marginal sacrifice* (*MS*) *curve* (see Figure 9.1). It is drawn as a

continuous function, indicating that there is no sharp line between a minor and major sacrifice, and indeed that particular avenues of conservation (for example home insulation, reducing commuting) can be varied continuously. The negative portion of the curve requires some explanation. At any particular time it is possible to find specific energy-saving measures which are justified on efficiency grounds quite apart from conservation motives. For example (at current energy prices), the costs of greater home insulation are outweighed by the financial benefits of reduced fuel bills. Such measures are sometimes referred to as *leak-plugging*, while measures which, deliberate conservation apart, are not worth while are dubbed *belt-tightening*.

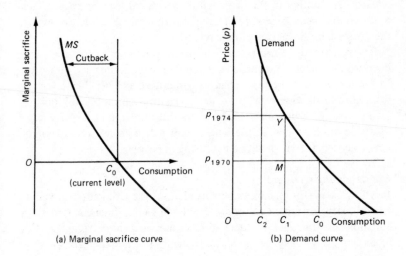

Figure 9.1   The sacrifice curve

Now, if revealed consumer preferences are accepted, the *MS* curve is closely related to the demand curve for energy (see Figure 9.1(b)). For example, at the 1970 price the preferred level of consumption is C_0, and the marginal sacrifice associated with a lower level, C, is the vertical distance YM. Hence the *MS* curve is obtained simply by re-labelling the vertical axis and setting the zero at the 1970 price. The effect of a rise in price may be seen either as a rise in the origin or, equivalently, as a fall in the sacrifice curve. Further, a particular level of energy saving may be associated with a price at which such energy savings would be justified. This may be referred to as the *shadow price* ('true social value') of energy, One method of conservation is of course to levy an energy tax, which may be chosen to equate the market price with the shadow price. This would make belt-tightening measures *appear* leak-plugging to the individual decision-maker.

In the long run it may be presumed that all available leak-plugging measures will have been taken. But response to changing conditions (for example technical advance) is slow, due both to simple inertia and to costs associated with over-rapid change (cf. Chapter 7); meanwhile it is possible to indicate and measure the potential for efficiency gains. Some of these gains involve energy savings (for example new steel-making processes) and may be described as 'plugging energy leaks'. However, the general run of technical advance has involved saving *labour*, frequently at the expense of increased energy usage. This tendency has been largely due to the steady increase in real wages and the decrease in the real cost of energy.

The recent large, abrupt change in energy prices has shifted the curve downwards, thereby creating a large reservoir of leak-plugging measures. In the longer term the price changes will induce a changed emphasis to research and development, a greater concentration on possibilities for saving energy. Hence it is likely in the medium term and, if energy prices continue to rise, in the longer term that a greater proportion of new technologies will involve a net saving in energy.

Evaluating the sacrifices

In a few cases (for example home insulation) the main costs and benefits of energy-saving measures are readily derived in financial terms as a function of the energy price. Other cases are more complex. For example, energy may be saved by reducing (or not increasing) room temperatures, or by people travelling to work by bus instead of car. The standard economist's approach is to accept individual evaluations of costs and benefits as indicated by their behaviour, specifically their 'willingness to pay'. If this principle is accepted, then the marginal sacrifice curve is simply a demand curve which may be estimated in the usual way.

However, many writers reject the evidence of consumer choice, and prefer to judge for themselves what is or is not a sacrifice. For example, Commoner (1971), in castigating the wastefulness of disposable metal beer containers, suggests that 'what contributes to human welfare is the beer not the can'; similarly, Chapman (1975) 'seriously doubt[s] whether many people would feel "deprived" or "worse-off" if the food they purchased had just one layer of packaging instead of two', and again, when advocating the encouragement of small cars, he writes 'It seems to me quite arbitrary that at the moment the "best" cars are simply the biggest. This value judgement on cars has been deliberately encouraged by advertising techniques used to sell cars.' Even the more conventional government reports (for example Central Policy Review Staff, 1974) give sympathetic consideration to smaller cars without even mentioning the possible welfare loss, and in discussion of modal switching seem less concerned with the welfare loss than the accompanying consumer and voter resistance.

Clearly, Commoner and Chapman are much too cavalier. The nuisance of returning beer containers is a relevant consideration and likewise there are very real advantages of large cars (more storage space, leg room, greater accessibility of parts, etc.). In some cases, however, consumer behaviour is distorted by recognised market failures. For example, it is widely thought that a switch to public transport would secure major gains quite apart from energy saving. In particular there would be a reduction in congestion, pollution and noise; these are external costs of motoring of which the motorist takes no account. There is thus a strong case for levying a charge on motorists for use of urban roads to internalise these costs. On this view such a charge represents a net current gain to society and is properly classified as a leak-plugging measures. It so happens that the leaks include a significant energy component. Conservation, implying a higher shadow price of energy, reinforces but does not create the argument for road pricing. However, it does justify a higher price for road use, and correspondingly a greater switch to buses.

However, road pricing, unlike home insulation, raises a host of complex and controversial issues. While the theoretical case for road pricing is established, the practical difficulties are considerable and the over-all desirability in dispute. Alternative measures of reducing congestion (for example parking taxes, subsidies to public transport, bus lanes), though administratively simpler, encounter other difficulties. All this may be a way of saying that the hidden costs of reducing congestion outweigh the theoretical benefits. If so, it would be misleading to present road pricing or modal switching as a clear case of leak-plugging or as an easy way of saving energy.

In other cases 'irrational' behaviour is implied and, more specifically, it is being suggested that tastes are influenced by advertising. These arguments were discussed in Chapters 5 and 6. The conflict of views may sometimes be less than at first sight appears. What are dismissed as 'no sacrifice' by these writers may be acknowledged to be rather slight sacrifices even by the conventional willingness to pay criterion. These cases will be covered by distinguishing a category of 'measures claimed to involve little or no sacrifice'.

Time scale

Few energy-saving measures can be implemented immediately in full. Often changes in capital are involved; modifications to existing capital may be expensive or even impossible, so that energy saving depends crucially on the rate of replacement. If the energy savings are very large, it may be worth bringing forward replacement dates, but in many cases replacement (for example of the housing stock) will be virtually un-affected by energy considerations, placing a limit on the rate at which savings can be introduced. Capacity constraints in the investment-goods industries may also be important. Sometimes new labour skills are re-quired; at best, retraining takes time and involves a 'wastage' of existing skills and the least-cost method of introducing new skills is to instil them in new entrants to the labour force. Measures requiring further research before they become fully operational involve even longer lead times. Even if operational measures have been developed, further technical development might render these obsolete and massive invest-ment based on a soon-to-be-superseded technology could prove an expensive mistake. Moreover, relatively untried techniques could be subject to unforeseen snags (well-known examples in other fields in-clude the side-effects of D.D.T. and the contraceptive pill); a slower introduction of new techniques reduces the risks associated with such teething troubles. Finally, there are human problems of adaptation, especially where sacrifices are involved. If consumer tastes are malle-able, malleability is a process in time, and in particular each genera-tion's tastes, attitudes and expectations are generated afresh.

All these considerations suggest that the costs of energy saving are crucially dependent on the rate at which they are introduced. This time dimension, suppressed in Figure 9.1, greatly complicates the analysis. An ideal procedure would involve deriving the *optimum* rate of intro-duction of each form of energy saving and relating the over-all energy saved to the over-all sacrifice using some appropriate discounting pro-cedure. In practice determination of optimum time paths has been treated rather casually in all the studies; most are content to search for a *feasible* path taking account of the more obvious constraints (for example the normal rate of replacement of capital stock). A great deal more work needs to be done.

The base-line from which to measure energy savings

Since conservation is never immediate but is, rather, a process in time, its effect should ideally be measured in terms of deviations from the future *path* of consumption. If, for cimplicity, it is decided to concentrate on a single year, this must be sufficiently far in the future to allow for the long lags in adjustment. (Here the year 2000 will be used.) Changes in the total and pattern of consumption may be estimated naively by extrapolating trends or by more sophisticated methods. However, one difficulty is that past trends incorporate significant leak-plugging (see Table 9.1 below): significant energy savings have been sought and found and, to some extent measures now proposed represent no more than a continuation of this process. Thus a 'no change in policies' projection embodies a considerable measure of energy conservation. To measure the gains of policies investigated from such a base-line would clearly involve double-counting. Three considerations somewhat reduce the force of this point. First, it applies only to leak-plugging; significant belt-tightening in the interest of energy conservation has not occurred so far. Second, in the past (energy) leak-plugging has taken place despite the continued drop in energy prices; now the incentive for energy leak-plugging is greatly increased by the much higher and probably rising level of energy prices. Third, and following from this, falling energy prices led to substitutions of energy for other inputs which outweighed the energy leak-plugging. In the future not only are such substitutions less likely but on the contrary a wide range of small-scale energy savings are to be expected which will not be picked up in any case-by-case study.

Technical progress

By the year 2000 significant changes in technology are to be expected. Indeed, all the studies indicate important opportunities for energy saving which depend on solving apparently rather minor technical problems. In other cases the difficulties are more considerable, but it is to be expected that at least some of these will prove successful. Even looking forward twenty-five years the possibility of technical progress involves a major element of uncertainty in the marginal sacrifice curve. Our discussion will be limited to indicating the major possibilities for imminent technical advance and their likely implications for energy conservation.

In the longer term technical progress is the dominant consideration. Possible innovations are probably as important and certainly much more varied than possibilities for increasing energy supply. It is to be expected that recent price increases and probable future price increases will significantly influence the emphasis of research and development towards energy saving, and that this may be reinforced by government encouragement. Indeed, one of the most important roles for the government in energy conservation is to encourage appropriate research. While this is crucially important, any attempt at detailed quantification of the long-term future is so problematic as to be of little use. Certainly, it will not be attempted here.

Indirect effects on energy consumption

So far consideration has been confined to the immediate effects of a conservation measure on energy consumption. However, other inputs, notably labour, will also be affected, with possible repercussions on energy. Additionally, there is an income effect to be considered.

The most instructive case is a leak-plugging measure through which, while energy is saved, labour input is increased. In the first instance total employment in the economy is increased. Now this increase may have further ramifications, depending on the reaction of the government (see Chapter 7). Since employment is substantially under the control of the government, the best general assumption is that, having regard for inflation and other considerations, employment will be restored to its original level. If, over the rest of the economy, labour and energy are complementary, the only way that employment can be maintained at its initial level is by a general depression of activity, involving a further reduction in energy use, over and above that initially calculated. The welfare gain from the leak-plugging measure is correspondingly reduced.

However, it is more reasonable (except in the very short term) to assume that full employment will be restored through the substitution of energy for labour (either directly by varying productive techniques or indirectly by varying product mix). This indicates an increase in energy consumption to be set against the initial savings. More of the welfare gain is retained.

The welfare gain implies a possible *income effect* on energy consumption. The benefits could be taken partly in the form of increased leisure or increased savings – the latter would spread the gains to future generations more widely than simple energy conservation. But some of the welfare gain will probably be *taken* in the form of increased consumption of energy, offsetting the initial saving. The effect may be termed a *buy-back effect* (cf. Sharp, 1966).

There are three other cases to be considered (see immediately below). Similar arguments may be applied and the analysis is left to the reader. The results (assuming substitutability) are as follows:

(i) *Leak-plugging*
   (a) Labour input *increased* initially. This results in extra resource use offsetting the initial saving.
   (b) Labour input *decreased* initially. The result is uncertain (opposing income and substitution effects).
(ii) *Belt-tightening*
   (a) Labour input *increased* initially. The result is uncertain (opposing income and substitution effects).
   (b) Labour input *decreased* initially. This results in a reinforcement of the initial resource saving.

With leak-plugging, (a) is the normal case, so that offsets (buy-back) are likely. With belt-tightening, buy-back is less likely (because the income effect works in reverse) and the effect of restoring full employment may even be to reinforce the initial resource savings.

International trade

The pattern of trade exerts a significant influence on energy consumption. A net exporter of energy-intensive commodities will, *ceteris paribus*, show a higher energy consumption than a net importer. The United Kingdom could indeed reduce energy consumption by displacing domestic production of energy-intensive commodities (for example glass, iron and steel, cement) by imports; production could be directed to less energy-intensive commodities which could be exported to maintain external balance. Clearly, there is little merit in such a policy; what is happening is that energy, instead of being imported as such, is being imported embodied in commodities, in which form it does not appear as 'energy' in the statistics. There is no gain either to the United Kingdom or the world, and indeed there could be considerable loss from such an arbitrary alteration in the pattern of trade. In the case of cement, imports would involve heavy transport costs including unnecessary consumption of energy.

In other cases global energy savings are obscured by accompanying changes in the pattern of trade. For example, recycling aluminium leads to substantial savings of energy (and bauxite). However, since aluminium is imported, the savings occur abroad, and indeed U.K. energy consumption is probably increased by additional recycling. For this reason Chapman (1975) excludes increased recycling from consideration, noting that 'An increase in recycling may well do a lot to help the balance of payments, but may slightly increase U.K. fuel consumption.' However, it is clear from the above discussion that recycling has as much claim to be regarded as an energy-saving measure as other measures which happen to be more adequately reflected in the statistics.

One way to avoid this anomaly would be to study, not U.K. energy consumption, but rather the *energy content of U.K. final expenditure*. However, this involves estimating the energy content of imports (and exports), which is difficult, except on the unsatisfactory assumption that foreign processes are identical to U.K. ones. U.K. energy consumption has the advantage of being a familiar published statistic, readily available for a long run of years. In the recent past the two measures appear to have moved very similarly. When considering policies, however, those which rely for their impact on U.K. energy consumption on changes in the pattern of trade will be disregarded. Conversely, policies like aluminium recycling which, though not benefiting U.K. energy consumption, would reduce the energy content of U.K. consumption will be included.

Energy units

Energy is heterogeneous; a variety of different fuels are derivable from a variety of primary energy sources. Substitutability is important but imperfect, since particular fuels have strong advantages in particular uses (for example petroleum in road transport). A full discussion of energy would treat each use and each fuel explicitly; such a discussion would be long, complex and expirically demanding. It is therefore common to treat *energy* as a whole, distinguishing particular fuels only where lack of substitutability is especially important. This is the approach adopted here.

Aggregation demands a *common unit* – at least if the discussion is to be quantitative. The unit usually chosen is a measure of the energy content, such as the joule (J). The gigajoule (GJ) equals 10^9 J, the exojoule (EJ) 10^{18} J. A ton of high-quality coal contains 32GJ, a gallon of petrol 0.16GJ. However, in extracting, processing, transporting and using the fuel much of the energy content is lost, while further energy is involved in running the associated equipment.

Typical energy losses associated with various forms of domestic heating are shown in Table 9.1. This table is intended to give a rough indication of magnitudes – there will in practice be considerable variation, depending on conditions and technologies employed.

Several lessons may be drawn, for example the apparently enormous

Table 9.1 Typical energy losses in domestic heating uses

Energy required to provide 100 units useful energy and per cent

Primary source / Use	(1) Coal (open fire)	(2) Coal (electric fire)	(3) Uranium* (electric fire)	(4) Natural gas (central heating)	(5) Petroleum (central heating)
(1) Original energy (energy in place)	850	582	71600	236	489
(2) Losses, etc., in extraction	260	174	3600	71	312
(3) Gross energy (energy extracted)	590	408	68000	165	171
(4) Losses, etc., in conversion, distribution, etc.	90	306	67898	22	17
(5) Net energy (energy supplied)	500	102	102	143	154
(6) Losses, etc., in use	400	2	2	43	54
(7) Useful energy	100	100	100	100	100
(8) Extraction efficiency (3/1)	70	70	95	70	35
(9) Conversion efficiency (5/3)	85	25	0.15	85	90
(10) Utilisation efficiency (7/5)	20	98	98	70	65
(11) Over-all efficiency (7/1)	11	18	0.14	42	21
(12) Efficiency excluding unconsumed fraction	17	25	10	61	58

*Converted to electricity by means of the burner reactor. The enormous losses largely represent unused uranium-238 (see text).

Sources: United Nations Economic Commission for Europe (1976); N.E.D.O. (1974).

potential for efficiency gains and the importance of looking at the whole process from extraction to use (thus the alleged advantages of electric heating over coal are greatly diminished when account is taken of conversion losses). However, our concern here is with *units*. Energy could in principle be measured at any one of the four stages distinguished in the table, and this choice greatly influences the relative weight given to different fuels. Since our concern is with supply limitations, it may seem most appropriate to work in terms of *original energy*. It appears that vast reductions in demand for original energy may be achieved by switching fuels (for example natural gas in place of nuclear electricity).

However, there are several reasons for questioning the wisdom of such switches. First, some of the 'losses, etc.' represent energy that is not dissipated as waste heat but is set aside as not worth recovering. The prime examples are oil, gas and coal left in the ground and uranium-238, which cannot be utilised in the burner reactor. (It is this last that accounts for the very low conversion efficiency in column 3.) In principle this energy is available for later recovery, and, in so far as it is not, it is doubtful if it should be included in original energy.[1] Consequently it is more appropriate to work in terms of gross energy, and moreover to disregard the uranium-238 rejected by the burner reactor. This in fact corresponds to our treatment on the supply side. Efficiencies on this basis are shown in row 12 of Table 9.1.

A comparison of the figures in row 12 indicates the superiority (from an energy-conservation viewpoint and in this particular context) of coal-based electricity over coal and of oil and natural gas over both. The former comparison is appropriate enough: both methods of heating are based ultimately on coal, which is conserved if it is first converted into electricity. But where different primary fuels are involved a simple efficiency comparison, though often presented with little or no qualification (see Chapman, 1975; United Nations Economic Commission for Europe, 1976; Department of Energy, 1976a) is barely relevant. The significance of energy efficiency lies in the prospect of eventual exhaustion (or the need to move to a lower grade). Here the exhaustion of one resource may be more serious or more imminent than that of another.

Specifically, gas and oil are specialised fuels, for which in many ('premium') uses coal could not be substituted (or only following liquification or gasification involving conversion losses and hence lower efficiency levels than indicated in the table). Using gas and oil for non-premium uses hastens their exhaustion, thereby precluding their employment in uses in which they have a much greater comparative advantage. At a zero discount rate and ignoring the complications of technical change, the analogy with international trade theory is indeed exact. Although gas and oil are more energy-efficient (and let us say more efficient over-all) in domestic heating, their superiority is greater in other uses, and their use should be reserved for these; for domestic heating coal is *absolutely* less efficient but *relatively* more efficient and should be used. At a positive discount rate (or on different assumptions about technology) less weight is given to future exhaustion of oil and gas, and the early use of these in a wider variety of uses may be indicated.

Another difficulty concerns some ambiguity over the concept of 'useful heat'. A coal fire is less flexible, it cannot be switched on and off according to whether the room is occupied. Hence its heat output may in fact be less 'useful'. Again, while the output of a light is normally measured in terms of illumination, the normal incandescent electric light gives off more heat than light. This heat may be 'useful' or the reverse depending for example on the time of year. Ranging more widely, a coal fire is dirty and involves more trouble; on the other hand, it is, to some, aesthetically preferable. However, such factors are reflected in the market *prices* of the fuels; these represent what, at the margin, they are worth to consumers, bearing in mind the side-effects; they represent also what at the margin they cost to produce. Turvey and Nobay (1965) argue convincingly for the use of prices rather than energy equivalences in combining different fuels. But there are various difficulties: first, as admitted by Turvey and Nobay, relative prices can change quite dramatically over time. A particularly sharp change, illustrated in Table 9.2, was brought about by the oil price rise of 1974. Second, a concern with conservation is necessarily associated with a distrust of markets in important respects. Market prices would not reflect externalities in extraction, processing or use. Nor, more centrally to the purposes of this book, do they necessarily reflect at all adequately the scarcity of the resources concerned.

Table 9.2 **Alternative equivalence ratios for conventional energy sources**

	Electricity	*Gas*	*Oil*	*Coal*
Net energy basis	1	1	1	1
Gross energy content (1970)	Range *c.* 2.5 − 20 Average 3.7	Town 1.22 Natural 1.04 Average 1.16	1.06	1
Price (United Kingdom)				
1965	7.9	3.07	0.76*	1
1970	7.6	1.80	0.88*	1
1975	7.5	0.75	n.a.	1
Shadow price (United States, 1970)†	1.24	0.68	2.16	1

* heavy fuel oil, excluding duty.

† Nordhaus (1973b) estimates; natural gas and oil measured at well-head, coal at pit-head, electricity at power-station. Correction for distribution costs would make little difference to these ratios. For a criticism of Nordhaus's study, see p. 174.

Sources: Digest of United Kingdom Energy Statistics 1976; Nordhaus (1973b).

Ideally a conservation-orientated exercise should work in terms of gross energy resources which should be brought to equivalence using *shadow prices* to correct for myopia. This would pick up the immediate resource conservation aspects of the problem, though it would neglect differences in non-energy costs including environmental impacts which a full analysis would include. This approach is beyond the scope of this study, though estimates of shadow prices (by Nordhaus, 1973b) are included in Table 9.2.

Table 9.2 shows some of the wide range of fuel equivalences one might use. We have opted to use 'gross' physical energy, measured in joules (J), as the least unsatisfactory of the readily available alternatives. It is particularly crucial to bear in mind the limitations of this (or any other) measure when *alternative policies* are being considered.

9.2 Past trends

Table 9.3 gives past trends and illustrative projections of energy consumption broken down into its main components. It will be seen that the main growth areas of the 1960s were road freight and travel by air and car. Several components, most notably rail transport and iron and steel, showed a decline in energy consumption. The fourth column gives the 1960–72 growth in energy consumption relative to a measure of the output of the sector, thus giving some indication of a change in energy efficiency. The limitations of the measures of both output and energy input must be borne in mind. The measure of output, particularly when a simple physical unit is used, may neglect important quality changes. Thus passenger-transport modal switching, from bus and train to car and air, has substantially reduced energy efficiency though this factor is outweighed by efficiency gains in individual modes, especially rail). These shifts stem partly from consumer preferences, for the latter modes are often faster or more convenient. The additional energy cost has to be weighed against these advantages, an issue which is taken up in more detail below (p. 210). On the input side the appropriateness of a gross physical measure of energy is somewhat doubtful in view of the large change in fuel mix (away from coal) that dominated the period (cf. p. 195).

In some sectors energy efficiency fell. This could be due to (i) the factors discussed in the previous paragraph, (ii) a substitution of energy for other inputs stemming from the falling relative price of energy as well as from technical changes, and (iii) improvements in the work environment (for example higher office temperatures). But it is interesting, in view of falling energy prices, how many sectors exhibit a a rise in gross energy efficiency. The most striking cases are those industrial sectors where energy is a major cost, for example the iron and steel industry, in which, in 1972, energy accounted for over 20 per cent of input costs. This gave a large incentive to save energy, thus stimulating major advances in furnaces (N.E.D.O., 1974). In other industries where energy is a major input, for example railways, paper, building

Table 9.3   U.K. energy consumption, 1960–2000

| | Past period | | | | Future period | |
| | Energy consumption (EJ) | | Growth (% p. a.) | Growth relative to stated indicator (% p. a.) | Consumption (EJ) | Growth (% p. a.) |
	1960	1972	1960–72	1960–72	2000	1972–2000
Domestic	2.10	2.55	1.7	−1.9[a] ('useful energy')	4.2	1.7
Government, commercial, etc.	0.89	1.16	2.2	−0.2 (output index)	1.7	1.4
Industry and agriculture	3.52	3.71	0.4	−2.6 (output index)	5.8	1.7
Agriculture	0.08	0.11	2.7	0.1 (output index)	0.1	1.3
Food, D and T	0.21	0.29	2.1	−0.4 (I.I.P.)*	1.1	1.9
Chemicals, etc.	0.39	0.57	3.2	−2.2 (I.I.P.)	1.1	2.4
Iron and steel	0.93	0.78	−1.5	−1.8[b](tons finished steel)	0.7	−0.5
Engineering, etc.	0.47	0.62	2.3	0.4 (I.I.P.)	1.1	1.9
Textiles, etc.	0.23	0.21	−0.8	−2.9 (I.I.P.)	0.2	−0.5
Building materials	0.33	0.34	0.3	−2.3 (I.I.P.)	0.4	0.6
Paper, etc.	0.16	0.20	1.9	−0.7 (I.I.P.)	0.3	1.0
Other	0.24	0.49	6.2	3.9 (I.I.P.)	1.5	4.0
Transport	1.01	1.41	2.8	0.4 (output index)	3.5	3.3
Road:						
car, etc.	0.31[c]	0.68	6.8	−0.7 (passenger-miles)	1.6	3.1
bus	0.06[c]	0.05	−1.5	–	0.05	0
freight	0.14[c]	0.34	7.9	3.1 (ton-miles)	0.8	3.0
Rail	0.34	0.08	−11.4	−8.8 (output index)	0.1	0
Air	0.09	0.21	7.3	−1.5 (output index)	0.9	5.3
Water	0.07	0.05	−4.6	–	0.05	0
All passenger[d]	0.73	0.98	2.7	−1.8 (passenger-miles)	2.4	3.2
All freight[d]	0.28	0.43	3.6	1.4 (ton-miles)	1.1	3.4
Total[e]	7.15	8.83	1.8	−0.7 (G.D.P.)	15.2	2.0

Notes: [a] 1963–75, from N.E.D.O. (1974) table 13. [b] N.E.D.O. (1974) table 31. [c] Breakdown of road transport not available. Estimated from figures for motor spirit and derv. [d] Own estimates. [e] Excludes petrochemical feedstocks and other non-energy uses of petroleum. * Index of Industrial Production.

Sources: *past* – Annual Abstract of Statistics, Transport Statistics in Great Britain, Digest of United Kingdom Energy Statistics, N.E.D.O. (1974); *future* – Department of Energy (1976a), Chapman (1975).

materials as well as non-ferrous metals (not shown separately), there have been significant gains in energy efficiency.

The rise in efficiency of the domestic sector is attributable partly to the increased efficiency of appliances, especially central heating and solid-fuel burners, partly to the displacement of the open fire, and partly to improved insulation in new houses.

The illustrative projections

The last two columns give projections to 2000, for use as a base-line from which to measure the impact of conservation. These projections are illustrative and not much weight should be attached to the details. To project twenty-five years ahead is inevitably an uncertain exercise for which precision is inappropriate. For our purpose orders of magnitude are all that are required. In fact the total is a Department of Energy (1976a) projection, and the breakdown represents our estimates based on past trends, various projections (for example Chapman, 1975) and sundry special considerations.

9.3   A modelling approach

In principle many of the difficulties discussed in Section 9.1 are avoided by constructing a model in which energy supplies and demands are related to various explanatory variables, including prices. The model may treat energy as an aggregate or distinguish different categories of energy and/or use. Ideally it would be estimated on past data and applied to predict energy consumption in the year 2000. It is then an easy matter to compute the effect of the recent oil price rise and also the impact of any energy tax. In 'ideal' circustances such a tax is the most efficient way of cutting energy consumption and the resultant sacrifice may readily be calculated. A model of this type has been constructed for the U.S. economy by Hudson and Jorgenson (1976) and similar work for the United Kingdom is being done under Professor Littlechild at the universities of Birmingham and Aston. A number of other studies are summarised by the Department of Energy (1977b).

While this work is valuable in aiding understanding of aspects of energy use, its reliability in the current context is questionable. First, it is difficult to separate the influence of various factors governing energy use, for example income and price over a period (up to 1974) when both have followed steady trends. Their influence is in fact likely to be distinguished by the effects of short-term fluctuations which may be wholly misleading as a guide to longer-term effects. Second, this period involved consistent reductions in the real price of energy and it is doubtful how far the effects are reversible when energy prices rise. In both cases the post-1974 period is potentially more indicative, but as yet insufficient evidence has accumulated. Third, it is difficult to see how the effect of technical advance can be handled satisfactorily, especially at a time when the direction of research is changed by a change in price trends. Fourth, an energy tax is not the only or even the best policy instrument (cf. Chapter 6); it would be difficult to incorporate the full range of policy variables in the model, and the impact of novel policies could hardly be estimated from past data. Fifth (cf. p. 188), sacrifice can be identified with demand only on the assumption of consumer rationality. For all these reasons, then, there is no satisfactory alternative to the more *ad hoc* approach adopted here.

It is worth noting the implications of available estimates of price elasticity. The short-term elasticity appears to be about 0.4, the long-term elasticity about 0.5 (Department of Energy, 1977b), though the latter seems rather low (cf. the first point in the previous paragraph). Using 0.5, the threefold energy price rise involves a cutback of 42 per cent. Such a cutback is leak-plugging and the associated welfare gain (cf. Figure 9.1) is approximately:

$$\tfrac{1}{2}\Delta p \,\Delta q = \tfrac{1}{2}(1 - 0.33)p_{74}(1.73 - 1)q_{74}$$
$$= 0.24 p_{74} q_{74}$$
$$= \pounds2290\text{m. (4 per cent G.D.P.)}$$

A further threefold price increase, secured by a 200 per cent tax on energy, would lead to a further cutback of 42 per cent, making 67 per cent in all. This further cutback is belt-tightening and the associated welfare loss is approximately:

$$\tfrac{1}{2}\Delta p \,\Delta q = \tfrac{1}{2}(3 - 1)p_{74}(0.42)q_{74}$$
$$= 0.42 \, p_{74} q_{74}$$
$$= \pounds4010\text{m. (7 per cent G.D.P.)}$$

The welfare loss arising from a rise in the *real* cost of obtaining fuels or in the price of fuel imports is of course much larger, specifically:

$$pq + \tfrac{1}{2} \Delta p \,\Delta q = \pounds13,560\text{m. (nearly 25 per cent G.D.P.).}$$

However, as emphasised above, the validity of these calculations depends on the reliability of the elasticity estimates and the acceptance of the demand curve as an indicator of sacrifice.

9.4 Simple leak-plugging

Home insulation

The Rothschild Report (Central Policy Review Staff, 1974) identifies only one clear case of leak-plugging, namely home insulation. The principles of the calculations are straightforward: higher insulation standards reduce the fuel input required to maintain any given level of room temperature, and the annual cost savings may be discounted and compared with the costs of installation. For a 'typical' new three-bedroomed semi-detached or end-terrace house maintained at 21°C downstairs and 18°C upstairs, it is worth while to install 'high' insulation[2], cutting fuel input by 26 per cent. Allowing for some increase in room temperatures, this is reduced to 20 per cent. No allowance is made for more generalised buy-back. On existing houses room temperatures may be lower and hence the buy-back effect will be stronger. Moreover, insulation costs are higher, reducing the optimum level. Our calculations are based on a 20 per cent (12GJ average) saving on all centrally heated housing, estimated at 16 million dwellings by the year 2000.

It is sometimes alleged (for example Chapman, 1975; N.E.D.O., 1974) that in calculating the energy implications of these measures account should be taken of the energy content of the investment involved. However, this investment is also subject to a buy-back effect (in reverse) in that it displaces other expenditure. It is only in so far as the energy intensity of the investment differs from that of the expenditure displaced that a correction is necessary (cf. p.192).

Other domestic

Other suggestions range from increased efficiency of appliances to lower standards of comfort. One obvious target, discussed extensively by the N.E.D.O. (1974) is solid-fuel burners. In 1970 such burners (excluding those for central heating) operated at 30 per cent efficiency on average, accounting for nearly 37 per cent of domestic energy consumption. If all burners were brought up to modern efficiency standards, i.e. about 60 per cent, 18½ per cent of domestic energy consumption (nearly 0.8EJ in the year 2000) could be saved. However, this is very much an upper estimate. First, for many the attractions of an open fire outweigh the additional heating costs. Second, replacement may be by burners using other fuels; while the energy gain is comparable (except where the switch is to electricity), the conservation value of burning scarce oil or gas is questionable (see p.196). Third, the buy-back effect is likely to be particularly strong, especially where old burners are replaced by central heating (for example where an old property is demolished and replaced by a new centrally heated house). Whatever gains remain are probably no more than a continuation of past trends.

N.E.D.O. also suggests greater insulation of refrigerators, care in the orientation and siting of houses to maximise solar input and minimise heat loss: 'Occupiers are likely to pay about 10 per cent more for heating for the privilege of a north-facing living room and south-facing bathroom.' The Rothschild Report (Central Policy Review Staff, 1974) recommends greater efficiency of light fittings. In addition there is widespread scope for general economy of behaviour, for example shutting doors and windows, switching off lights and appliances when not in use, and accepting lower standards of comfort (lower room temperatures, lower-powered lights, fewer and shallower baths, and so on. Such measures may appear to constitute belt-tightening, but if at current prices householders consider them worth while, they come under our definition of leak-plugging (except perhaps where they are adopted as a personal contribution to conservation). The Department of Energy (1976a) estimates that the consumption of *useful* energy in the year 2000 will be '10 per cent below what it would otherwise have reached . . . without the recent escalation in energy prices' (saving 0.40EJ). Otherwise no attempt has been made to quantify these economies.

Government and commercial

Large economies may be made by installing sophisticated heating-control systems. N.E.D.O. report a survey of 300 such installations in large offices at a total cost of £458,000. This led to fuel savings ranging from 30 to 50 per cent and financial savings of £262,000 p.a., a net present value of £2.62 million, a return of nearly 600 per cent. A 40 per cent saving applied to all commercial, etc., energy consumption for heating amounts to about 0.28EJ in the year 2000. Admittedly the scope for gains is less in smaller establishments, but on the other hand greater gains may be possible where the methods are installed *ab initio* in new offices. Other sources of savings include lower standards of comfort (estimated by the Department of Energy (1976a) at 10 per cent), better insulation, improved light fittings and great energy-consciousness on the part of employees.

Industry

Traditionally the main industrial user has been iron and steel, currently accounting for 10 per cent of total energy consumption (however, this percentage is falling due to fuel economies and slow growth of the industry). The N.E.D.O. report includes a long discussion of potential savings. These comprise (i) increasing use of higher-grade imported ore (1GJ/tonne), (ii) various improvements in blast-furnace operations (not quantified), (iii) changeover from obsolete Bessemer converters to basic oxygen converters (0.4GJ/tonne), (iv) extension of continuous casting operations (1.5GJ/tonne eventually), (v) construction of further integrated mills eliminating cooling and reheating between processes (2GJ/tonne), and (vi) replacement of older iron-making plant (2GJ/tonne).

The total savings amount to 7GJ/tonne, (or 1.3EJ over-all). However, the industry has experienced large energy savings in the past, amounting to 1.6 per cent p.a. per tonne produced; these savings have been stimulated by the unusually high fraction of costs (over 20 per cent) represented by energy costs. The further savings envisaged represent no more than a continuation of these trends. The impact of the energy price rise has not been calculated.

The N.E.D.O. report discusses briefly the other major energy-using industries, aluminium, cement, chemicals and packaging. Apart from the introduction of pre-heaters to the cement-making process and more paper recycling (the impacts of which are not quantified), no specific conservation measures are suggested. In fact these industries, like iron and steel, have always made efforts to economise on their large energy input (cf. Table 9.3). Further economies are therefore likely to be not much more than a continuation of past trends. Possibly, if one seeks departures from past trends in energy use, one should examine industries where, until now, energy costs have not been an important consideration. In this context a survey by the Advisory Council for Energy Conservation (1977) indicates savings of about 10 per cent from simple 'good housekeeping' measures. Applying this to all industry except iron and steel gives savings of 0.5EJ in the year 2000.

Transport

Car, freight and air transport are major growth areas where economies are particularly worth while. Up to 1973 the number of cars, average engine size and car mileage all rose rapidly. In 1973 these trends were halted abruptly. This was partly a direct consequence of higher petrol prices, but the 5 per cent fall in incomes was probably more important (cf. p.166). Probably only in the changing size composition of cars was the price effect predominant. This change could gather momentum as more cars become due for replacement and as the availability of small cars increases.[3] On past trends average engine size might have reached nearly 2000 c.c. by the year 2000 (Chapman, 1975); here we assume that higher petrol prices restrict the rise to 1500 c.c., just a little above the current level. The direct energy saving is about 0.33EJ. (Chapman derives much higher savings in such calculations by including *indirect* savings, for example in car production. However, such activities are not especially energy-intensive and savings are likely to be matched by 100 per cent buy-back effects.) Further opportunities for energy saving include fewer, shorter journeys (partly through a reversal in the trend to longer journeys to work), car pooling, modal switching, more energy-conscious driving and more frequent servicing. Vehicle design could also be improved to reduce energy loss. The over-all saving could be very considerable. Here it is set somewhat arbitrarily at a further 0.33EJ. This may be taken to include similar savings on the freight side.[4]

Air transport is increasing rapidly and could account for nearly 30 per cent of all transport fuel consumption by the year 2000. The Department of Energy (1976a) considers that, by increasing load factors from their scandalously low current levels and by depressing cruising speeds, savings of 20–25 per cent (0.2EJ) could be achieved. Additionally production could be concentrated on low-energy planes and in particular supersonic transport should be avoided.

Over-all leak-plugging

These estimates are brought together in Table 9.4. The inevitable limitations should again be stressed. At best the figures provide a crude indication of the more obvious possibilities available with given tech-

Table 9.4 Primary energy saving from leak-plugging and belt-tightening by sector

	Domestic		Government and commercial		Industry and agriculture		Transport		Total
Economies from leak-plugging	Insulation	0.19[R]	Heating control	0.28[N]	Good housekeeping	0.51[E]	Cars engine capacity	0.33[C]	
	Less 'useful energy'	0.40[E]	Less 'useful energy'	0.14[E]			other	0.33	
							Aircraft	0.20[E]	
	Total	0.59	Total	0.42	Total	0.51	Total	0.86	2.38
Additional economies claimed to involve 'little sacrifice' ('belt-tightening')	Insulation	0.27[R]	Insulation	0.07	Recycling Al.	0.02[N]	Cars engine capacity	0.33[C]	
	Double-glazing	0.07[B]	District heating and C.H.P.	0.32[E]	Returnables	0.08	speeds	0.12[C]	
	District heating and C.H.P.	0.16[E]	Heat pumps	0.12[E]	Durability	0.41	occupancy	0.30[C]	
	Solar panels	0.65[C]	Room temps	0.05	Paper and packaging	0.07	Lorry schedules	0.08	
	Heat pumps	0.28[E]	Lighting	0.02	Pesticides and fertilisers	0.14[L]	Aircraft modal switch	0.07	
	Room temps	0.27			Hydrolysis of straw	0.07[C]	other	0.10	
	Other	0.21			Other agriculture	0.17[L]	Vehicle-miles	0.35	
					Product mix	0.48	Maintenance	0.12	
							Modal switch	0.76[C]	
Less Interactions		−0.54	Interactions	−0.17	Interactions	−0.24	Interactions*	−1.07	
	Total	1.37	Total	0.41	Total	1.20	Total	1.16	4.14

Primary energy consumption (level and per cent p. a. 1972–2000)

	Domestic		Government and commercial		Industry and agriculture		Transport		Total	
1972	2.55		1.16		3.71		1.41		8.83	
2000 trend	4.2	*1.7*	1.7	*1.4*	5.8	*1.7*	3.5	*3.3*	15.2	*2.0*
with LP	3.6	*1.3*	1.3	*0.4*	5.3	*1.3*	2.6	*2.2*	12.8	*1.4*
with BT	2.2	*−0.5*	0.9	*−0.9*	4.1	*0.4*	1.5	*0.2*	8.7	*−0.1*

* Includes a deduction for the 'other' energy savings associated with car travel already included as leak-plugging.

Sources: [B] = Building Research Establishment (1975); [C] = Chapman (1975); [E] = Department of Energy (1976a); [L] = Leach (1976); [N] = N.E.D.O. (1974); [O] = O.E.C.D. (1976); [R] = Central Policy Review Staff (1974).

nology. Over-all leak-plugging reduces consumption by 2.38EJ, a useful but modest figure. Even with these savings consumption at 12.8EJ is nearly 50 per cent above its 1972 level and the growth rate over the period 1.4 per cent p.a.

9.5   Measures claimed to involve little or no sacrifice

A large number of measures have been suggested. Some would be stimulated by a significant further rise in energy prices. Others might encounter more resistance and it is more in the nature of a social judgement (cf. p. 188 above) that the sacrifice involved is negligible. In yet other cases (especially in the transport field) considerable savings can be achieved by measures which have strong justification quite apart from energy conservation. The savings attainable by these measures depends on the intensity with which they are applied.

Home insulation

For the standard house, considered in the previous section, the 'extra high' standards become worth while at about three times[5] current energy prices (they are also worth while at current prices if energy prices are expected to rise at 6 per cent p. a. or if a 4 per cent discount rate is used). The associated energy saving is 0.27EJ. Double-glazing is also worth while, saving a further 0.07EJ.

Other domestic

Large savings of non-renewable energy could be made by adapting new forms of heating, notably district heating, solar collectors and heat pumps. All are subject to considerable cost variations but are generally considered to be financially justified at current prices only in the most favourable conditions. A threefold price rise would justify district heating in all dense new developments; installation in existing dwellings is costly and disruptive but might sometimes be worth while. District heating might be used in at most 4 million dwellings by the year 2000, saving a potential 0.04EJ. Where district heating can be supplied from combined heat and power (C.H.P.) much larger gains are possible (0.12EJ if 50 per cent use C.H.P.: see Department of Energy, 1976a, 1977c; Central Policy Review Staff, 1974).

The potential of solar collectors is controverial. The official (Department of Energy, 1976a) view is that 'retrofitting of old houses may never become economic' and their productivity in new houses depends strongly on house design and technical advances in heat pumps. They envisage a maximum contribution by the year 2000 of 0.18EJ and consider this relatively insensitive to energy prices. However, Chapman (1975) suggests that most houses which are not supplied with district heating should be fitted with solar panels, thus meeting 70 per cent of the demands for space and water heating. By 2000 half the housing stock could be converted, saving 0.65EJ. While the economics are in dispute there is no doubt that such a programme is technically feasible.

A doubling of energy prices would be sufficient to justify the installation of heat pumps in most new housing. In existing homes, however, the central heating system would require conversion, increasing the cost and inconvenience. The Department of Energy (1976a) envisages that some 10 per cent of demand for space heating could be met by heat pumps, with minor technical developments but little increase in energy prices. Using this same 10 per cent figure as appropriate to a threefold price increase but no technical change gives savings of 0.28EJ.

In all cases the possibility that lower current costs of heating will lead to higher consumption of useful energy is ignored. In fact this is particularly likely with district heating, where in the absence of a satisfactory heat meter individual householders are not charged according to use, so that there is no incentive to economise.

Householders could adopt lower standards of comfort (cf. Section 9.4, p. 202), most notably lower room temperature. Any drop should be viewed against the rising trend in room temperatures. The 1½°C drop assumed in Table 9.4 (saving 0.27EJ) is from a base-line 3°C above the current level. Additional economies can be achieved by greater care (for example switching off lights). The table includes a modest 5 per cent reduction from such sources, which is perhaps the most that can be expected from a threefold rise in energy prices.

The various savings interact. For example, solar heating or lower room temperatures reduce the gains from any given level of insulation. (They also reduce the optimum level of insulation. No allowance has been made for this, and hence the price required to stimulate the stated economies is slightly understated.) The individual figures are derived without allowing for interactions and an explicit deduction (amounting to about one-third of total savings) is shown separately. Over-all, additional savings from belt-tightening amount to 1.37EJ, reducing domestic energy consumption to a little below the 1972 level.

Government and commercial

The big leak-plugging opportunity is to instal heating control. At even higher prices this could possibly be made even more sophisticated and it would probably be profitable to extend such methods to smaller offices. This possibility is ignored as no information is available. Gains are credited for insulation (following Department of Energy, 1976a), district heating and C.H.P. (as discussed above), heat pumps and for some reduction in heating and lighting standards. It is possible that employees could be induced to become more energy-conscious, but no allowance has been made for this in view of the lack of incentive (cf. p.144).

Industry

Opportunities for energy saving are highly specific and generally dependent on technical advance. The available studies are unrevealing, and it would take a major research programme to estimate the potential for saving. However, a number of possibilities for 'eliminating waste' have been put forward by conservationists. Recycling is often canvassed, but the reader is referred to the critical discussion in Chapter 6. Aluminium recycling is the most promising, since this uses one-eighth of the energy required for production from bauxite. However, availability of scrap is the most critical factor; a 20 per cent increase in usage of scrap could save 0.02EJ. Some other recycling operations, for example copper and paper, may produce significant energy savings. In the case of glass secondary recycling is mostly unpromising but re-use of bottles could make a significant contribution. This could be encouraged by greater standardisation (see p.138). But it should be noted that the energy content of glass is high. A glass bottle would have to be used at least ten times to beat a disposable plastic container on energy grounds (see Over and Sjoerdsma, 1974), so that unless a very efficient returning system can be evolved it may be preferable to encourage the trend to disposable containers.

Products could also be made to last longer. Built-in obsolescence is a notorious phenomenon, encouraged by advertising (see Packard, 1957); social critics suggest that frequent replacement brings little welfare gain. A 50 per cent increase in the lives of all consumer goods would save 0.82EJ. However, this would be achieved partly by increased expenditure on servicing and repair, which would use some energy; there would also be a buy-back effect. These factors might reduce the energy saving by about one-half. It should be noted that durable products 'lock in' existing technology, including in some cases technology that is extravagant in energy use. For example, the durability of houses, industrial plant and vehicles is a major barrier to energy saving.

Paper products are energy-intensive and it is often suggested that consumption is extravagant. Particular targets for criticism are packaging and advertising (the latter being condemned also for the stimulus it gives to aggregate demand). Smaller economies could also be made by, for example, re-use of envelopes, writing on both sides of the paper and reducing the circulation of memoranda. The major difficulty here is that extravagance is most likely in large organisations where employee behaviour is difficult to control. A 25 per cent cut has been assumed, after allowing for the buy-back effect.

Substantial savings could be made by variations in product mix. In particular, goods tend to be much more energy-intensive than services. A switch of 20 per cent of current expenditure on goods (excluding food, drink, tobacco and fuels) to services would save 0.48EJ.[6] At first sight such a switch may seem ambitious; but it must be seen in the context of growth − thus 100 per cent growth in consumption of goods would be reduced to 60 per cent. Also, no allowance has been made for switches from more energy-intensive to less energy-intensive items within each broad category.

Another important substitution possibility occurs in the food sector. The proportion of meat and the degree of processing have increased, steadily, though *nutritionally* these changes represent little improvement and indeed present some dangers for health. Nutritutional needs can be met at least as well as at a fraction of the cost in energy (and land) from a diet involving no meat and less processing. Leach (1976) shows that through such a diet protein output could be increased by over 50 per cent (leading to self-sufficiency in temperate foodstuffs and energy consumption for food production cut by nearly 60 per cent). Such a diet is not especially cheap, indicating a minimal buy-back effect. The calculations are offered as illustrative and it is admitted that the scenario is 'rather absurd': diet is not simply a question of nutrition −taste and convenience are also important. However, attitudes are crucial and it could plausibly be maintained that a significant move in this direction would involve little sacrifice. A 15 per cent saving (0.12EJ) has been assumed. This includes indirect savings in supplier industries (some of which are highly energy intensive, for example fertiliser production).

Leach has other suggestions for savings in agriculture: (i) reductions in the use of inorganic fertilisers, partly through increased care in application to reduce run-off − fertiliser production is energy-intensive and the gains could be substantial (0.07EJ); (ii) reduced wastage, as products are often discarded because they are small, misshapen or suffering from attacks by pests which often have no effect on the taste of the product; additionally attempts to avoid such attacks increase the use of pesticides (a 10 per cent reduction in wastage is assumed saving 0.07EJ); (iii) out-of-season products grown in greenhouses are very extravagant in energy use, and discontinuing such products would save 0.05EJ; (iv) Chapman (1975) claims that all energy needs on the farm could be met by hydrolysis of straw, and a threefold increase in the energy price would almost certainly make this process cost-effective (0.07EJ would be saved).

Over all, allowing for interactions, savings in the industrial sector amount to 1.33EJ.

Transport

There are three broad strategies for reducing energy consumption in transport. The first is to reduce total transport. (The rapid increase in transport means that very large — 60 per cent — gains could be made by simply arresting current trends. This does not mean that this is a desirable programme, or even that this is the best way of achieving this scale of economies.) If it is to be done without sacrifice, then the *need* for transport must be reduced; more housing could be provided in the central cities, and jobs and other facilities provided in villages and residential areas. Provision of as many facilities as possible within walking distance of people's homes would dramatically reduce the need for mechanised travel. On the freight side transport needs would be reduced by smaller-scale production for local markets. In both cases the advantages would have to be set against losses of economies of scale (but notice that this would increase the energy gain — a negative buy-back effect). These developments would be encouraged automatically by a rise in energy prices; but in view of the interconnection between location decisions (cf. Chapter 7) the role of land-use planning is crucial. A modest 10 per cent reduction in vehicle mileage is assumed, saving 0.35EJ. This is very small compared with the savings implicit in, for example, the *Blueprint* for *Survival* (Goldsmith, 1976), where, with communities of 100,000, transport could be cut by nearer 90 per cent.

A second strategy is to influence modal choice. Chapman (1975) includes in his preferred low-energy-growth scenario a reduction in the proportion of passenger-miles travelled by car by 50 per cent. This saves 0.76EJ. This includes some switching from car to bicycle or foot (as recommended in official reports, for example N.E.D.O., 1974). A 10 per cent switch of passengers from air to train and boat saves 0.07EJ. The return of some freight to the railways is frequently advocated (see O.E.C.D., 1976), but it is doubtful if this would either save energy or reduce congestion, given the existing transport networks and pattern of journeys: few journeys begin or end near a railhead, hence the choice is between road and road–rail–road and transhipment costs must be taken into account (see Pryke and Dodgson, 1975). However, if new industrial building were sited near railheads or new railheads established at existing industrial estates, the situation could be transformed. As it is industrial estates tend to be sited near motorways on the grounds that, if roads are to be used social and resource costs anyway, such siting will minimise both.

Finally, the efficiency of individual modes could be increased. A major inefficiency arises from low loadings. Chapman (1975) suggests a 22 per cent increase in car occupancy, saving 0.31EJ. Utilisation of lorries could also be increased by more careful scheduling; a 10 per cent improvement would save 0.08EJ. In the case of air transport further increases in load factors and reductions in speeds might save 0.10EJ. A 50 m.p.h. speed limit on roads, as adopted in the energy crisis, would save 5 per cent of road fuel (0.12EJ). Comparable savings could be achieved more satisfactorily by the two-pressure accelerator – a device to make motorists aware of the sharp increase in petrol consumption as the cruising speed is exceeded (see Advisory Council for Energy Conservation, 1977). (Reducing speeds of buses and trains, though saving energy, would make modal switching more difficult.)

Vehicle efficiency may also be increased by better standards of maintenance (saving up to 5 per cent i.e. 0.12EJ) and above all by a reduction to average engine size (to 1000 c.c., saving 0.33EJ over and above the saving assumed under leak-plugging: see Chapman, 1975).

One by-product of these changes is much lower road congestion. Assuming no additional travel, the consequent rise in speeds in towns will yield further energy savings. But in the absence of specific deterrents the improved conditions will generate additional journeys, reducing the above savings very substantially. It is assumed these are somehow prevented (for example less road building or by direct road pricing).

Over all the potential for savings is very substantial, amounting to 1.16EJ (45 per cent), allowing for interactions.

These savings (especially on the passenger side) are controversial. Empirical work suggests strongly that such changes would not be brought about by a threefold rise in energy prices. However, the externalities associated with some journeys are such as to justify much greater price rises without any reference to conservation.[7] Moreover, the interactions between various transport and locational decisions are such that the market system cannot be expected to work very well in reflecting preferences. Finally, it is plausibly suggested (cf. p.189) that consumer decisions in this area are ill-informed (for example ignorance of the marginal costs of motoring) and 'irrational', or subject to strong relative consumption effects (for example large fast cars acting as prestige symbols).

Thus a convincing case can be made for strong interventions. However, this case rests mainly on external costs (especially motorists' time) rather than conservation. This is important because it indicates a rather different *pattern* of cutbacks concentrating on trips where external costs are highest; for example driving on congested urban roads merits strong discouragement, but the case for influencing inter-city travel is generally weaker.

An effective programme would meet with great hostility. This is partly because of strong vested interests, partly because of undoubted difficulties in achieving a smooth transition (cf. Chapter 7). However, the crucial factor is perhaps the widespread ignorance of the massive inefficiency involved in the present arrangements. Until this is dispersed an effective transport policy is infeasible.

9.6   An assessment

The economies described above were brought together in Table 9.4 (p. 205). The over-all impact is substantial; between them, leak-plugging and belt-tightening cut energy consumption by nearly 50 per cent to a little below the 1972 level.[8]

However, it is important to realise that some of the economies, especially in transport, are very controversial. Their desirability is questioned by many – and this affects their feasibility. On the other hand, the investigation has been largely confined to identified economies, and there are doutbless many more, each perhaps insignificant, but adding up to something substantial.

Moreover, no account has been taken of technical progress, which is likely to become an increasingly important source of energy conservation, following the rise in price. Probable fields of advance include heat meters, insulation materials and methods, ventilation systems, heat pumps, vehicle design, battery technology, new forms of mass transit, new braking systems, new methods of transporting heat and techniques for waste conversion; this list makes no mention of the very varied opportunities in industry (see N.E.D.O., 1974; Over and Sjoerdsma, 1974).

The analysis illustrated clearly the long lags involved in implementing conservation measures. For example, nearly all the energy-saving measures in buildings are cheaper, more effective and less disruptive when incorporated *ab initio* in new building. In the United Kingdom under 0.5 per cent of the housing stock is replaced each year, so that in the twenty-five year span here examined only 10 per cent has been replaced. A further constraint is the capacity of the industries supplying and installing solar panels, etc. In industry too energy conservation often depends on the installation of new plant, and in transport on a web of interacting locational decisions (cf. Chapter 7). Further lags are involved in research and development. This underlines the importance of anticipating any crisis in supply by several decades.

9.7   A note on less-developed countries

In developed countries cheap and abundant energy, combined with affluence, has led to extravagance and it is relatively easy to find cutbacks which, provided they are phased in over a long period, cause only minor inconvenience. In a developing country energy productivity may be low due to lack of capital or knowledge, but extravagance is comparatively rare. There is very limited opportunity to cut back on energy consumption without real hardship.

However, as these countries develop it is tempting for them to emulate the modes of living of rich countries, and suggestions that this may be undesirable or unwise are apt to be resented. Nevertheless it should be borne in mind that high energy consumption, while it has doubtless contributed to the comfort, power and culture of the rich countries, has also rendered them very vulnerable to possible future scarcity. Indeed, a major theme of this book is how extravagant life-styles, once acquired, are very difficult to throw aside, especially quickly. Developing countries, not having yet acquired these life-styles, have a great opportunity to avoid the potential dangers of future energy scarcity.

NOTES

Chapter 1

1. Henceforth 'natural resource' will be shortened to 'resource' in those instances where there is no danger of misunderstanding.

2. Leading Pessimist writings include the following: Boulding (1970), Common and Pearce (1973), Commoner (1971), Daly (1971, 1972), Ehrlich and Ehrlich (1970), Goldsmith (1976), Heilbroner (1974), Meadows *et al.* (1972), Mesarovic and Pestel (1974), Mishan (1977) and Ophuls (1977).

3. Commoner (1971) is, however, a striking exception.

4. Leading Optimist writings include the following: Barnett and Morse (1963), Beckerman (1972, 1974), Cole (1973), Fischman and Landsberg (1972), Kay and Mirrlees (1975), Maddox (1972), Nordhaus (1973a, 1973b) and Nordhaus and Tobin (1972).

Chapter 2

1. The world has indeed already experienced numerous local examples of disastrous overcropping in the face of such limits, leading to erosion and the creation or extension of deserts (Dale and Carter, 1955; Ehrlich and Ehrlich, 1970).

2. However, the new finds are often of less accessible or lower-grade ores. In the absence of technical change this would cause a rise in resource prices (see pp. 29–32).

3. The terms 'Malthusian' and 'Ricardian' were first used in this context by Barnett and Morse (1963).

4. See previous note.

5. The question of quality also arises in comparing cars which use metal of different thicknesses.

6. For convenience the argument is set out in terms of a specific non-renewable resource, i.e. oil. However, it is applicable, with minor and obvious modifications, to a renewable resource, or to all natural resources. The reader should convince himself of this.

7. Oddly, Barnett and Morse's account omits mention of the opportunity cost of resources *in situ* – which is a further element in the cost, and hence, in perfect markets, the price of resource products. These opportunity costs or resource rentals should rise at a rate equal to the return of other assets (see p. 48). The opportunity costs arise

Bacharach, 1967). From an ethical viewpoint the claims of future generations are perhaps especially strong and have indeed been supported by a number of economists (see Ramsey, 1928; Pigou, 1924; Page, 1976).

However, the scope for government discretion is severly limited by potential public opposition. Thus the U.K. government might safely impose a modest tax on resources, especially if this was justified largely as a cheap and convenient source of revenue; but a heavier tax, involving noticeable current sacrifices, would almost certainly lead to defeat at the next election. In short, the *overriding* limitation to government action in defiance of preferences is not one of ethics but of political feasibility.

It is for this reason that the conservationist must address his analysis less to the government than to the people. He must seek to dispel ignorance and facile optimism, to make the public more fully aware of the risks associated with unrestrained resource use. He must try to put these issues vividly to counteract myopia. He must appeal to the hearts of the current generation to ponder afresh the ethics of exposing future generations to substantial risk. In this way individuals may be led both to modify their own behaviour and to support appropriate collective action through the government.

10 GOVERNMENT POLICY AND THE PUBLIC

In this book the suggested response to excessive resource depletion was appropriate action by the government. In so far as the problem results from market failure — the failure of the market to reflect the preferences of the people — this is appropriate enough. Market failure is very pervasive and extensive action can be justified under this head. Devising the most appropriate action is rarely straigthforward, especially when account is taken of distribution, enforcement costs (both economic and psychic and transitional problems. It should also be borne in mind that enforcement costs depend to a considerable extent on the degree of *voluntary* compliance with the rules. But at least the remedy, since it conforms with public preferences, should receive political support.

However, there is another possible source of excessive resource depletion — namely 'wrong-headed' preferences. This could arise from (i) 'facile optimism', ignorance of the risks associated with high resource depletion; (ii) 'irrationality', in particular myopia, especially where more distant effects are uncertain, and (iii) generational selfishness. These problems raise more fundamental difficilties. To many, especially economists, preferences are sacrosanct — to reject them is dictatorial and elitist.

In fact there are many precedents for government action to protect individuals from their own folly and from the 'tyranny of the majority'. Examples of the first are laws requiring motor-cyclists to wear crash helmets, regulations concerning product quality, laws against drug-taking and taxes on tobacco; examples of the second are the abolition of the death penalty and relaxation on the laws on homosexuality, both passed in defiance of majority opinion as expressed in public-opinion polls. Sometimes public opinion may be transformed by decisive government action (for example U.K. entry to the E.E.C.). Political mechanisms, even in the most democratic societies, are imperfect vehicles for translating popular preferences into public action; governments may take advantage of such imperfections to 'improve on' public preferences, while unrepresentative pressure groups often advocate such action and wield considerable influence. The propriety of such behaviour (both by government and pressure groups) is controversial (see from eventual exhaustion. If resource owners consider this a remote possibility, these costs will be ignored and resources *in situ* will be treated as free goods.

8. The statistics, though capable of considerable refinement, are much better than the nineteenth-century data which Barnett and Morse were forced to employ.

9 Nordhaus and Tobin note that 'in general, resources might be renewable and augmentable, like capital or exhaustible, like stocks of minerals. But we shall confine ourselves to the case typified by "land" where the stock is constant — neither augmentable nor destructible.' This limitation is not mentioned again and the authors speak of 'land' and 'resources' interchangeably (see p. 27).

10. See previous note.

11. This follows a standard procedure for estimating CES production functions (see Heathfield, 1971). A variable z is defined as the ratio of the share of the composite $L-K$ factor to the share of resources in national income, and on the assumption that factors are paid their marginal products the following expression is derived:

$$z = (a_1/a_2)\,(R/N)^{\rho}\,\exp(\lambda\,\rho t),$$

where $\lambda = (\dot{A}_R/A_R) - \epsilon\,(\dot{A}_K/A_K) + (1-\epsilon)\,(\dot{A}_L/A_L)$. Logarithms are taken to give $\ln z = \text{constant} + [\rho\ln(N/K) + \lambda t]$, which is estimated by ordinary least squares. This gives $\rho = 0.5046$ (SE = 0.35), $\lambda = -0.319$ (SE = 0.017), $R^2 = 0.98$. The Durbin–Watson statistic is not given.

12. In view of Nordhaus's (1973a) severe criticisms of the Meadows model on precisely these grounds, it is odd that he and Tobin should fall into the same trap. They appear to have been lulled by the widespread use by economists (in the neoclassical tradition) of Cobb–Douglas and C.E.S. production functions embodying exponential trends in technical progress. The sole justification is that this 'follow[s] a considerable body of economic investigation'. By contrast, *World Dynamics* (Forrester 1971) (a forerunner of *Limits to Growth*) is taken to task for 'differ[ing] significantly from other studies of economic systems'.

13. See also note 9.

14. Many writers (for example Heilbroner, 1974; Ehrich and Ehrlich, 1970) have stressed the possibility that a severe shortage of resources or severe pressure of population such as feared by the Pessimists could easily provoke a nuclear war.

15. Clearly, very difficult ethical issues are involved here. Situations

could be envisaged in which the pressure of population on resources was so great that 'race survival' could be ensured only by a policy of mass slaughter. The point made here is that the primacy of the 'race-survival' objective over a 'minimum current death rate' objective is not obvious. It is even less so when it is borne in mind that the *certain* sacrifice of *current* lives affects only the *probabilities* of race survival to certain dates and in addition that the *eventual* demise of the human race is a certainty.

Chapter 3

1. Falling catches are not *conclusive* evidence of overfishing. High initial catches could represent culling of a superabundant stock to reduce it to the optimal level; falling catches could also reflect belated awareness of limits. However, some of the collapses are evidently too severe to be explained in this way. In most other cases more detailed study (for example Crutchfield and Pontecorvo, 1969) show overfishing to be the main factor.

2. This formula generalises to models embodying a variety of real world complications; the notion of user cost must be generalised correspondingly (see for example, Kuller and Cummings, 1974).

3. Differentiation of an integral expression needs justification which is not attempted here. As an intuitive justification consider differentiating the analagous Σ expression in discrete time with respect to q_t.

Chapter 4

1. A planning horizon is often introduced by mathematical economists as a *device* for making a problem more tractable; however, such an artefact is illegitimate except as an opening gambit. If the horizon is infinite, the solution to the corresponding finite horizon programme is totally irrelevant.

2. However, it does not follow that future resource use exceeds current resource use.

3. However, operational growth models often introduce the constraint $\Delta C \geqslant 0$ to deal with precisely this problem.

4. Drawn for $v > 0$ (inelastic *MUC* function). The analysis is not materially affected by $v < 0$.

Chapter 5

1. However, the idea that the price mechanism renders self-seeking harmless is dangerous indeed. At best, the market mechanism covers some kinds of activities, and these very imperfectly. Altruism and group

loyalty are still important in promoting the public good (see Hirsch, 1976).

2. For convenience the discussion employs the familiar concept of income and its distribution. Our concern is more properly with the distribution of *welfare*; the same principles apply but measurement is more difficult.

3. This argument is not conclusive, however. It is widely argued (see p. 109) that welfare depends as much on relative as on absolute income. If so, a simultaneous increase in relative and decline in absolute income may be reckoned a gain. This is the most promising justification for the otherwise excessive concern recently shown with distribution.

4. An alternative proposal for rendering consistent decisions affecting the future is the 'indicative plan', But such plans as have been drawn up are generally too broad and insufficiently binding on the participants to ensure consistency and, besides, are related to comparatively short time periods. For an excellent discussion of forward markets, insurance markets, indicative planning and their interrelationship, see Meade (1971).

5. With a lower discount rate the change in trend occurs much earlier (if at all) and is much more gradual. Resource rentals rise much more slowly and do not acquire dominance with such suddenness. For example, for $i = 3$ per cent p.a. it takes sixty years for the trend in product prices to change from a *fall* of 1 per cent p.a. to a *rise* of 1 per cent p.a.

6. This analysis is based on my recent paper 'The Isolation Paradox' (Lecomber, 1977). This includes a discussion of the complications to the argument introduced by overlapping generations, heterogeneous preferences and the possibility of other forms of giving.

7. Bequests must be viewed widely. Various forms of market failure could lead to an unbalanced portfolio of bequests − too much productive capacity and a degraded environment. If this failure is sufficiently extreme, an increase in bequests could actually damage future generations. An otherwise valid partial analysis can always be overturned in this way in a second-best situation.

8. If contraceptives are not completely reliable and are sold without restriction according to normal commercial criteria, then a couple face a choice between (i) sex without contraceptives, or (ii) sex with contraceptives, or (iii) no sex. The pleasures of sex (with or without contraceptives) must now be taken into account, together with the probability of conception and the costs and benefits of such an outcome. This is an example of decision-making under uncertainty, and provided the

couple react 'rationally' and the prices encountered represent social costs and benefits, the decision will be socially optimal. In fact the same distortions are present and in addition it is possible that the couple are myopic in their relative evaluation of immediate pleasures and possible longer-term effects.

9. This analysis compares the cost and benefits to the couple with those to society *ex ante*. The welfare of the child is not considered (cf. p. 70).

10. From *Economic Trends* (Dec. 1976). For example, in the original income range £2116–2561, two-adult families pay (on average) taxes net of benefits of £344, while families of two adults plus four children receive net benefits of £1146. Thus four children appear to reduce net tax liability by £1490, or 70 per cent of the post-tax and post-benefit income of the two-adult group. While this calculation could be greatly refined, it gives a crude indication of the extent of subsidy.

11. The short-term impact of advertising on aggregate demand is confirmed by empirical studies (for example Cowling *et al.*, 1975).

12. But even on this view there are other issues, for example marketed fripperies versus essential public services ('private affluence and public squalor' Galbraith, 1958), and versus environmental quality (see Lecomber, 1975), and fripperies in rich countries versus necessities, even survival, in poor ones.

Chapter 6

1. Fishing zones can be established but this only partially meets the problem as many types of fish will move across the boundaries.

2. Though note that the present system approximates much more closely to an expenditure tax than is often realised on account of the exemptions given to 'approved' forms of savings and the tax concessions granted to 'approved' forms of investment (see Meade *et al.*, 1978). But see p. 113, where, *inter alia*, it is suggested that these concessions operate very erratically, in particular discriminating against conservation of natural resources.

3. It is sometimes suggested that instead of a tax advertising expenditure should be disallowed as a business expense. However, since (clearly) advertising *is* a business expense, this obscures the objective of the tax and, moreover, ties the effective rate of tax on advertising to the corporation-tax rate.

4. However, some countries, for example Tunisia and Singapore, do disciminate against large families.

5. A possible exception to this is to pay relatively small subsidies to

people undertaking sterilisation. This has been done in India, transistor radios being used as subsidies. Essentially the authorities are trading on people's myopia, inducing them to take virtually irrevocable decisions they may later deeply regret.

6. Simple output taxes are not generally appropriate to renewable resources since depletion is not closely related to the level of output. It is generally more related to particular production processes (for example destruction of hedgerows, inorganic fertilisers) and is difficult to assess. In practice taxes would need to be related to particular depleting processes and regulations would often be more appropriate.

7. The case of pollution taxes is more difficult. Where the externality is related to *production*, the tax should be related to production (not consumption) and rebates should not be given for exports.

Chapter 7

1. Note that innovations need not be of this character. They might be of a resource-saving kind, allowing the same Y to be produced with less R and the same L. Then the opposite problem of excess demand for labour appears; this may also be dealt with by adjustments in the mix of products or processes, as described in the text.

2. The ratio of the post-tax to the pre-tax price in year n would be given by $(1.03)^n$ and the corresponding tax ratio would be $(1.03)^n - 1$.

3. Notice, for example, that some movements are associated with an *increase* in resource use. Notice also the arguments against easy mobility advanced by Mishan (1967) and Hirschman (1970).

4. However, change is multi-dimensional and some caution is needed. For example, halting the growth of car ownership, while reducing changes in public-transport provision and the physical environment of the city, involves a *fall* in vehicle production, a significant change, likely to involve serious structural unemployment.

Chapter 8

1. Likewise electricity is irreplaceable but can be produced from a wide variety of primary sources.

2. A further disadvantage of the Nordhaus programme is that, eventually, the breeder is envisaged as the sole source of energy supply. Reliance on a single, centralised, capital-intensive source places unprecedented power in the hands of workers in the industry.

3. By 2170 roughly 65 per cent of the original energy base remains, but 11 per cent of this is being consumed each year. Thus even if growth is stopped at this point, these resources last only a further nine

years. Nordhaus does not give the rate of growth of energy consumption implied by his model and it may be lower than recent rates. But this does not materially affect the above argument. For example, at 3 per cent p.a. growth, resources last about 350 years, or 760 years if growth is halted in 2170.

4. The simpler applications of solar heating (for example living-rooms facing south) are most naturally regarded as means of reducing demand for (public-produced) energy. More elaborate solar energy systems may be regarded equally as means of increasing supply or of reducing demand.

Chapter 9

1. However, the possibility of future recovery may be jeopardised by current techniques, for example a mine once closed may be expensive to reopen, and disposal of uranium-238 would effectively preclude its later use in breeder reactors. Arguably, fuel thus lost should be included in original energy and regarded as a genuine processing loss.

2. The inner leaf of the cavity wall is made of insulating concrete blocks, the cavity filled with insulant, and 200 mm. of glass fibre placed between the ceiling joists in the roof. Double-glazing is not cost-effective (Building Research Establishment, 1975). Simple devices like draught-proof strips around doors and windows probably are, but no one seems to have computed the savings.

3. With massive injections of public funds government attitudes are crucial. Much depends on how far goverment funds are tied to the development of small cars.

4. The Department of Energy (1976a) considers the 'resulting savings in petroleum could be as high as 40%'. This is about 1.0EJ, compared with 0.66EJ given in the text. However, the Department assumes a number of successful technical developments which are, in principle, excluded from our calculations.

5. 'Extra high' standards are better than 'high' standards at approximately double the current prices. However, the *optimal* standard is then about half-way between the two.

6. This is the net gain. In fact energy saving in industry would be more than this but energy consumption in services would rise.

7. The *extent* of the distortion seems little appreciated. For a congested urban road, where the rate of flow is 7 m.p.h., the Ministry of Transport (1964) estimated the marginal external cost from congestion alone at 42p per mile. Allowing for increases in the cost of petrol and the value of time (the latter assumed to rise with the wage rate), an

equivalent figure for 1977 was £2 per mile. This is some six times the private cost (including time), and some seventy times the private petrol cost. Adding in external costs (for example noise, pollution, severance) could double this figure. (Naturally appropriate policies would reduce the congestion and hence the marginal external cost substantially.)

8. However, it should be noted that the cutbacks are smaller than those obtained using an elasticity of 0.5 (Section 9.3).

REFERENCES

T. AARONSON (1971) 'The Black Box: The Fuel Cell', *Environment*, vol. 13, no. 10 (reprinted in B. Commoner *et al.*, 1975).

M. A. ADELMAN (1971) *The World Petroleum Market* (Baltimore, Johns Hopkins University Press).

ADVISORY COUNCIL FOR ENERGY CONSERVATION (1977) *Road Vehicle and Engine Design: Short and Medium Term Energy Considerations*, Energy Paper No. 18 (London, Advisory Council for Energy Conservation).

R. C. ANDERSON *et al.* (1977) 'U.S. Federal Tax Policy: The Evolution of Percentage Depletion for Minerals', *Resources Policy*, vol. 3, no. 3.

K. J. ARROW (1970) *Essays in the Theory of Risk-Bearing* (Harvard University Press).

K. J. ARROW and R. C. LIND (1970) 'Uncertainty and the Evaluation of Public Investment Decisions', *American Economic Review*, vol. 60, no. 3.

LORD ASHBY (1972) *Pollution in Some British Estuaries: Third Report of the Royal Commission on Environmental Pollution* (Chairman, Lord Ashby) (London, H.M.S.O.).

R. U. AYRES and A. V. KNEESE (1971) 'Economic and Ecological Effects of a Stationary Economy', *Annual Review of Ecology and Systemics*, vol. 2.

P. BACHARACH (1967) *The Theory of Democratic Elitism: A Critique* (Boston, Little, Brown).

F. E. BANKS (1976) *The Economics of Natural Resources* (New York, Plenum).

H. J. BARNETT and C. MORSE (1963) *Scarcity and Growth: The Economics of Natural Resource Availability* (Baltimore, Johns Hopkins University Press).

W. BECKERMAN (1971) 'The Desirability of Economic Growth', in *Conflicts Among Policy Objectives*, ed. N. Kaldor (Oxford, Blackwell/British Association for the Advancement of Science).

W. BECKERMAN (1972) 'Economists, Scientists and Environmental Catastrophe', *Oxford Economic Papers*, vol. 24, no. 3.

W. BECKERMAN (1974) *In Defence of Economic Growth* (London, Cape).

Y. BEN PORATH (1974), Economic Analyses of Fertility in Israel', in *Economics of the Family*, ed. T. W. Schultz (Chicago University Press).

R. J. H. BEVERTON and S. J. HOLT (1957) *On the Dynamics of Exploited Fish Populations*, Ministry of Agriculture, Forestry and Fishing (London, H.M.S.O.).

M. R. BONE (1973) *Family Planning Services in England and Wales* (London, H.M.S.O.).

K. BOULDING (1970) 'The Economics of the Coming Spaceship Earth', in *Agenda for Survival*, ed. H. W. Helfrich (Yale University Press).

G. M. BRANNON (1975) 'U.S. Taxes on Energy Resources', *American Economic Review*, Paper and Proceedings, vol. 45.

J. BRAY (1972) *The Politics of Environment*, Fabian Tract No. 412 (London, Fabian Society).

U. BRONFENBRENNER (1971), *Two Worlds of Childhood, U.S. and U.S.S.R.* (London, Allen & Unwin).

W. BROWN (1962) *Piecework Abandoned* (London, Heinemann).

BUILDING RESEARCH ESTABLISHMENT (1975) *Energy Conservation: A Study of Energy Consumption in Buildings and Possible Means of Saving Energy in Housing* (Watford, Building Research Establishment).

R. CARSON (1962) *Silent Spring* (Boston, Houghton Mifflin).

CENTRAL POLICY REVIEW STAFF (1974) *Energy Conservation* (Rothschild Report) (London, H.M.S.O.).

P. F. CHAPMAN (1975) *Fuel's Paradise: Energy Options for Britain* (Harmondsworth, Penguin).

C. J. CICHETTI (1972), *Alaskan Oil: Alternative Routes and Markets* (Washington, D.C., Resources for the Future).

C. W. CLARK (1976) *Mathematical Bio-economics* (New York, Wiley).

M. CLAWSON (1975) *Forests, for Whom and for What?* (Baltimore: Johns Hopkins University Press).

A. CODDINGTON (1972) 'The Cheermongers or How to Stop Worrying and Love Economic Growth', *Your Environment*

H. S. D. COLE et al. (eds) (1973) *Thinking About the Future* (Brighton, Chatto & Windus/Sussex University Press).

M. S. COMMON and D. W. PEARCE (1973) 'Adaptive Mechanisms, Growth and the Environment: The Case of Natural Resources', *Canadian Journal of Economics*, vol. 6, no. 3.

B. COMMONER (1971) *The Closing Circle* (London, Cape).

B. COMMONER et al. (eds) (1975) *Energy and Human Welfare: A*

Critical Analysis, Vol. II Alternative Technologies for Power Production (New York, Macmillan).

CONSERVATION SOCIETY (1973) *The Economics of Conservation: An Outline Plan for the United Kingdom* (Walton on Thames, Conservation Society).

M. CORDEN (1963) *A Tax on Advertising* (London, Fabian Society).

K. COWLING *et al.* (1975) *Advertising and Economic Behaviour* (London, Macmillan).

J. A. CRUTCHFIELD and G. PONTECORVO (1969) *The Pacific Salmon Fisheries* (Baltimore, Johns Hopkins University Press).

T. DALE and V. G. CARTER (1955), *Topsoil and Civilization* (Oklahoma University Press).

J. H. DALES (1968) *Property Pollution and Prices* (Toronto University Press).

H. E. DALY (ed.) (1971) *Essays Toward a Steady-State Economy* (Cuernavaca, Mexico, Centro Inticultural de Documentation).

H. E. DALY (1972) 'In Defence of a Steady State Economy', *American Journal of Agricultural Economics*, vol. 54.

R. C. d'ARGE and K. C. KOGIKU (1973) 'Economic Growth and the Environment', *Review of Economic Studies*, vol. 16.

P. DASGUPTA (1969) 'On the Concept of Optimum Population', *Review of Economic Studies*, vol. 36.

P. DASGUPTA and G. HEAL (1975) 'The Optimal Depletion of Exhaustible Resources', *Review of Economic Studies,* 'Symposium on Natural Resources',

P. DAVIDSON (1963) 'Public Policy Problems of the Domestic Crude Oil Industry', *American Economic Review*, vol. 53, no. 1.

DEPARTMENT OF ENERGY (1976a) *Energy Research and Deverlopment in the United Kingdom*, Energy Paper No. 11 (London, H.M.S.O.).

DEPARTMENT OF ENERGY (1976b) *Geothermal Energy: The Case for Research in the United Kingdom*, Energy Paper No. 9 (London, H.M.S.O.).

DEPARTMENT OF ENERGY (1977a) *Tidal Power Barrages in the Severn Estuary: Recent Estimates on their Feasibility,* Energy Paper No. 23 (London, H.M.S.O.).

DEPARTMENT OF ENERGY (1977b) *Report of the Working Group on Energy Elasticities,* Energy Paper No. 17 (London, H.M.S.O.).

DEPARTMENT OF ENERGY (1977c) *District Heating Combined with Electricity Generation in the United Kingdom*, Energy Paper No. 20 (London, H.M.S.O.).

DEPARTMENT OF ENERGY (1977d) *The Prospects for the Generation of Electricity from Wind Energy in the United Kingdom*, Energy Paper No. 21 (London, H.M.S.O.).

DEPARTMENT OF THE ENVIRONMENT (1977) *Housing Policy : a Consultative Document*, Cmnd 6851 (London, H.M.S.O.).

D. DICKSON (1974) *Alternative Technology and the Politics of Technical Change* (London, Fontana).

R. DORFMAN (1969) 'An Economic Interpretation of Optimal Control Theory', *American Economic Review*, vol. 59, no. 3.

A. DOWNS (1957), *An Economic Theory of Democracy* (New York, Harper & Row).

J. S. DUESENBERRY (1949) *Income, Saving and the Theory of Consumer Behavior* (Cambridge, Mass., Harvard University Press).

R. A. EASTERLIN (1974) 'Does Economic Growth Improve the Human Lot? Some Empirical Evidence', in *Nations and Households in Economic Growth*, ed. P. A. David and M. W. Reder (New York, Academic Press).

M. EDEL (1973) *Economic and the Environment* (Englewood Cliffs, N.J., Prentice-Hall).

P. EHRLICH and A. H. EHRLICH (1970) *Population, Resources, Environment: Issues in Human Ecology* (San Francisco, Freeman).

J. ELLUL (1965) *The Technological Society* (London, Cape).

M. T. FARVAR and J. P. MILTON (eds) (1973) *The Careless Technology: Ecology and International Development* (New York, Double-day/Natural History Press).

L. L. FISCHMAN and H. M. LANDSBERG (1972) 'Adequacy of Nonfuel Minerals and Forest Resources', in *Population, Resources and the Environment*, Commission on Population Growth and the American Future (Washington, D.C., U.S. Government Printing Office).

B. FLOWERS (1976) *Nuclear Power and the Environment: Sixth Report of the Royal Commission on Environmental Pollution* (London, H.M.S.O.).

FORD FOUNDATION (1974) *A Time to Choose: America's Energy Future* (Cambridge, Mass., Ballinger).

J. W. FORRESTER (1971) *World Dynamics* (Cambridge, Mass., Wright Allen).

M. GAFFNEY (ed.) (1967) *Extractive Resources and Taxation* (Madison, University of Wisconsin Press).

J. K. GALBRAITH (1958) *The Affluent Society* (London, Hamilton).

N. GEORGESCU-ROEGEN (1971) *The Entropy Law and the Eco-*

nomic Process (Cambridge, Mass., Harvard University Press).

A. GILBERT (1976) 'The Arguments for Very Large Cities Reconsidered', *Urban Studies*, vol. 13.

E. GOLDSMITH (1976) *A Blueprint for Survival* (Harmondsworth, Penguin). (reprinted from the Ecologist, vol. 2, no. 1, 1972).

H. S. GORDON (1954) 'Economic Theory of a Common-property Resource: The Fishery', *Journal of Political Economy*, vol. 62.

W. C. GOUCH and B. J. EASTLUND (1971) 'Energy, Wastes and the Fusion Torch', in H. E. Daly (ed.) (1971).

J. de V. GRAAF (1957) *Theoretical Welfare Economics* (Cambridge University Press).

P. HALL (ed.) (1977) *Europe 2000* (London, Duckworth).

R. HANNESON (1975) 'Fishery Dynamics: A North Atlantic Cod Fishery', *Canadian Journal of Economics*, vol. 8.

R. HARRIS and A. SELDON (1959) *Advertising in a Free Society* (London, Institute of Economic Affairs).

A. J. HARRISON (1974) *The Economics of Transport Appraisal* (London, Croom Helm).

R. M. HAVEMAN (1977) 'The Economic Evaluation of Long-run Uncertainties', *Futures*, vol. 9, no. 5.

G. HAWTHORN (1970) *The Sociology of Fertility* (London, Collier-Macmillan).

F. A. HAYEK (1963) 'The Non-sequitur of the Dependence Effect', in *Private Wants and Public Needs*, ed. E. S. Phelps (New York, Norton).

G. HEAL (1976) 'The Relationship Between Price and Extraction Cost for a Resource with a Backstop Technology', *Bell Journal of Economics*, vol. 7, no. 2.

D. F. HEATHFIELD (1971) *Production Functions* (London, Macmillan).

R. L. HEILBRONER (1974) *An Inquiry into the Human Prospect* (New York, Norton).

O. C. HERFINDAHL (1967) 'Depletion and Economic Theory', in M. GAFFNEY (ed.) (1967).

O. C. HERFINDAHL and A. V. KNEESE (1974) *The Economic Theory of Natural Resources* (Columbus, Ohio, Merrill).

F. HIRSCH (1976) *The Social Limits to Growth* (Cambridge, Mass., Harvard University Press).

A. O. HIRSCHMAN (1970) *Exit, Voice and Loyalty* (Cambridge, Mass., Harvard University Press).

H. HOTELLING (1931) 'The Economics of Exhaustible Resources', *Journal of Political Economy*, vol. 39, no. 1.

R. W. HOUGHTON (ed.) (1970) *Public Finance* (Harmondsworth, Penguin).

K. HUBBERT (1969) 'Energy Resources', in *Resources and Man,* National Academy of Sciences and National Research Council (San Francisco, Freeman).

E. A. HUDSON and D. W. JORGENSON (1976) 'Tax Policy and Energy Conservation', in *Econometric Studies of Energy Policy,* ed. D. W. Jorgenson (Amsterdam, North-Holland).

I. ILLICH (1971) *Deschooling Society* (London, Calder & Boyars).

A. INGHAM and P. SIMMONS (1975) 'Natural Resources and a Growing Population', *Review of Economic Studies*, vol. 42.

INSTITUTE OF FISCAL STUDIES (1976) *Taxation and Incentives* (London, Institute of Fiscal Studies).

M. D. INTRIGILATOR (1971) *Mathematical Optimization and Economic Theory* (Englewood Cliffs, N.J., Prentice-Hall).

D. C. ION (1976) *Availability of World Energy Resources, First Supplement* (London, Graham & Trotman).

M. JAHODA (1973) 'Postscript on Social Change', in H. S. D. COLE *et al.* (eds.) (1973), (reprinted from *Futures*, vol. 5, no. 2., 1973).

B. JOHNSON (1977) 'Nuclear Power Proliferation: Problems of International Control', *Energy Policy*, vol. 5, no. 3.

N. KALDOR (1955) *An Expenditure Tax* (London, Allen & Unwin).

K. W. KAPP (1963) *Social Costs of Business Enterprise* (Bombay, Asia Publishing House).

J. A. KAY and J. A. MIRRLEES (1975) 'The Desirability of Natural Resource Depletion', in *The Economics of Natural Resource Depletion*, ed. D. W. Pearce (London, Macmillan).

W. KEIZER (1971) *The Soviet Quest for Economic Rationality* (Rotterdam University Press).

A. V. KNEESE (1976) 'Natural Resources Policy 1975–1985', *Journal of Environmental Economics and Management* vol. 3, no. 4.

A. V. KNEESE (1977) *Economics and the Environment* Harmondsworth, Penguin).

J. V. KRUTILLA and A. C. FISHER (1975) *The Economics of Natural Environments* (Baltimore, Johns Hopkins University Press).

R. G. KULLER and R. G. CUMMINGS (1974) 'An Economic Model of Production and Investment for Petroleum Reserves', *American Economic Review*, vol. 64.

K. LANCASTER (1969) *Introduction to Modern Microeconomics*

(Chicago, Rand McNally).

L. B. LAVE and L. C. FREEBURG (1974) 'Health Costs to the Consumer per Megawatt-hour of Electricity', in *Energy, the Environment and Human Health*, ed. A. J. Finkel (Acton, Mass., Publishing Sciences Group).

G. LEACH (1976) *Energy and Food Production* (Guildford, I.P.C. Science and Technology Press).

J. R. C. LECOMBER (1970) 'Government Planning, With and Without the Cooperation of Industry', *Economics of Planning*, vol. 10, nos. 1–2.

J. R. C. LECOMBER (1974) *The Growth Objective*, International Institute of Social Economics, Monograph No. 3 (Humberside, Emmasglen).

J. R. C. LECOMBER (1975) *Economic Growth Versus the Environment* (London, Macmillan).

J. R. C. LECOMBER (1977) 'The Isolation Paradox', *Quarterly Journal of Economics*, vol. 91, no. 3.

J. R. C. LECOMBER and J. FISHER (1978) *Tax Reform and Conservation* (London, Institute of Fiscal Studies).

M. LEIBENSTEIN (1974) 'An Interpretation of the Economic Theory of Fertility, Promising Path or Blind Alley?', *Journal of Economic Literature*, vol. 12, no. 2.

D. M. LEIPZIGER and J. L. MUDGE (1976) *Seabed Mineral Ores and the Economic Interests of Developing Countries* (Cambridge, Mass., Ballinger).

M. LIPTON (1968a) *Assessing Economic Performance* (London, Staples).

M. LIPTON (1968b) 'Strategy for Agriculture: Urban Bias and Rural Planning', in *The Crisis of Indian Planning*, ed. P. Streeten and M. Lipton (London, Oxford University Press).

T. S. LOVERING (1969) 'Mineral Resources from the Land', in *Resources and Man*, National Academy of Sciences and National Resource Council (San Francisco, Freeman).

A. B. LOVINS (1975) *World Energy Strategies* (New York, Friends of the Earth).

S. L. McDONALD (1971) *Petroleum Conservation in the United States: An Economic Analysis* (Baltimore, Johns Hopkins University Press).

S. L. McDONALD (1976) 'Taxation System and Market Distortion', in *Energy Supply and Government Policy*, ed. R. J. Kalter and W. E. Tyner (Ithaca, Cornell University Press).

V. E. McKELVEY (1972) 'Mineral Resource Estimates and Public Policy', *American Scientist*, vol. 60.

J. MADDOX (1972) *The Doomsday Syndrome* (London, Macmillan).

S. A. MARGLIN (1963) 'The Social Rate of Discount and the Optimal Rate of Investment', *Quarterly Journal of Economics*, vol. 77.

S. A. MARGLIN (1967) *Public Investment Criteria: Benefit–Cost Analysis for Planned Economic Growth* (London, Allen & Unwin).

MASSACHUSETTS INSTITUTE OF TECHNOLOGY (1970) *Man's Impact on the Global Environment: Assessment and Recommendations for Policy* (Cambridge, Mass., M.I.T. Press).

J. E. MEADE (1971) *The Controlled Economy* (London, Allen & Unwin).

J. E. MEADE (1973) 'Economic Policy and the Threat of Doom', in *Resources and Population*, ed. B. Benjamin *et al.* (London, Academic Press).

J. E. MEADE *et al.* (1978) *The Structure and Reform of the Direct Tax System* (London, Allen & Unwin/Institute of Fiscal Studies).

D. H. MEADOWS *et al.* (1972) *The Limits to Growth* (London, Earth. Island).

M. D. MESAROVIC and E. C. PESTEL (1974) *Mankind at the Turning Point* (New York, Dutton).

MINISTRY OF TRANSPORT (1964) *Road Pricing: The Economic and Technical Possibilities* (Smeed Report) (London, H.M.S.O.).

J. A. MIRRLEES (1971) 'An Exploration into the Theory of Optimal Taxation', *Review of Economic Studies*, vol. 38.

E. J. MISHAN (1967) *The Costs of Economic Growth* (London, Staples).

E. J. MISHAN (1977) *The Economic Growth Debate: An Assessment* (London, Allen & Unwin).

NATIONAL ECONOMIC DEVELOPMENT OFFICE (1974) *Energy Conservation in the United Kingdom* (London, H.M.S.O.).

W. D. NORDHAUS (1973a) 'World Dynamics: Measurement without Data', *Economics Journal*, vol. 83, no. 4.

W. D. NORDHAUS (1973b) 'The Allocation of Energy Resources', *Brookings Papers on Economic Activity*.

W. D. NORDHAUS (1974) 'The 1974 Report of the President's Council of Economic Advisers: Energy in the Economic Report', *American Economic Review*, vol. 64.

W. D. NORDHAUS (1977) 'Economic Growth and Climate: The Carbon Dioxide Problem', *American Economic Review*, Paper and Proceedings, vol. 47.

W. D. NORHAUS and J. TOBIN (1972) 'Is Growth Obsolete?', in *Economic Growth*, (New York, Columbia University Press/National

Bureau of Economic Research).

M. OLSON (1965) *The Logic of Collective Action* (Cambridge, Mass., Harvard University Press).

W. OPHULS (1977) *Ecology and the Politics of Scarcity* (San Francisco, Freeman).

ORGANISATION FOR ECONOMIC CO-OPERATION AND DEVELOPMENT (1976) *Energy Conservation in the International Agency* (Paris, O.E.C.D.).

J. A. OVER and A. C. SJOERDSMA (1974) *Energy Conservation: Ways and Means* (The Hague, Future Shape of Technology Foundation).

V. PACKARD (1957) *The Hidden Persuaders* (New York, David McKay).

T. PAGE (1976) *Conservation and Economic Efficiency: An Approach to Materials Policy* (Baltimore: Johns Hopkins University Press).

D. W. PEARCE (1971) *Cost—Benefit Analysis* (London, Macmillan).

D. W. PEARCE and I. WALTER (1977) *Resource Conservation: the Social and Economic Dimensions of Recycling* (New York University Press).

F. R. PENNANCE and H. GRAY (1968) *Choice in Housing* (London, Institute of Economic Affairs).

E. S. PHELPS (1965) *Fiscal Neutrality Toward Economic Growth* (New York, McGraw-Hill).

E. C. PIELOU (1969) *An Introduction to Mathematical Ecology* (New York, Wiley).

A. C. PIGOU (1924) *The Economics of Welfare* (London, Macmillan).

N. POLE (1973) *Oil and the Future of Personal Mobility* (Cambridge, Eco Publications).

C. PONTECORVO (1967) 'Optimization and Taxation in an Open-access Resource: The Fishery', in M. GAFFNEY (ed.) (1967).

R. W. PRYKE and J. DODGSON (1975) *The Rail Problem* London, Martin Robertson).

I. RAJARAMAN (1976) 'Non-renewable Resources. A Review of Long-term Projections', *Futures*, vol. 8, no. 3.

F. P. RAMSEY (1928) 'A Mathematical Theory of Saving', *Economic Journal*, vol. 38.

J. A. RAWLS (1971) *A Theory of Justice* (Cambridge, Mass., Harvard University Press).

H. W. RICHARDSON (1973) *The Economics of Urban Size* (Farnborough, Saxon House).

H. W. RICHARDSON (1975) *Economic Aspects of the Energy Crisis* (Farnborough, Saxon House).

J. ROTHENBERG (1970) 'The Economics of Congestion and Pollution, an Integrated View', *American Economic Review*, vol. 60, no. 2.

J. W. F. ROWE (1965) *Primary Commodities in International Trade* (Cambridge University Press).

H. E. RYDER and G. M. HEAL (1973) 'Optimal Growth with Intertemporally Dependent Preferences', *Review of Economic Studies*, vol. 40.

M. RYLE (1977) 'Economics of Alternative Energy Sources', *Nature*, vol. 267.

E. F. SCHUMACHER (1973) *Small is Beautiful* (London, Blond & Briggs).

T. SCITOVSKY (1976) *The Joyless Economy, an Inquiry into Human Dissatisfactions* (London, Oxford University Press).

A. K. SEN (1961) 'On Optimising the Rate of Saving', *Economic Journal*, vol. 71.

C. SHARP (1966) 'Congestion and Welfare — an Examination of the Case for a Congestion Tax', *Economic Journal*, vol. 76, no. 4.

J. SHOREY (1976) 'An Inter-industry Analysis of Strike Frequency', *Economia*, vol. 43.

D. A. SINGER (1977) 'Long-term Adequacy of Metal Resources', *Resources Policy*, vol. 3, no. 2.

D. V. SMITH (1975) 'New Seeds of Income Distribution in Bangladesh', *Journal of Development Economics*, vol. 11, no. 2.

V. L. SMITH (1977) 'Control Theory Applied to Natural and Environmental Resources. An Exposition', *Journal of Environmental Economics and Management*, vol. 4.

R. M. SOLOW (1975) 'Intergenerational Equity and Exhaustible Resources', *Review of Economic Studies*, 'Symposium on Natural Resources'.

J. E. STIGLITZ (1975a) 'Growth with Exhaustible Natural Resources: Efficient and Optimal Growth Paths', *Review of Economic Studies*, 'Symposium on Natural Resources.'

J. E. STIGLITZ (1975b) 'Monopoly and the Rate of Extraction of Exhaustible Resources', *American Economic Review*, vol. 65, no. 4.

J. M. STYCOS (1971) 'Opinion, Ideology and Population Problems: Some Sources of Domestic and Foreign Opposition to Birth Control', in *Rapid Population Growth* (Washington D.C., National Academy of Sciences).

M. SURREY and W. PAGE (1975) 'Some Issues in the Current Debate about Energy and Natural Resources', in *The Economics of Natural*

Resource Depletion, ed. D. W. Pearce (London, Macmillan).

J. TOBIN (1964) 'Economic Growth as an Objective of Policy', *American Economic Review,* Papers and Proceedings, vol. 54, no. 3.

G. TULLOCK (1964) 'The Social Rate of Discount and the Optimal Rate of Investment: Comment', *Quarterly Journal of Economics,* vol. 78.

R. TURVEY and A. R. NOBAY (1965) 'On Measuring Energy Growth', *Economic Journal,* vol. 75.

UNITED NATIONS ECONOMIC COMMISSION FOR EUROPE (1976) *Increased Energy Economy and Efficiency in the ECE Region* (New York, U.N.E.C.E.)

UNITED STATES DEPARTMENT OF THE INTERIOR, BUREAU OF MINES AND GEOLOGICAL SURVEY (Annually) *Mining and Minerals Policy* (Washington, D.C., U.S. Government Printing Office).

T. VEBLEN (1899) *The Theory of the Leisure Class* (New York, Macmillan).

R. VERNEY (1976) *Aggregates: The Way Ahead, Report of the Advisory Committee on Aggregates* (London, H.M.S.O.).

W. VICKREY (1967) 'Economic Criteria for Optimum Rates of Depletion', in M. GAFFNEY (ed.) (1967).

N. VOUSDEN (1973) 'Basic Theoretical Issues of Resource Depletion', *Journal of Economic Theory,* vol. 6, no. 2.

WORLD ENERGY CONFERENCE (1974) *Survey of Energy Resources* (New York, World Energy Conference).

WORLD HEALTH ORGANISATION (1976) *Health Hazards from New Environmental Pollutants* (Geneva, United Nations).

G. WUNDERLICH (1967) 'Taxing and Exploiting Oil: The Dakota Case', in M. GAFFNEY (ed.) (1967).

M. YOUNG and P. WILLMOTT (1957) *Family and Kinship in East London* (London, Routledge & Kegan Paul).

NAME INDEX

SUBJECT INDEX